GW01608035

FRANCIS FRITH'S

ISLE OF MAN

PHOTOGRAPHIC MEMORIES

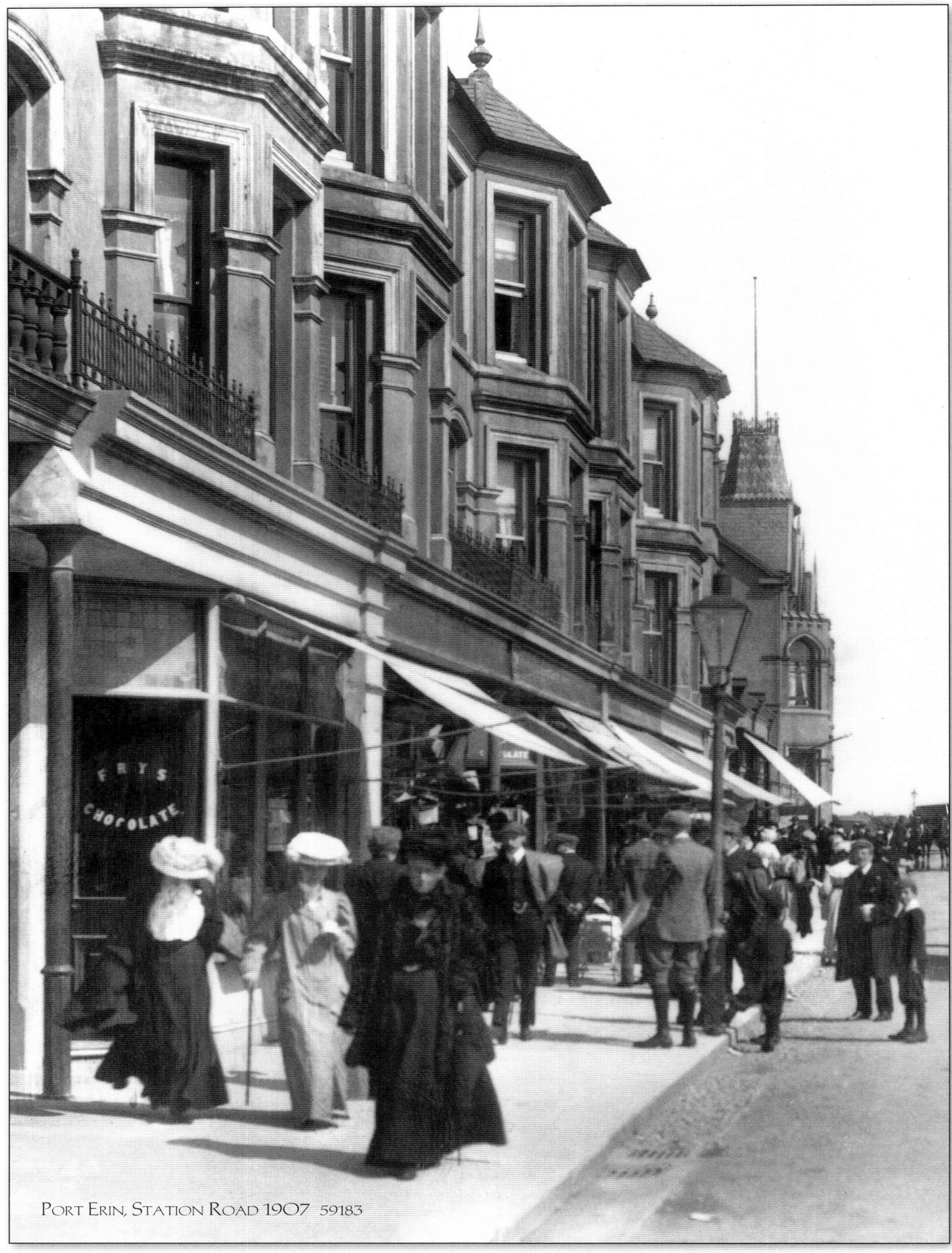

Port Erin, Station Road 1907 59183

ISLE OF MAN
PHOTOGRAPHIC MEMORIES

CLIVE HARDY

First published in the United Kingdom in 1999 by The Francis Frith Collection®

Paperback Edition 2001 ISBN 1-85937-268-6
This edition published exclusively for Dorrigo in 2009 ISBN 978-1-84589-447-4

Text and Design copyright © The Francis Frith Collection®
Photographs copyright © The Francis Frith Collection®
except where indicated

The Frith® photographs and the Frith® logo are reproduced under licence from Heritage Photographic Resources Ltd, the owners of the Frith® archive and trademarks. 'The Francis Frith Collection', 'Francis Frith' and 'Frith' are registered trademarks of Heritage Photographic Resources Ltd.

All rights reserved. No photograph in this publication may be sold to a third party other than in the original form of this publication, or framed for sale to a third party. No parts of this publication may be reproduced, stored in a retrieval system, or transmitted, in any form, or by any means, electronic, mechanical, photocopying, recording or otherwise, without the prior permission of the publishers and copyright holder

British Library Cataloguing in Publication Data

Isle of Man Photographic Memories
Clive Hardy
ISBN 978-1-84589-447-4

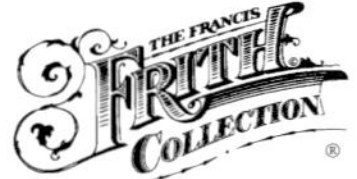

The Francis Frith Collection®
Frith's Barn, Teffont,
Salisbury, Wiltshire SP3 5QP
Tel: +44 (0) 1722 716 376
Email: info@francisfrith.co.uk
www.francisfrith.com

Aerial photographs reproduced under licence from Simmons Aerofilms Limited
Historical Ordnance Survey maps reproduced under licence from Homecheck.co.uk

Printed and bound in Malta

Front Cover: **DOUGLAS, DERBY CASTLE TERMINUS 1896** 38771t
The colour-tinting in this image is for illustrative purposes only, and is not intended to be historically accurate

Every attempt has been made to contact copyright holders of illustrative material. We will be happy to give full acknowledgement in future editions for any items not credited. Any information should be directed to The Francis Frith Collection.

AS WITH ANY HISTORICAL DATABASE, THE FRANCIS FRITH ARCHIVE IS CONSTANTLY BEING CORRECTED AND IMPROVED, AND THE PUBLISHERS WOULD WELCOME INFORMATION ON OMISSIONS OR INACCURACIES

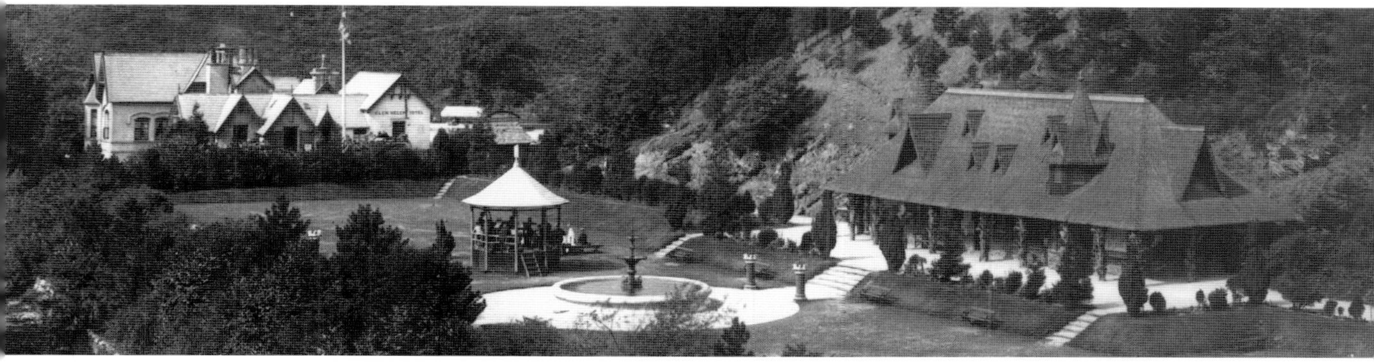

Contents

THE MAKING OF AN ARCHIVE

FRANCIS FRITH

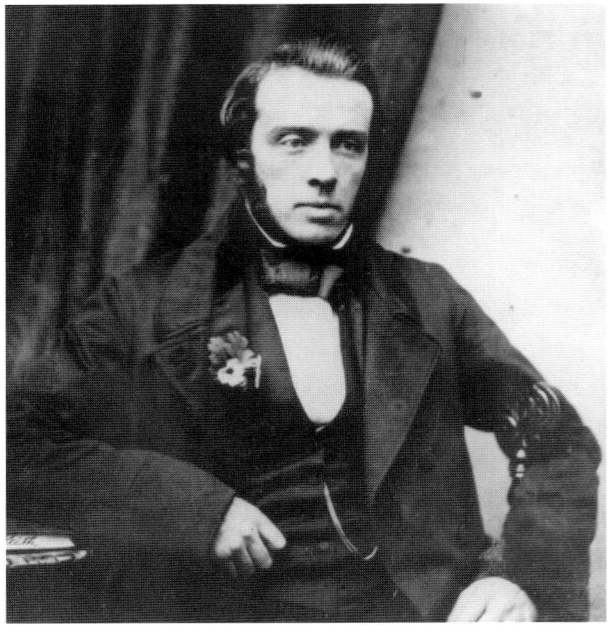

Francis Frith, Victorian founder of the world-famous photographic archive, was a devout Quaker and a highly successful Victorian businessman. By 1860 he was already a multi-millionaire, having established and sold a wholesale grocery business in Liverpool. He had also made a series of pioneering photographic journeys to the Nile region. The images he returned with were the talk of London. An eminent modern historian has likened their impact on the population of the time to that on our own generation of the first photographs taken on the surface of the moon.

Frith had a passion for landscape, and was as equally inspired by the countryside of Britain as he was by the desert regions of the Nile. He resolved to set out on a new career and to use his skills with a camera. He established a business in Reigate as a specialist publisher of topographical photographs.

Frith lived in an era of immense and sometimes violent change. For the poor in the early part of Victoria's reign work was a drudge and the hours long, and ordinary people had precious little free time. Most had not travelled far beyond the boundaries of their own town or village. Mass tourism was in its infancy during the 1860s, but during the next decade the railway network and the establishment of Bank Holidays and half-Saturdays gradually made it possible for the working man and his family to enjoy holidays and to see a little more of the world. With characteristic business acumen, Francis Frith foresaw that these new tourists would enjoy having souvenirs to commemorate their days out. He began selling photo-souvenirs of seaside resorts and beauty spots, which the Victorian public pasted into treasured family albums.

Frith's aim was to photograph every town and village in Britain. For the next thirty years he travelled the country by train and by pony and trap, producing fine photographs of seaside resorts and beauty spots that were keenly bought by millions of Victorians.

THE RISE OF FRITH & CO

Each photograph was taken with tourism in mind, the small team of Frith photographers concentrating on busy shopping streets, beaches, seafronts, picturesque lanes and villages. They also photographed buildings: the Victorian and Edwardian eras were times of huge building activity, and town halls, libraries, post offices, schools and technical colleges were springing up all over the country. They were invariably celebrated by a proud Victorian public, and photo souvenirs – visual records – published by F Frith & Co were sold in their hundreds of thousands. In addition, many new commercial buildings such as hotels, inns and pubs were photographed, often because their owners specifically commissioned Frith postcards or prints of them for re-sale or for publicity purposes.

In order to gain some understanding of the scale of Frith's business one only has to look at the catalogue issued by Frith & Co in 1886: it runs to some 670 pages. By 1890 Frith had created the greatest specialist photographic publishing company in the world, with over 2,000 stockists! The picture on the right shows the Frith & Co display board on the wall of the stockist at Ingleton in the Yorkshire Dales (left of window). Beautifully constructed with a mahogany frame and gilt inserts, it displayed a dozen scenes.

POSTCARD BONANZA

The ever-popular holiday postcard we know today took many years to appear, and F Frith & Co was in the vanguard of its development. Postcards became a hugely popular means of communication and sold in their millions. Frith's company took full advantage of this boom and soon became the major publisher of photographic view postcards.

Francis Frith died in 1898 at his villa in Cannes, his great project still growing. His sons Eustace and Cyril continued their father's monumental task, expanding the number of views offered to the public and recording more and more places in Britain, as the coasts and countryside were opened up to mass travel. The archive Frith created continued in business for another seventy years. By 1970 it contained over a third of a million pictures of 7,000 cities, towns and villages. The massive photographic record Frith has left to us stands as a living monument to a special and very remarkable man.

This book shows the Isle of Man as it was photographed by this world-famous archive at various periods in its development over the past 150 years. Every photograph was taken for a specific commercial purpose, which explains why the selection may not show every aspect of the island's landscape. However, the photographs, compiled from one of the world's most celebrated archives, provide an important and absorbing record of the Isle of Man.

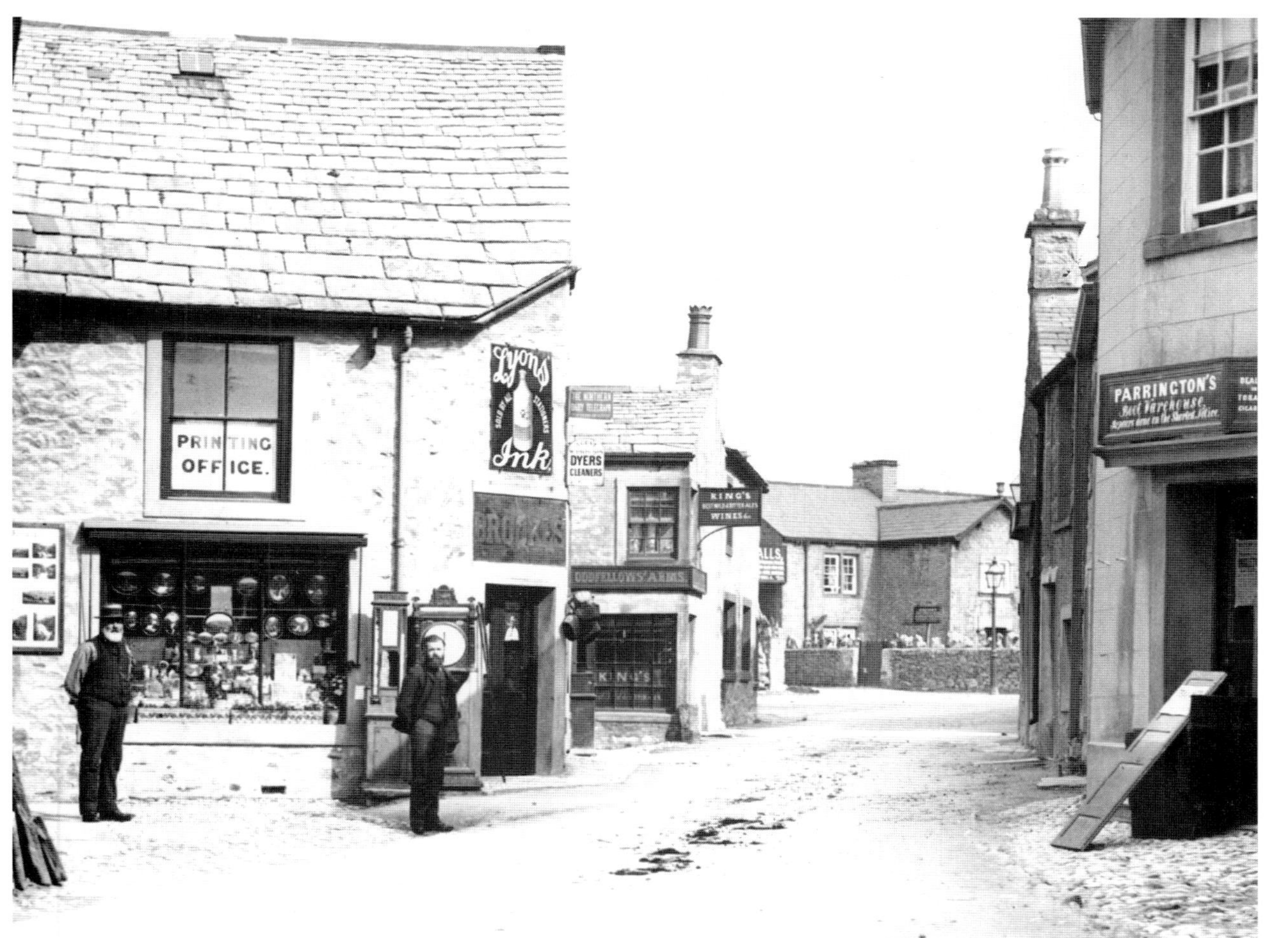

Douglas from the air

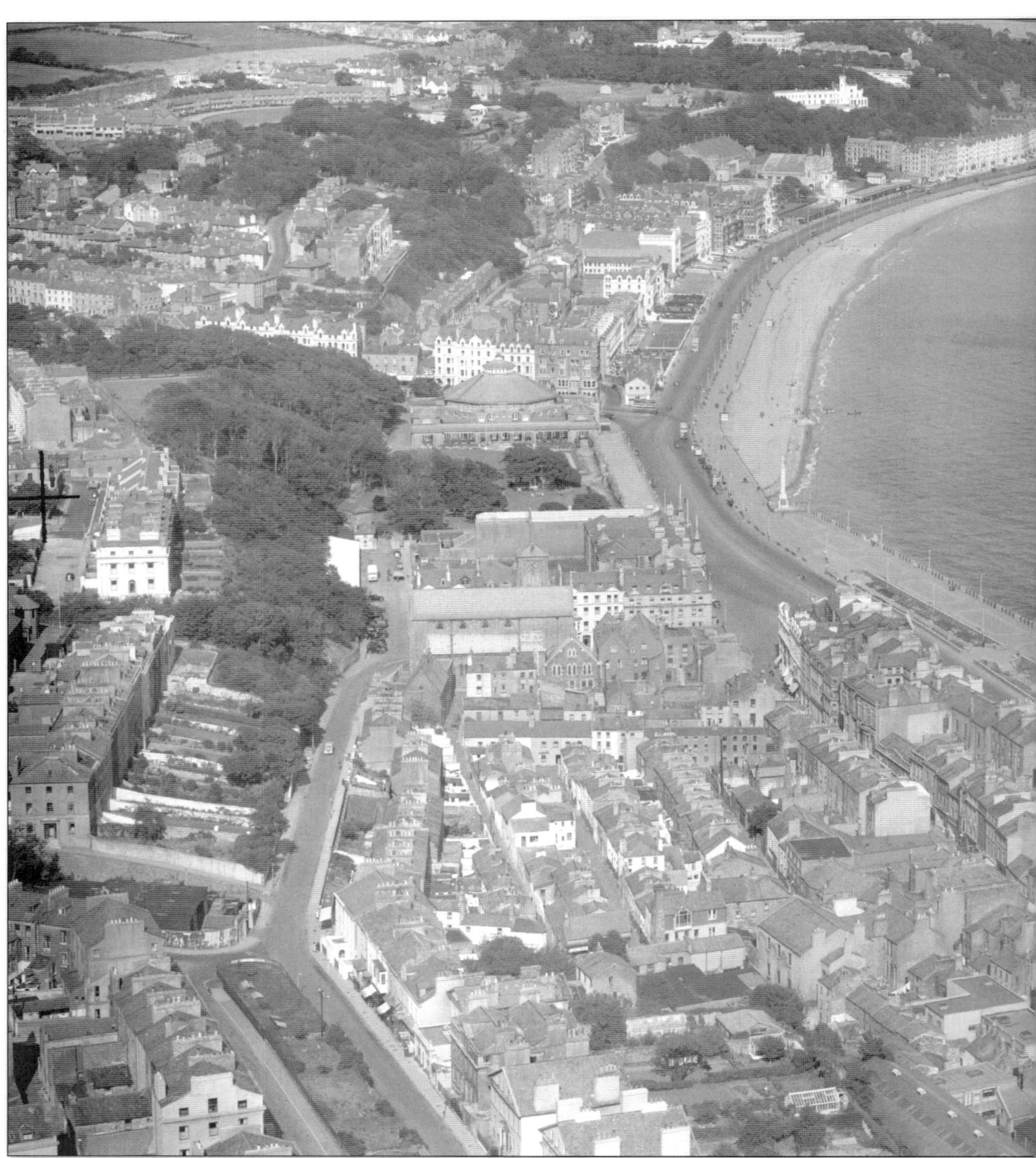

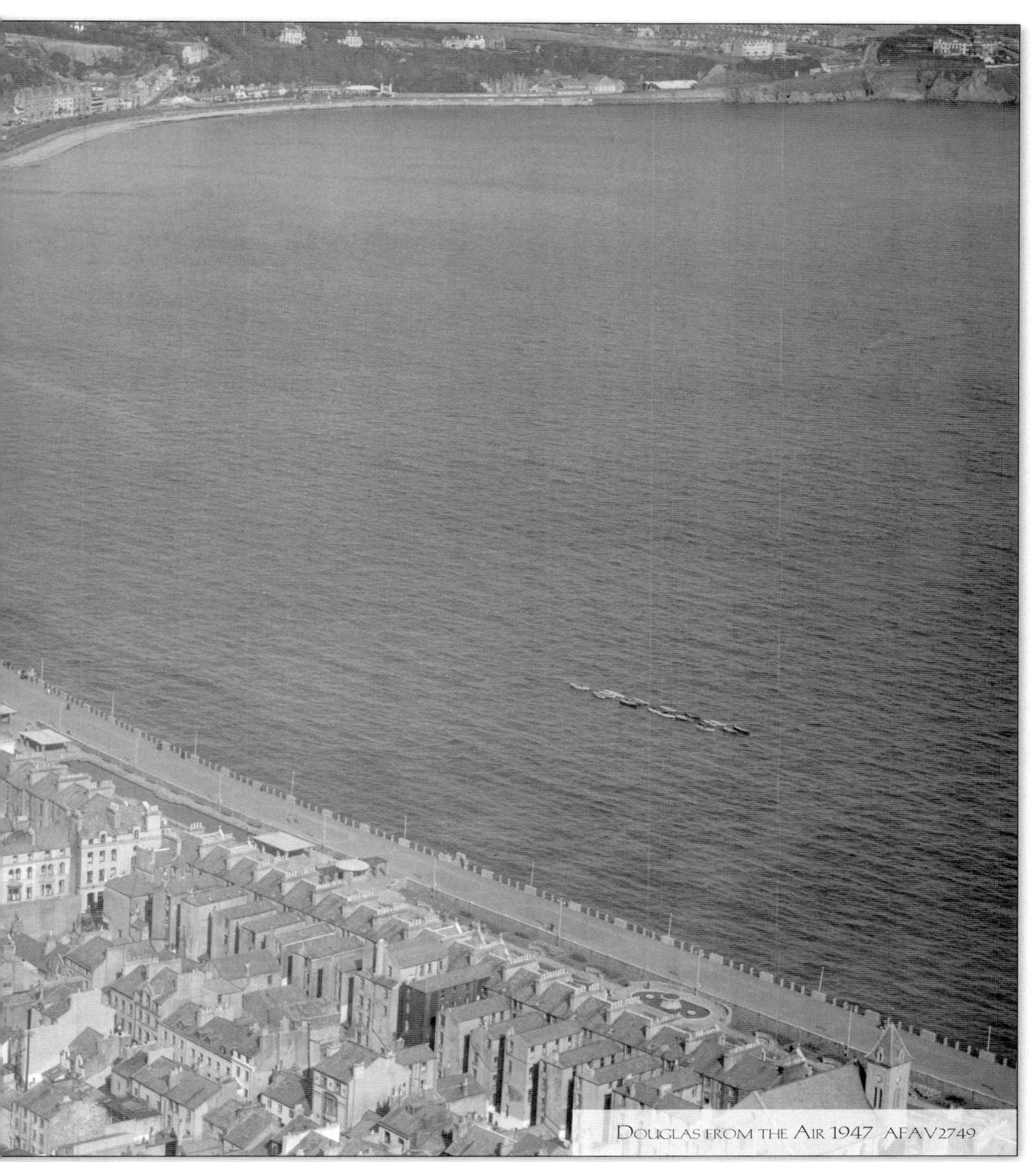

DOUGLAS FROM THE AIR 1947 AFAV2749

The Isle of Man - An Introduction

Much of the island's early history is entwined with that of the Western Isles and the Vikings. In 1066 Harald Hardrada, King of Norway, launched his ill-fated invasion of England and met his death at Stamford Bridge. One of Harald's allies was a chieftain named Godred Crovan, who following the defeat is said to have sought refuge on Man prior to moving to Islay in the Western Isles. After two abortive attempts, Crovan succeeded in mounting a successful invasion of Man in 1079 and reigned there for another sixteen years. It was Crovan who created the Keys, which then consisted of 32 members, sixteen each from Man and the Western Isles. After 1156 only Lewis and Skye continued to send members, four from each island. Following the sale of the Western Isles to Scotland in 1266 only the sixteen Manx members remained, so a further eight members were elected to bring the total back up to twenty-four.

Following Crovan's death the island was plunged into a bloody civil war as two rival chieftains, Ottar and Macmarus, fought each other for supremacy. In a battle at a place called Santwat (which tradition places near Peel), both chieftains were killed, and the island fell into the hands of Magnus Barefoot who arrived in 1098 with 160 longships. Magnus himself was killed in Ireland in 1103; there followed yet more years of confusion until Crovan's youngest son Olaf gained the throne around 1113.

Brought up at the court of Henry I, Olaf reigned for about forty years, during which time the great Cistercian monastery at Rushen Abbey was founded. When Olaf was murdered in 1153 his son Godred was in Norway. Godred's first campaign as King of the Western Isles was to launch an attack against Dublin, but the expedition ended in turmoil when a number of chiefs led by his brother-in-law Somerled, ruler of Argyll, rose in rebellion. In 1156 Godred was defeated in a sea battle off Colonsay and forced to cede territory to Somerled. Two years later Somerled invaded Man and drove out Godred. In 1164 Somerled was killed whilst campaigning against the Scots, and with Norwegian assistance Godred regained Man. He reigned until his death in 1187; the following year his body was taken to Iona for burial.

Norse rule continued until 1265 when King Magnus declared his allegiance to Alexander III of Scotland. The Scots ruled Man for less than a hundred years, for in 1333 it was taken by Edward III. In 1399 the unpopular Richard II was campaigning in Ireland when his cousin Henry took advantage of the situation and seized the throne for himself, reigning as Henry IV. It would be a reign marked by wars against Scotland and the Welsh, and open rebellion from the barons, notably the Percy family. At Shrewsbury on 21st July 1403 Henry IV fought a combined English and Scottish army led by Henry Percy. Taking part in the battle on the king's side were Sir Hugh and Sir John Stanley. Sir John was lord lieutenant of Ireland, and it was he who secured the Isle of Man for Henry in 1405. Subsequently Henry IV appointed Stanley Lord of Man on condition that he would present Henry with two falcons on Coronation Day. In order to secure his lines of communication, Stanley was authorised by Henry to fortify the Tower of Liverpool.

The Isle of Man - An Introduction

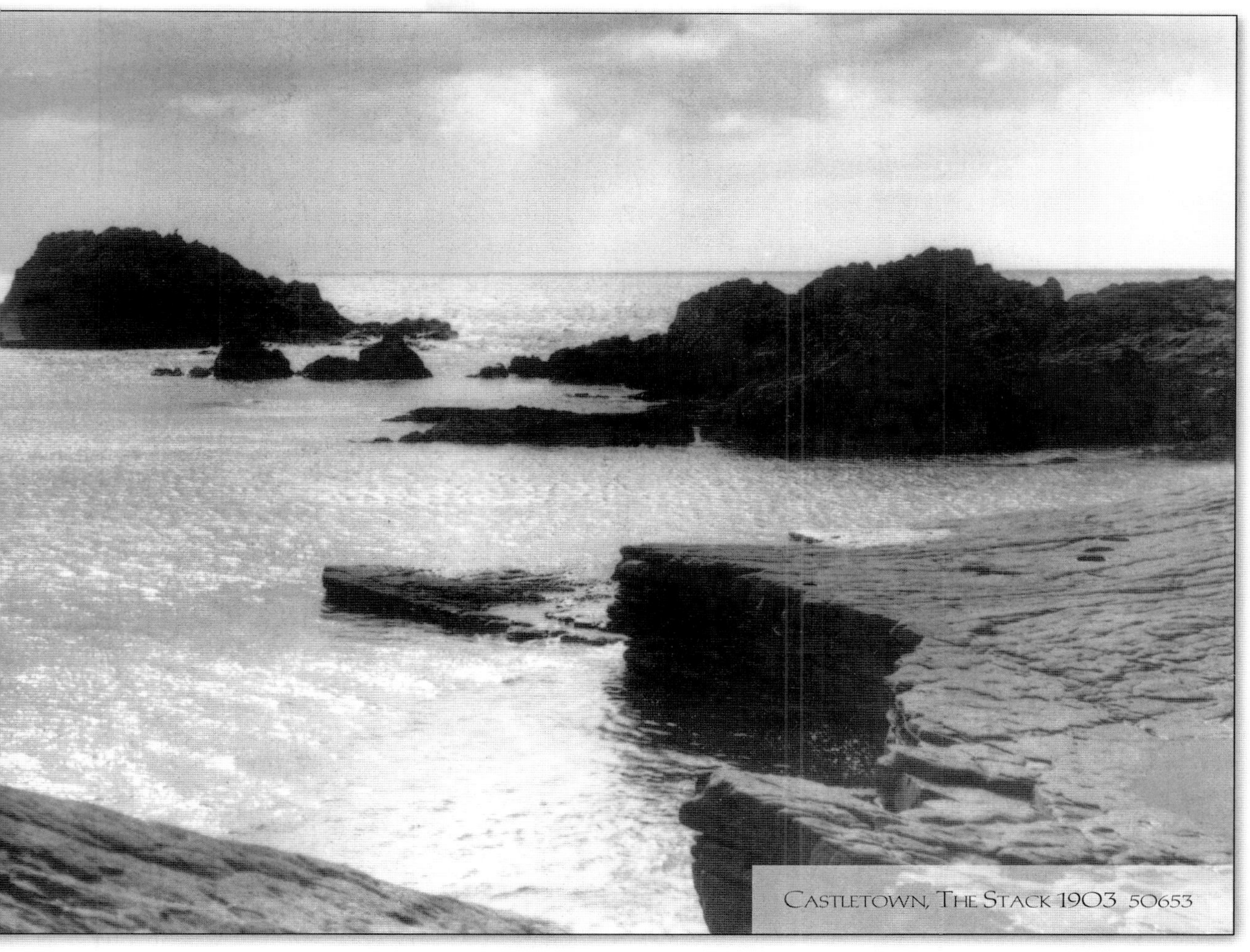
Castletown, The Stack 1903 50653

At Liverpool the Earls of Derby were treated like princes. On one occasion the weather was so bad that the fourth Earl was forced to wait two weeks in the Tower of Liverpool before he could embark for Man. It that time he was entertained to banquets, firework displays and morris dancing; it is also said that he attended church wearing a purple cloak. The Earl's household at the Tower was around 140; it included eight gentlemen waiters, eight grooms of the bedchamber, a chaplain and gentlemen ushers. There were also brewers, bakers, a slaughterman, stablehands and so on.

The Stanley family would rule the Man until 1736. Following the death of James II, tenth Earl of Derby, the Lordship of Man passed to his distant relative James Murray, second Duke of Atholl. James Murray took his responsibilities to heart; it was he who granted a series of reforms that culminated in 1737 with what in effect was a Bill of Rights - the right to trial by jury. In 1765 the Revestment Act led to King George III becoming the first regal Lord of Man. The Atholls were compensated for their losses. The third Duke received £70,000 plus an annuity of £2000, and in 1828 the fourth Duke received a further £417,000.

The Isle of Man and the English Civil War

James Stanley, seventh Earl of Derby, became one of the most popular Lords of Man, earning the title 'Y Stanlagh Moar' - The Great Stanley. It was he who changed the island's land laws. At the beginning of Stanley rule, all land was considered to belong to the king and there were no rights of inheritance. James changed the system: all lands were to be leased for periods of three lives, or 21 years, giving tenants and land-owners some measure of security.

Derby was a devout Royalist; when in 1651 Charles II invaded England from Scotland with an army of 8000 foot and 2000 horse, he obeyed his sovereign's wish that he should join up with him in Lancashire. With Sir Thomas Tyldesley, he sailed from the island on 17 August and landed at the mouth of the Wyre, where Fleetwood is now situated, with a force of about three hundred troops. Parliamentarian warships were sent to blockade the Wyre and cut off Derby's escape route, but the Earl had already left the area and was marching through Catholic Lancashire attempting to raise the county. The response was not great.

Derby reached Wigan where his force was routed, and Sir Thomas Tyldesley killed, by Parliamentarian troops commanded by Robert Lilurne. Derby, though wounded, escaped. He was cared for by Richard Penderel at Boscobel manor before making his way to Worcester, where he joined the king on 31st August. Though the city was well fortified, Charles was betrayed by his cavalry commander Alexander Leslie, who with his men remained inactive throughout the battle. Forced to flee, the king, accompanied by the Duke of Buckingham, Lord Wilmot, the Earl of Derby and about sixty others escaped to Stourbridge. Derby suggested that the king might find shelter with the Penderel family, and he was taken there.

It was at Boscobel that the king put on his disguise, still intent on walking to London 'in a country fellow's habit'. Derby advised him to rub soot on his face and hands and Lord Wilmot cut off his hair. The King was left in the safe hands of the Penderels and Derby and Wilmot made their own escapes. On the day that Charles and Lord Wilmot arrived at Fecamp in France, they learned that the Earl of Derby had been captured and sentenced to death for treason. He was beheaded at Bolton.

Industry and Tourism

Fishing has always been a dangerous occupation. Customs officer David Robinson made a number of visits to Man in the 1780s and 90s, and in 1794 his book 'A Tour Through The Isle of Man' was published. David relates how in 1786 Douglas lighthouse had been all but destroyed in a storm, and all that there was to replace it was a

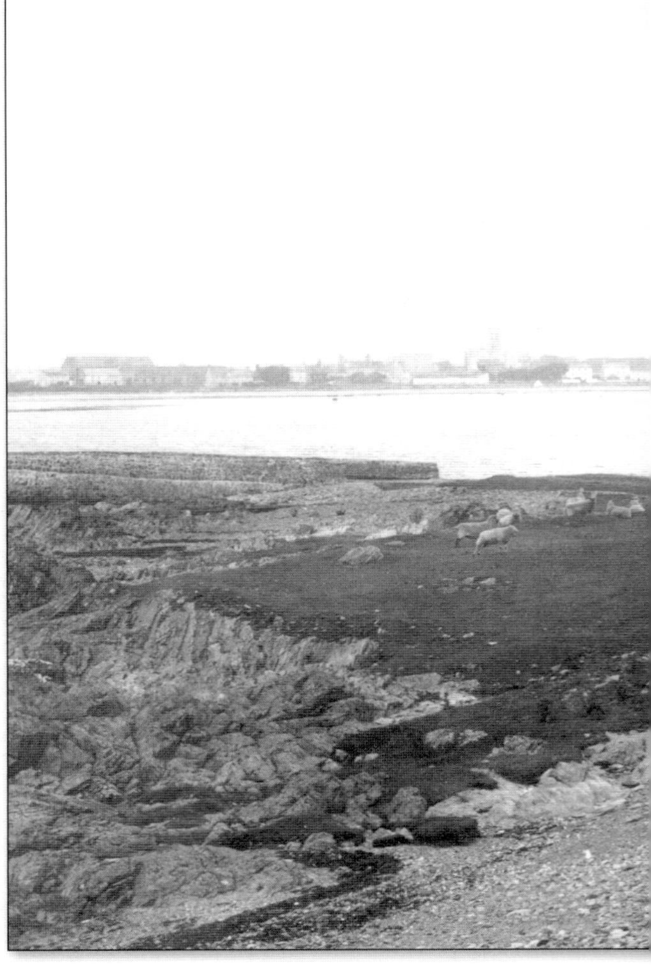

small lantern fixed to a post. In September 1787 David was once again in Douglas. It was the height of the herring season and he estimated that around 400 boats were working the grounds off Clayhead and Laxey. When the fleet had set out the weather had been perfect, but without warning a gale developed forcing the fishermen to head back to Douglas. By the time the first boats were approaching the harbour, high winds and waves were making boat handling difficult. According to David one of the first boats into the harbour somehow managed to dislodge the light, leaving the following craft blind. All hell broke loose. Boats were smashed against rocks and by daybreak the beach was littered with wreckage and bodies.

To encourage exports the British Government offered a bounty

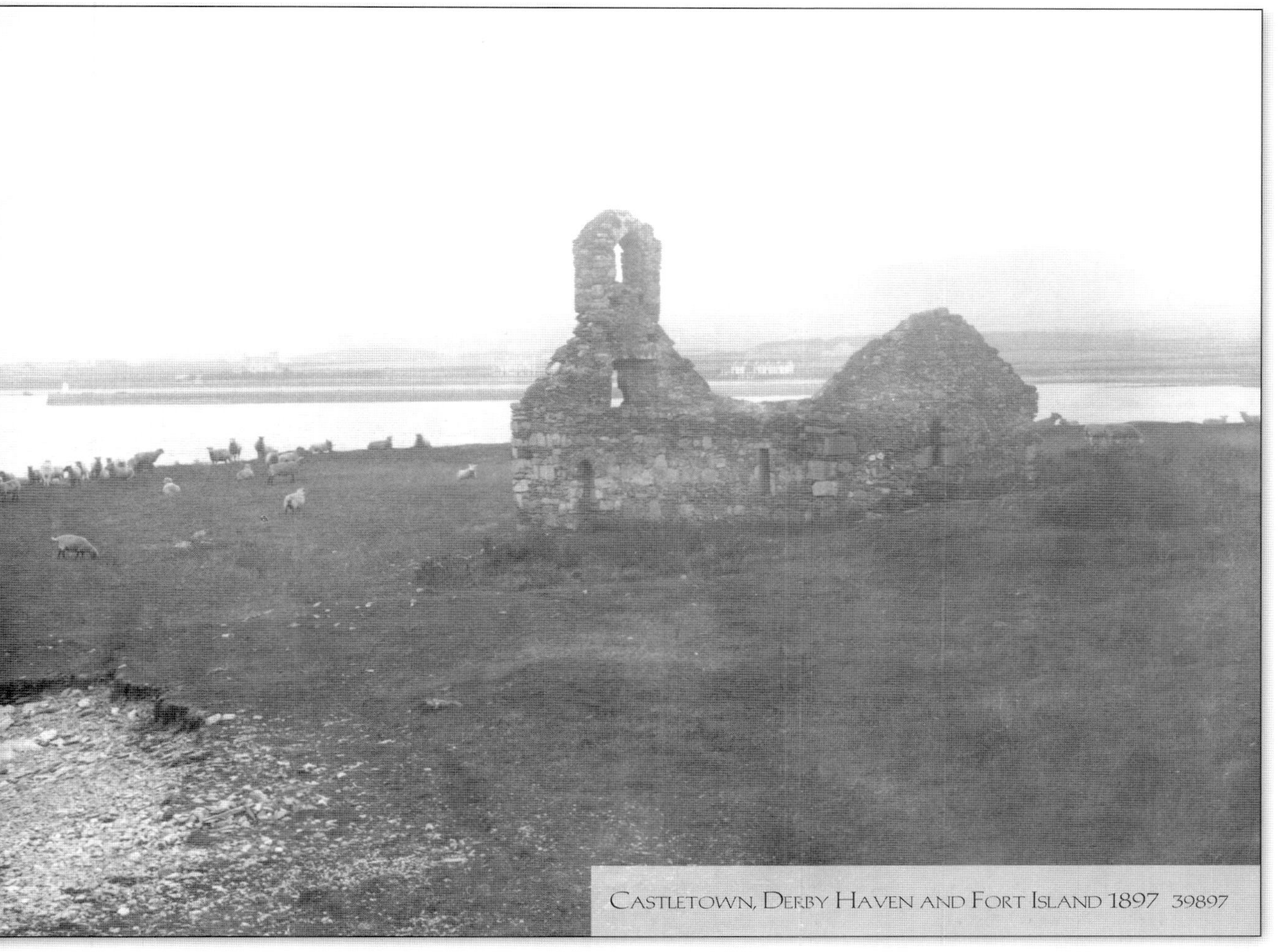

CASTLETOWN, DERBY HAVEN AND FORT ISLAND 1897 39897

of 1s a barrel on herrings destined for the British market, and 2s 6d overseas. The trade was always sensitive to prices. At the beginning of the season, cured white herring would fetch around 3s per hundred - but once the market had been flooded, curers would be lucky to get 1s 6d per hundred. A barrel held about 600 herring; the total cost to the curer was about 12s, and the price at Liverpool docks ranged between £1. 1s and £1. 5s. The art of curing red herring was introduced from Yarmouth in 1771.

A large proportion of the Manx herring catch was sent to Liverpool where it was cured and then shipped to the West Indies as food for slaves. When abolition came in 1834, demand for Manx herrings went into a sharp decline. During the second half of the 19th century it became common practice for boats to go into south-east Irish waters and fish for mackerel from March to June, return to Man for the herring season, and then from October follow the herring into Scottish waters.

The Mischief Act of 1765 attempted to put paid to at least one Manx pastime, smuggling. At least fifty officers and two or three revenue cutters were deployed accordingly. Any inroads they made were soon lost, as smuggling was rife again after 1767 following an Act passed in London setting higher duty levels than those announced by Tynwald. The Act allowed for the import of limited amounts of tea, spirits and tobacco from England, but with smugglers operating to and from the Wirral and remote landing places in Lancashire and

The Isle of Man - An Introduction

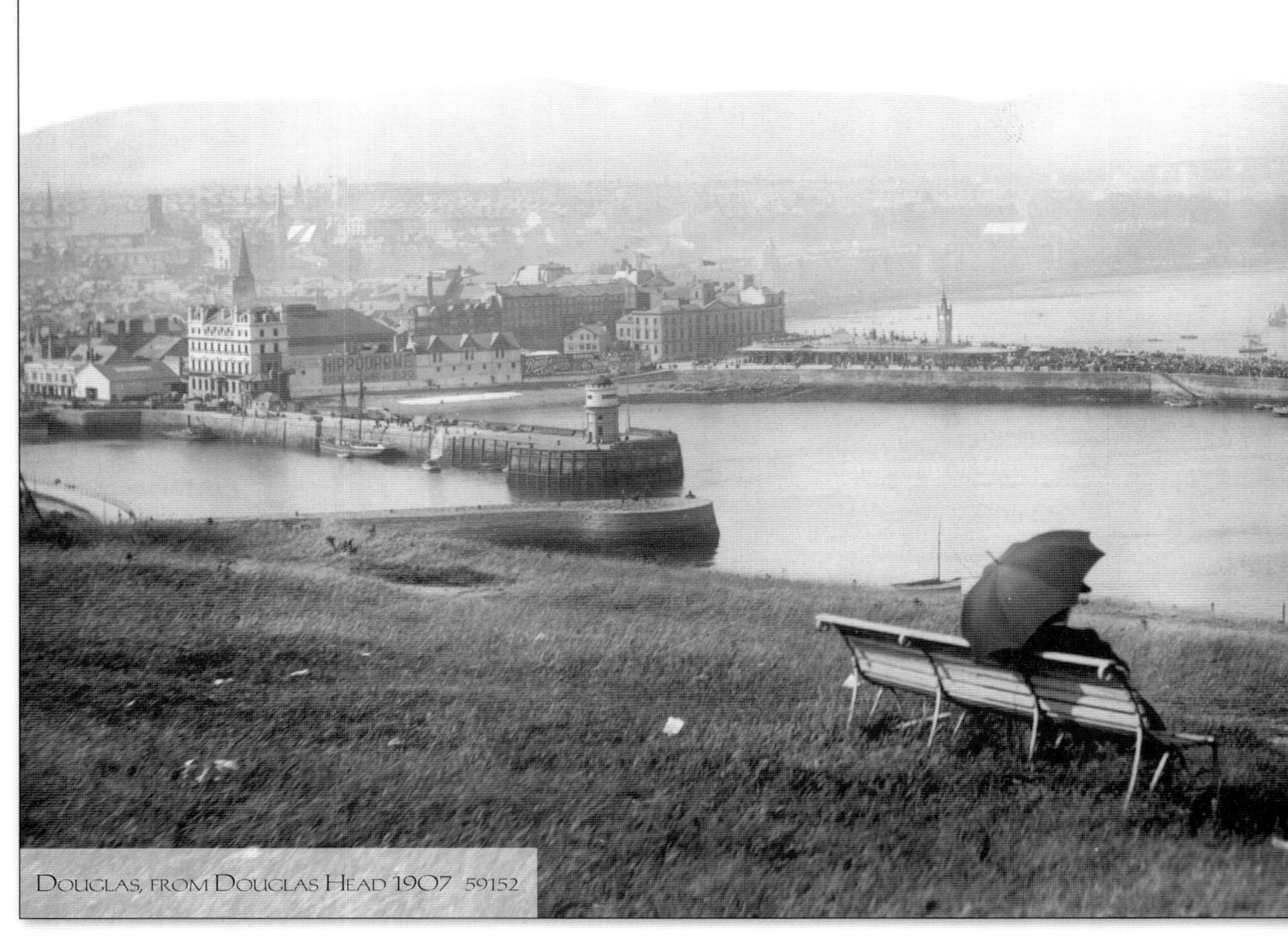

Douglas, from Douglas Head 1907 59152

Scotland, the Manx received all the tea, spirits and tobacco it could handle. No tea or spirits duties were paid to the English for years.

The Manx proved adept at giving the English Government a run for its duty. Around 1823, some bright spark hit on the idea of using the Manx privilege of importing foreign corn duty-free. Corn was bought from bonded warehouses in Liverpool, and no duty was paid. Shipped over to Man, it was ground into flour and then re-exported to England as Manx flour. This scheme worked for six or seven years before customs and excise rumbled it, by which time the shipments totalled about 25,000 quarters a year. Another venture for a little duty-free involved the importation of machinery into the island on false documentation, claiming that it was for use on Man. The machinery was then exported to customers throughout Europe.

The history of mining on Man, like almost anywhere else, is a tale of boom and bust. Over the years mining operations have been carried out at various locations with varying degrees of success. Foxdale was mined for silver and lead; Laxey for lead, silver and some copper; Ballasherlogue, Ballacorkish and Bradda Head for lead and silver; Maughold Head for haematite, and Langness for copper.

One of the earliest references to mining is a license granted by Edward I to John Comyn, Earl of Buchan, to dig for lead on the Calf of Man. Edward was desperate for lead; he needed it for the string

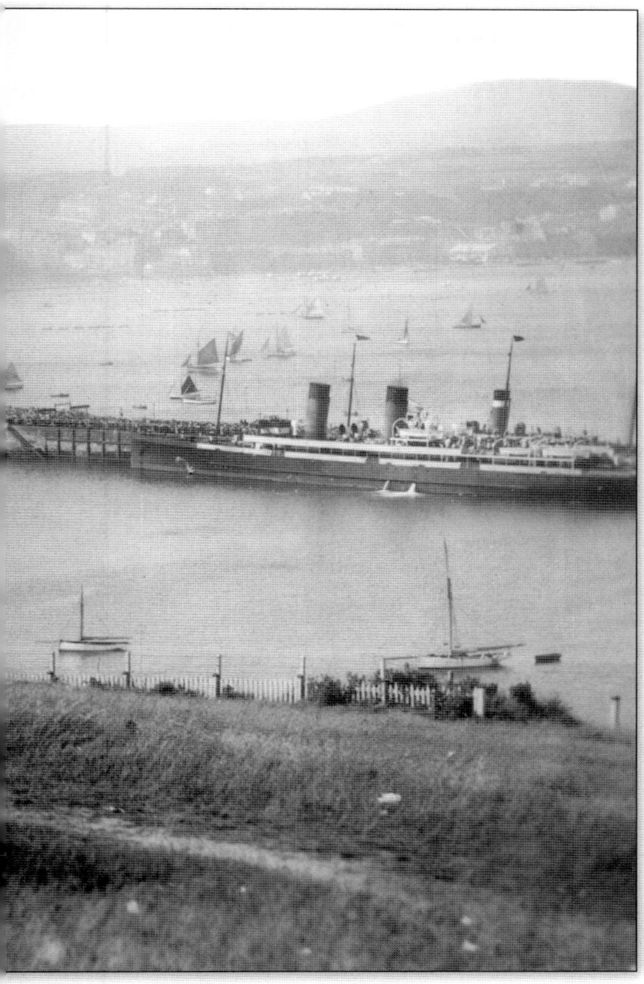

of castles he was building to subjugate Wales. In 1708 John Murray held leases from the Lord of Man on all Manx lead and copper mines on a royalty payment of £3 a tonne. Murray seems to have mined around thirty to forty tonnes a year, but by 1715 he had given up his leases and from then on mining appears to have been carried out on an ad hoc basis.

In 1823 both Laxey and Foxdale were reopened, and the haematite mine at Maughold in 1837. The 1830s and 40s were prosperous years for the Manx mining industry, and from 1870 to the 1880s lead and silver production remained at record levels. During these latter years the industry as a whole was employing over 1000 people, and the Laxey mine was shipping ore worth around £90,000 a year.

Cotton spinning was introduced on Man in 1779 when a mill was opened at Ballasalla, and all went well until 1791 when customs officials at Liverpool realised that it was operating in violation of an Act of 1765 which prohibited the importation of foreign goods, except for flax and hemp, into Britain via Man. The mill was forced to close, though by 1798 cotton yarns or cotton cloth from Man were being landed at mainland ports free of duty.

There was also a limited amount of shipbuilding on the island. The Bath Yard at Douglas was capable of building vessels up to 500 cwt, and the steamer King Orry was built there in 1841. Small yards were opened at Ramsey (1834) and Peel (1835), turning out fishing boats and schooners.

During the 19th century tourism grew to such an extent that it dominated the island's economy. In the 1830s, around 25,000 tourists a year braved the unpredictable Irish Sea to visit the island, making the crossing in the ships of the Isle of Man Steam Packet Co and the St George Steam Packet Co. By the 1860s the figure had risen to about 60,000 a year and was still climbing; the 100,000 barrier was broken in the early 1870s. By the beginning of the 20th century well over 400,000 visitors a year came to the island, and a new record was set during the 1913 summer season when the total reached 600,000.

In 1906 visitors could travel to the island from a number of ports. From Liverpool there were two sailings a day with additional services on Fridays and Saturdays. The fares were 3s 6d, or 6s single, 10s 6d return, and the same fare was charged to both Douglas and Ramsey. Other ports offering services were Fleetwood, Heysham, Barrow, Glasgow via Ardrossan, and Silloth via Whitehaven. The sailings from Silloth were twice weekly during the summer season; the Whitehaven route was one sailing per fortnight, but during July and August it was increased to three times weekly. In addition there were regular steamer services to Belfast and Dublin.

The 1948 season produced a record 625,000 visitors; it seemed as if the tourist industry had simply picked up the ball from where it had been dropped at the start of the Second World War. Tourism continued to be the mainstay of the economy for a number of years, but by the mid-1950s the decline was noticeable. The real slump came in the 1960s as people's expectations changed. Package holidays, the popularity of holidays abroad, and the massive growth in private car ownership all influenced people's choice of holiday. By the mid-1980s the number of visitors to the island was about the same as it had been in the 1880s, and the provision of financial services had become the island's principal source of income.

THE TRANSPORT REVOLUTION

Improved communications both to and from Man, and within Man itself, played a vital role in the economic growth of the island. Prior to 1767 there were few scheduled shipping services between Man and the mainland, apart from a monthly freight run operated by two sixty-tonne sloops. However, following the transfer of the island's sovereignty to the Crown of England, communications were improved with the introduction of a weekly mail packet service between Douglas and Whitehaven. Trade expanded, and by the early 19th century scheduled freight and packet services linked the island with a number of west coast ports.

Regular steamship services between Douglas and Liverpool were begun in 1822 by the St George Steam Packet Co, and throughout the summer service was adequate. Winter sailings appear to have been sporadic. West coast steamship companies may have been either unable or unwilling to provide the level of year-round services that Man required, a direct result of which was the formation of the Manx-owned Mona's Isle Company in December 1829. The StGSPC retaliated by starting a price war, and soon both companies were slashing fares; the lowest ever advertised by the StGSPC was just 6d each way. The StGSPC also transferred their fast steamer St George from their Irish route to the Isle of Man run in the hope of speeding up the crossing time between Douglas and Liverpool, but unfortunately she was wrecked on Conister Rock a few weeks later, having lost her lost her cable while attempting to ride out a storm. In July 1831 the StGSPC threw in the towel and abandoned all services to Man.

In 1832 the Mona's Isle Co changed its name to the Isle of Man United Steam Packet Co, and bought a second vessel. Three years later the company changed its name once more by dropping the 'United' from its title. Over the next hundred and fifty years the IOMSPCo would not only play a major role in the development of the island, but its ships would serve with

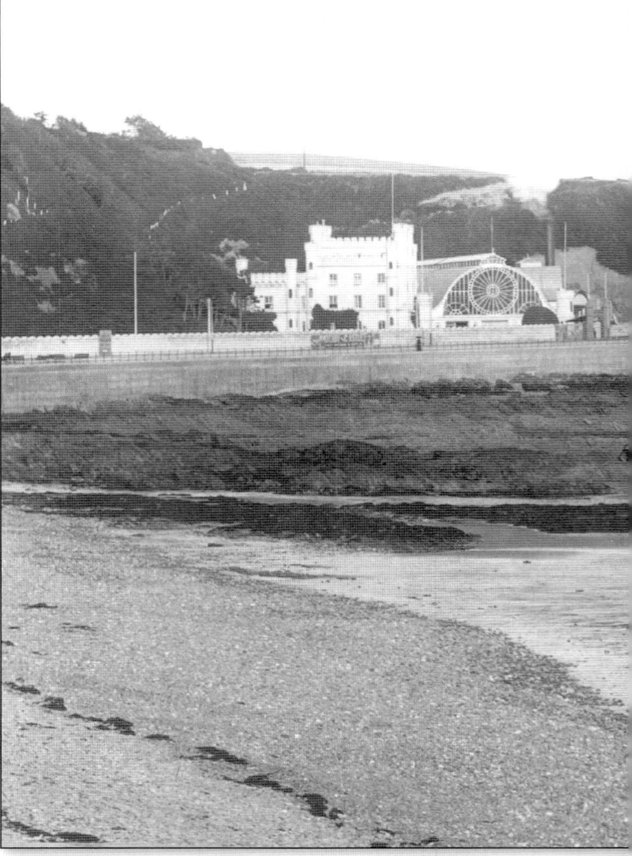

distinction in two world wars. By 1880 Manx shipping comprised 185 sailing vessels totalling 9344 grt, and nine steamers totalling 2816 grt; by 1895 the fleet stood at 103 sailing vessels of 7953 grt and 22 steamers of 4897 grt. Another Manx shipping company, the Ramsey Steamship Co, was founded in 1914 to take advantage of a niche in the market for coastal traffic using the smaller Manx and other Irish Sea ports.

The Isle of Man Railway Company was registered in 1870, the aim being to provide rail links between the island's principal towns and Douglas. The line between Douglas and Peel opened for traffic on 2 July 1873, and was followed by the Douglas to Port Erin line on 1 August 1874. The railway adopted the 3 ft gauge used extensively in Ireland, which was cheaper to construct per track mile than the standard gauge used on the mainland. Traffic returns for 1878 included 526,546 passengers and 23,374 tons of freight carried,

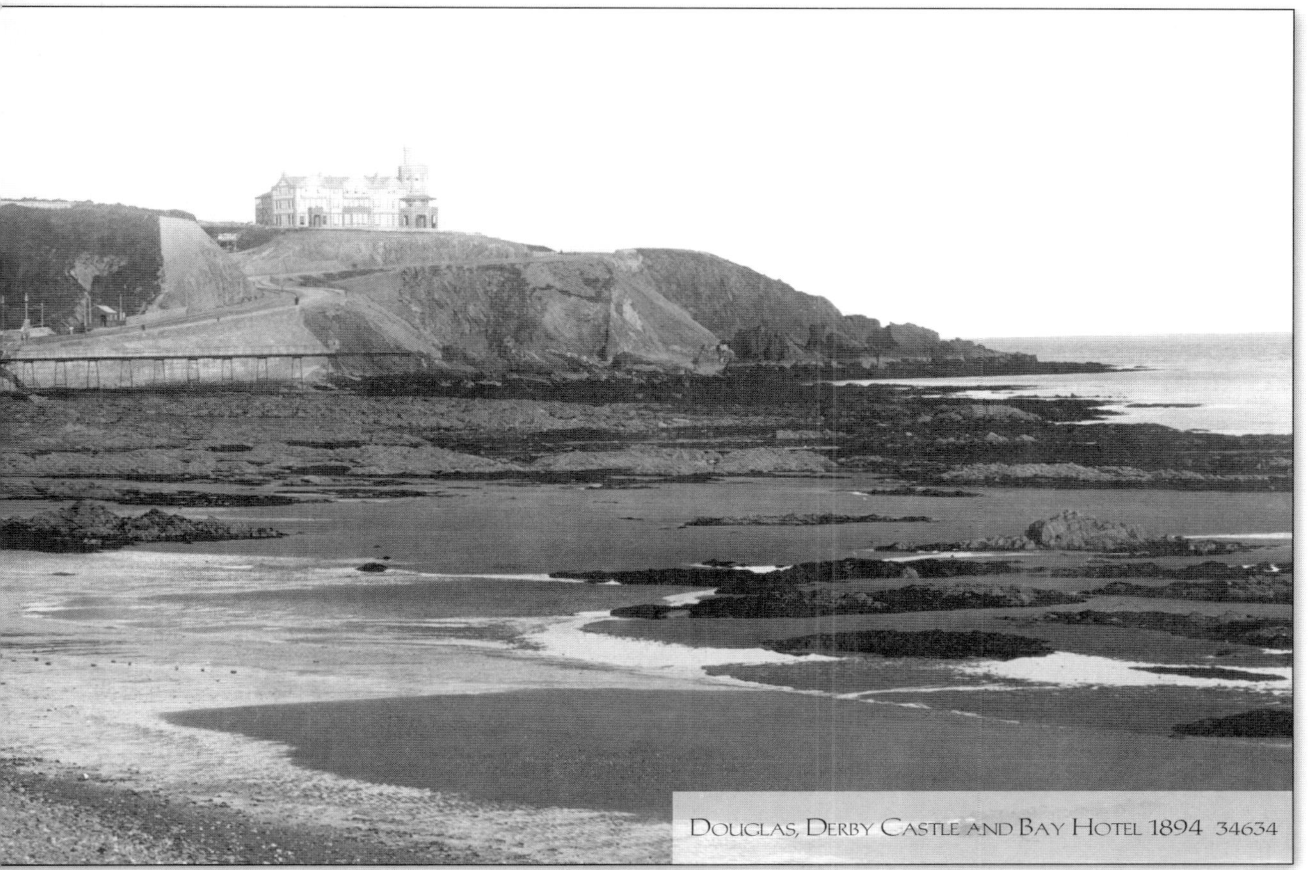

DOUGLAS, DERBY CASTLE AND BAY HOTEL 1894 34634

giving net receipts of £10,454. Even so, the company was strapped for cash, and the proposed line from St John's to Ramsey looked doubtful. In 1877 a new company, the Manx Northern Railway, had stepped into the breach, their line opening for traffic in September 1879. The MNR also leased the Foxdale Railway (which had been promoted in 1882 by Charles Forman, a civil engineer) primarily to provide rail access for the mines at Foxdale, though a passenger service was later added. Having signed a fifty year lease, the MNR were expecting a good return - but the Foxdale line never lived up to expectations. Cheaper ores were becoming available from overseas, and in April 1911 the mining company went into liquidation. The Foxdale Railway was such a drain on the resources of the MNR that by the beginning of the 20th century it was in serious financial trouble. In 1904 the Isle of Man Railway Co absorbed both the MNR and the Foxdale Railway.

On 7 September 1893, services began on a two-and-a-half-mile single-track electric light railway linking Derby Castle with Groudle Glen. The line was based on the American-type interurban, using single-deck bogie cars running on a reserved track. Within a short time the Douglas & Laxey Coast Electric Tramway was formed, the intention being to take control of the line and to finance the building of a double-track extension to Laxey. Construction was soon under way, and the original Douglas to Groudle Glen section was also double-tracked, services commencing throughout on 28 July 1894. Work then began on a further extension from Laxey to Ramsey, but rugged terrain and heavy civil engineering led to slow going and a strain on the company's financial resources. However, the new extension opened as far as Ballure in August 1898 and to Ramsey in July 1899.

Douglas

Douglas, Port Skillion, the Lighthouse 1895 36730

Douglas Head Lighthouse was erected in 1892, replacing the sixty year old Red Pier light. In 1786 Douglas harbour lighthouse had been destroyed during a storm and not rebuilt. The following year disaster struck the local herring fleet when the temporary light was somehow dislodged during a storm, leaving many of the boats blind. The following morning the beach and rocks were littered with wreckage and bodies.

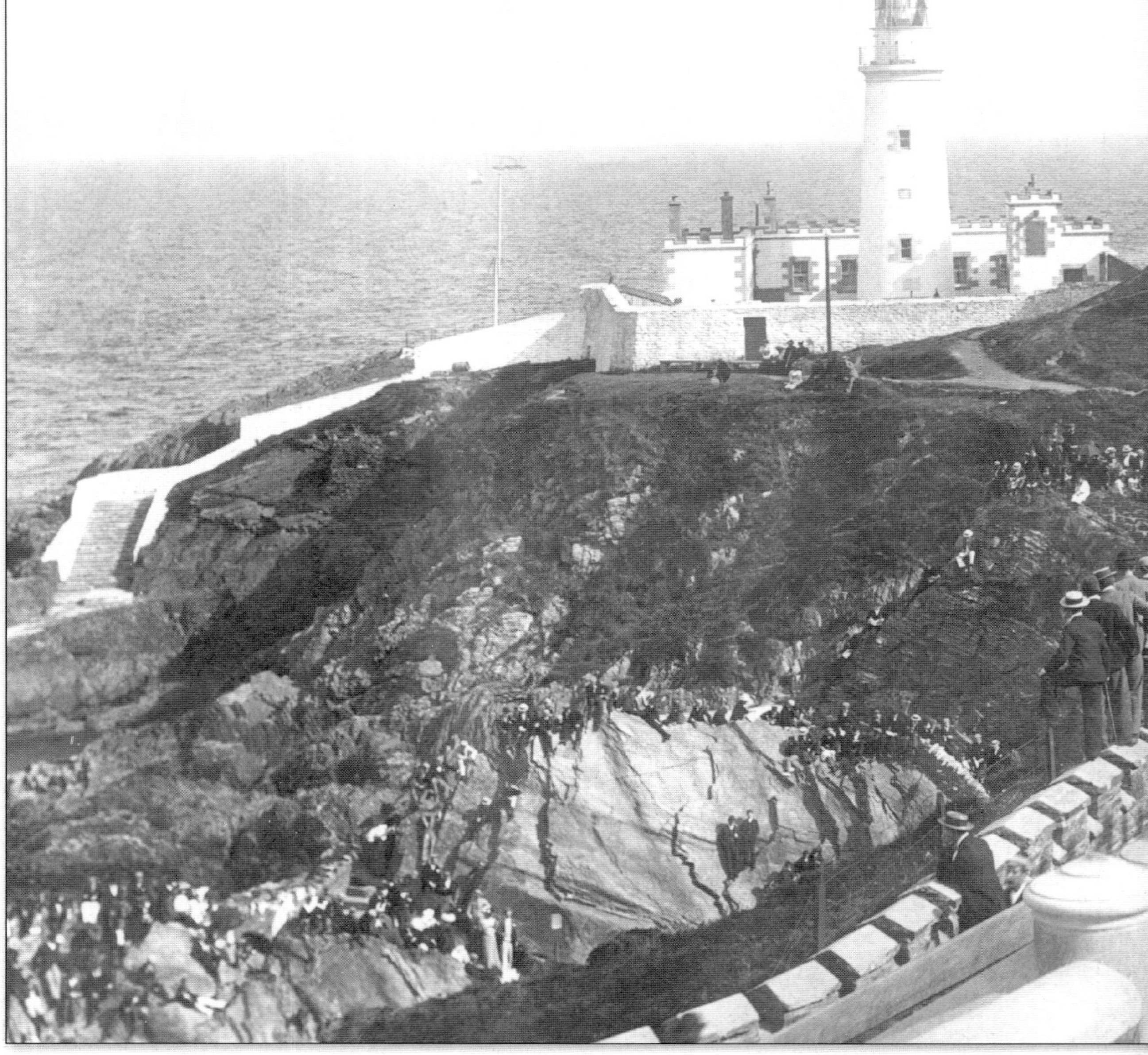

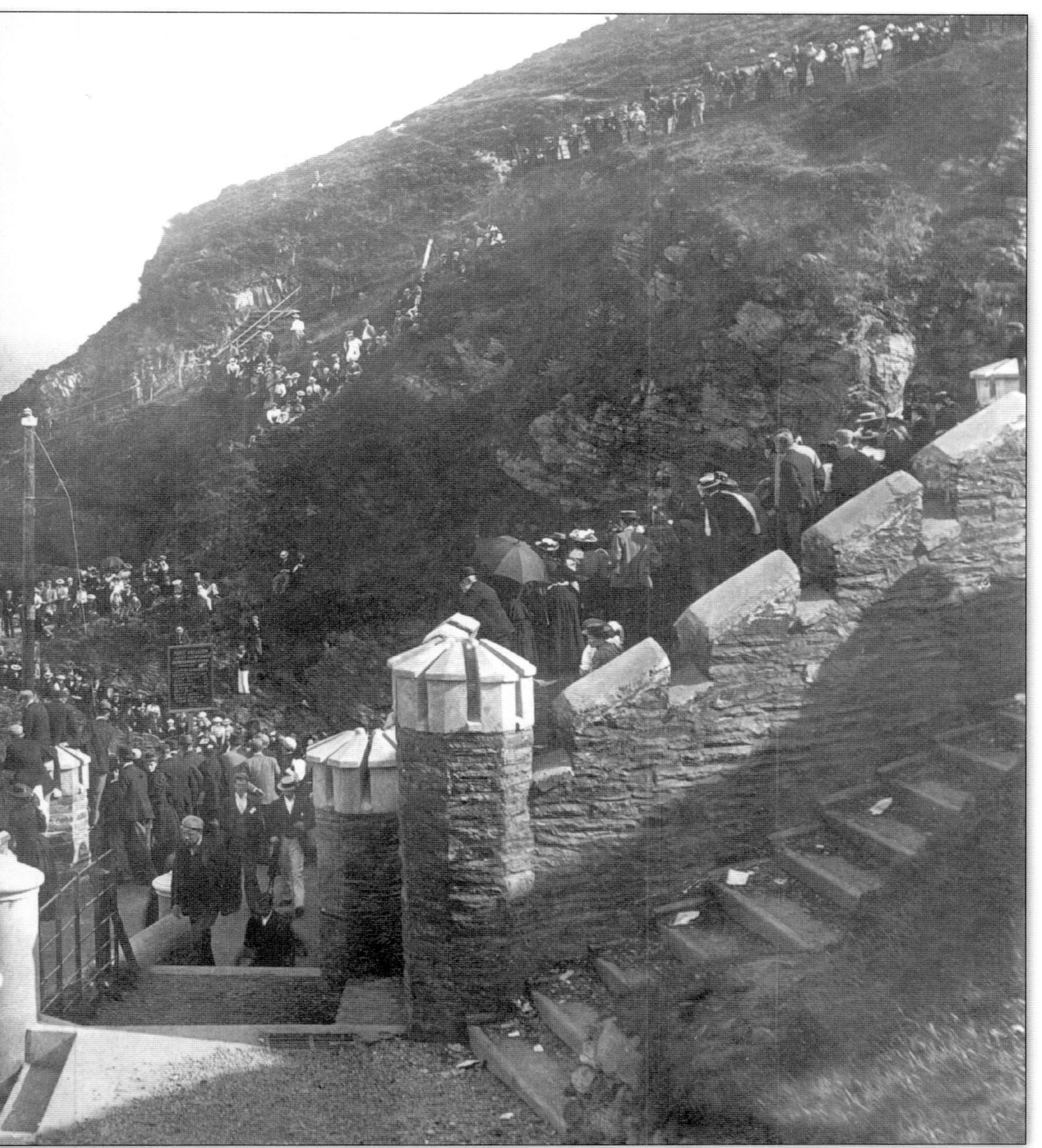

DOUGLAS

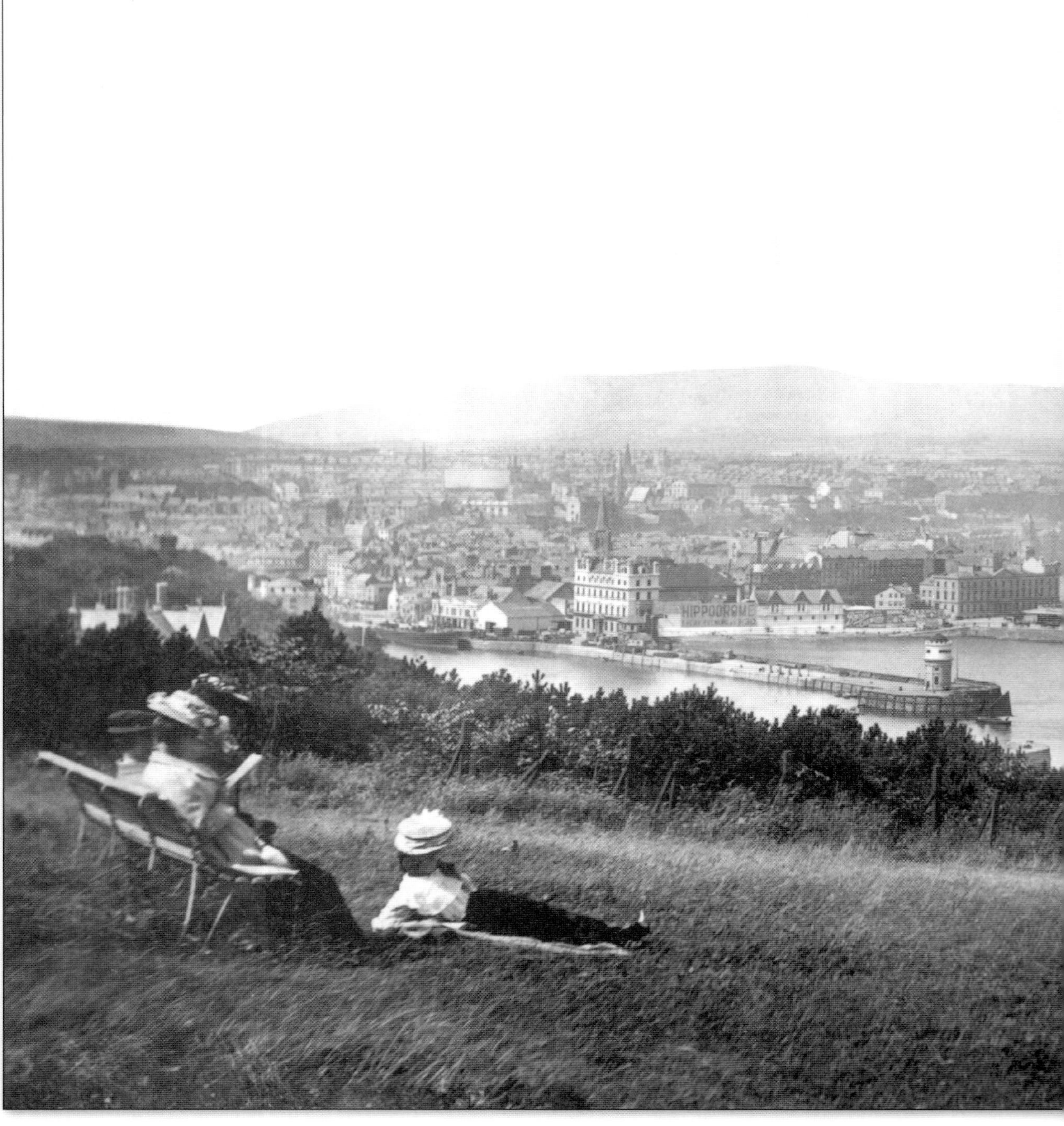

DOUGLAS

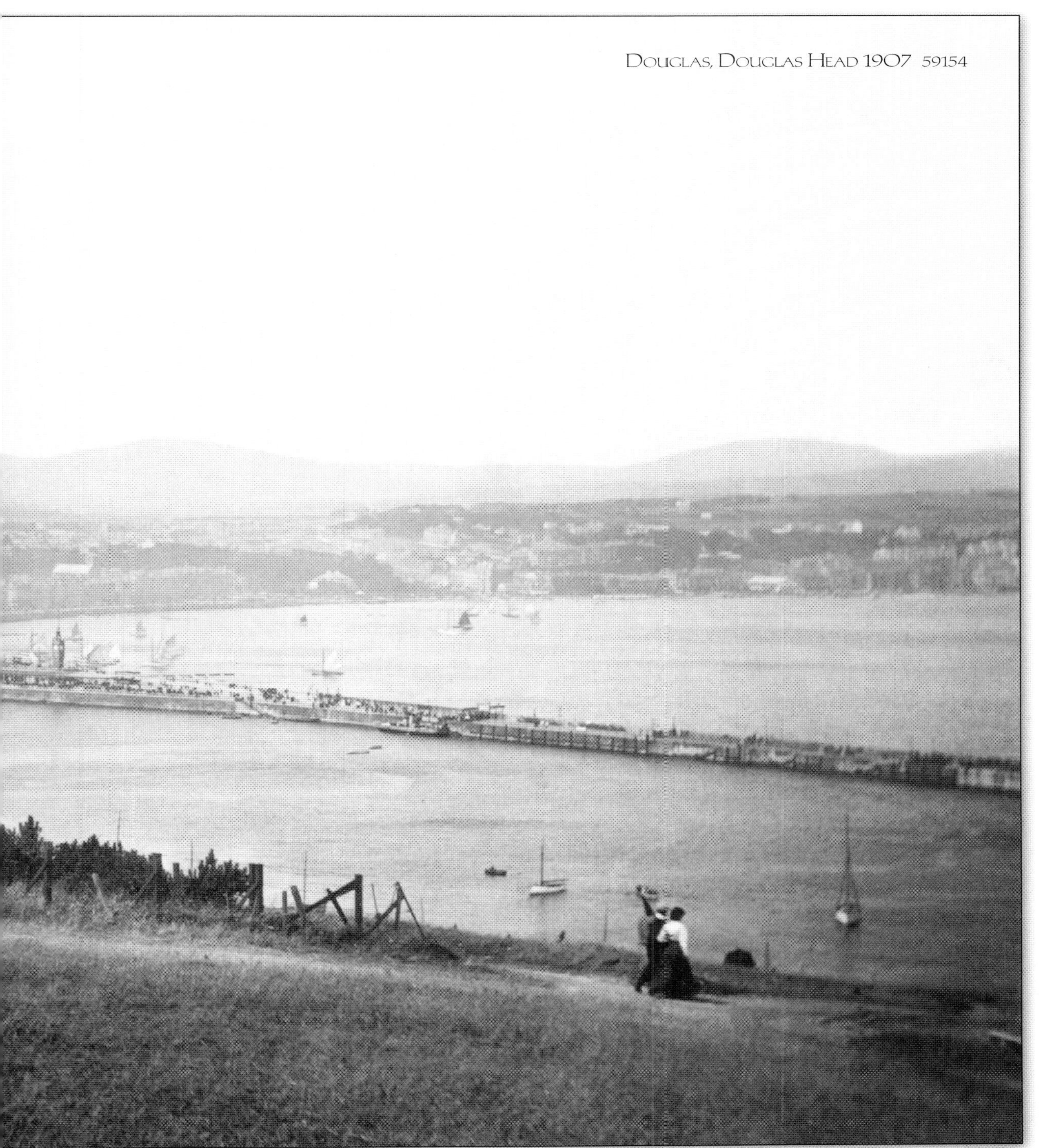

DOUGLAS, DOUGLAS HEAD 1907 59154

Douglas

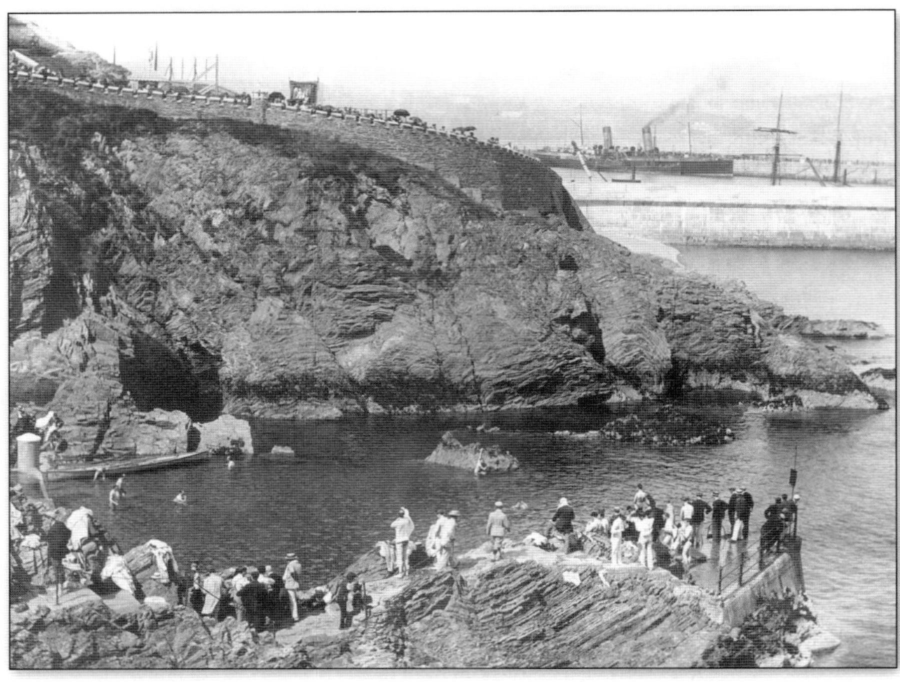

Douglas, Douglas Head 1893 33003

Port Skillion at the foot of Douglas Head was reached by ferry from the harbour, fare 1d, and was used by gentlemen only for open-air bathing. Ladies wishing to avail themselves of the efficacious pleasures to be experienced from sea-bathing were expected to engage the use of a bathing machine.

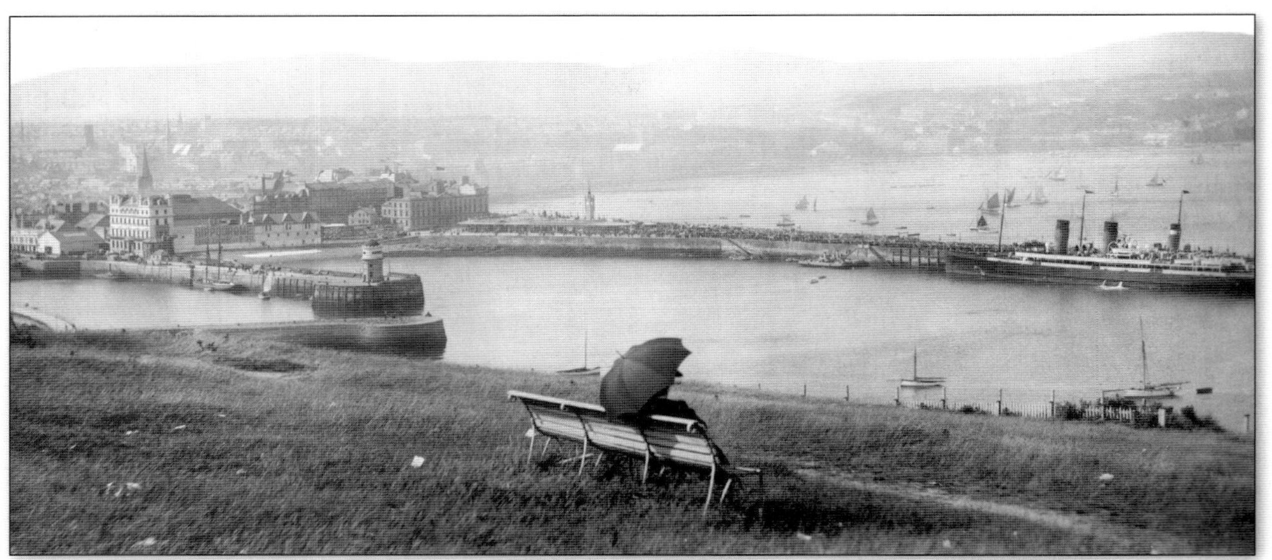

Douglas, From Douglas Head 1907 59152

Between May and September 1887, steamers brought nearly 348,000 visitors to the island, though the IOMSPCo. was forced to slash its fares to beat off competition from two new shipping companies who were trying to muscle in on the ever growing Manx holiday traffic. During the 1900 season over 400,000 visitors landed at Douglas.

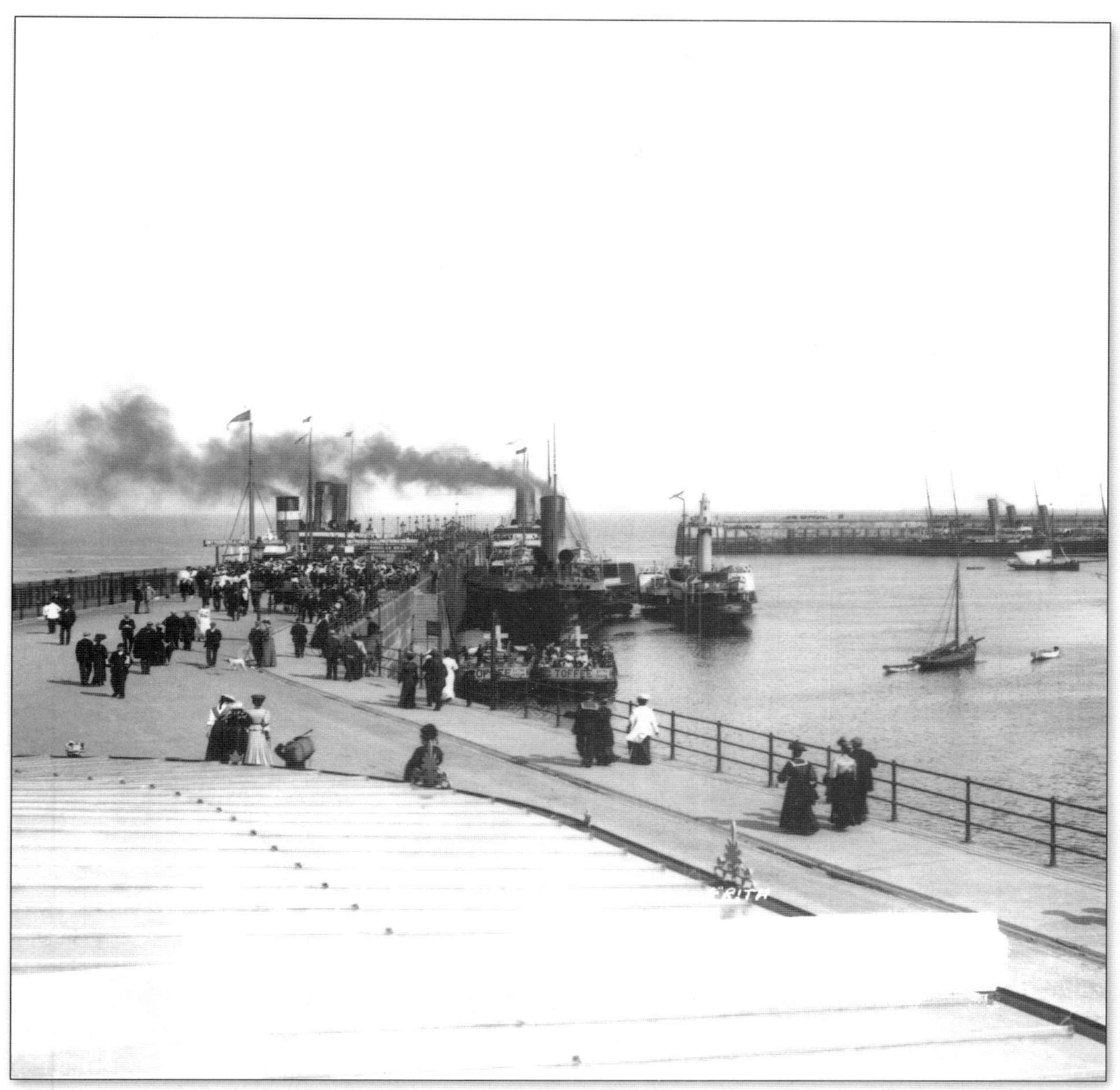

DOUGLAS, VICTORIA PIER 1907 59160A

When the Victoria Pier was completed in 1872 it gave Douglas the facility to handle steamers regardless of the state of the tide. To increase handling capacity the pier was extended in 1888 to a length of 1620 ft. The two small ferries berthed alongside the pier are the 'Rose' and the 'Thistle', which were used on the Douglas Head service. In 1896 the Liverpool & North Wales Steamship Co introduced a summer service from Llandudno.

Douglas

VILLIERS
HOTEL
VILLIERS BUFFET
VILLIERS BUFFET
VILLIERS BUFFET
BALLAQUAYLE RD & BROADWAY
74

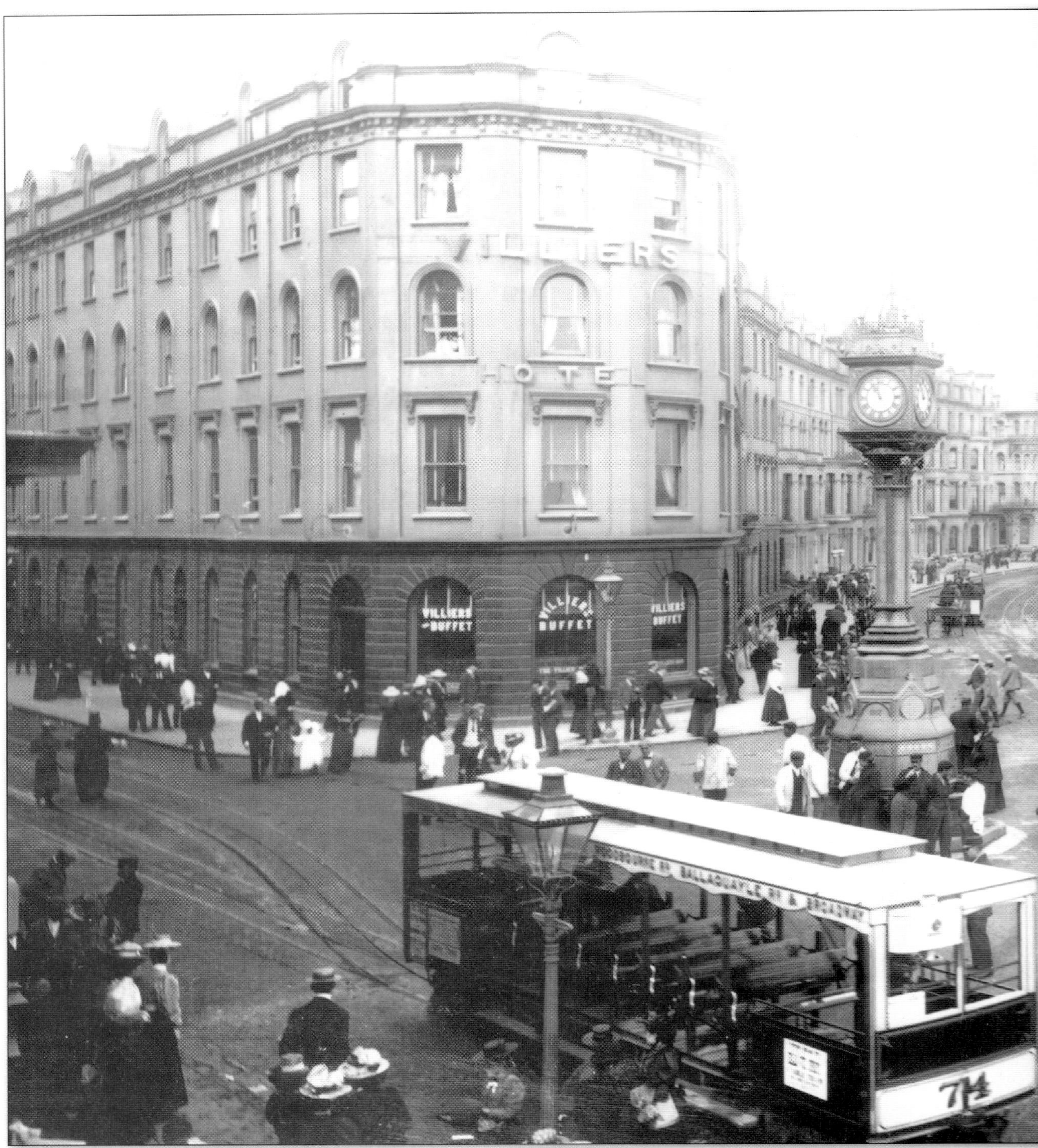

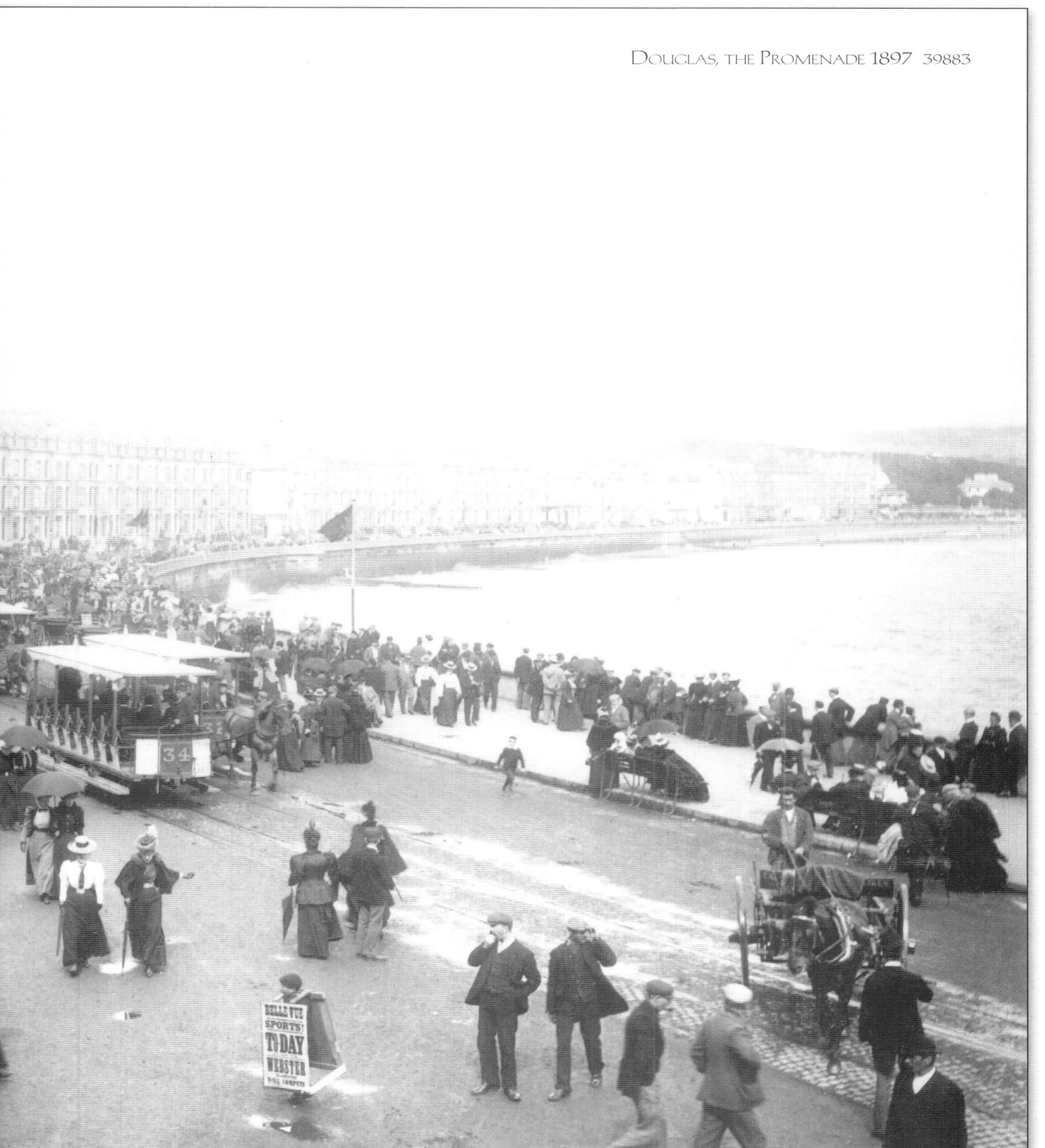

DOUGLAS, THE PROMENADE 1897 39883

DOUGLAS

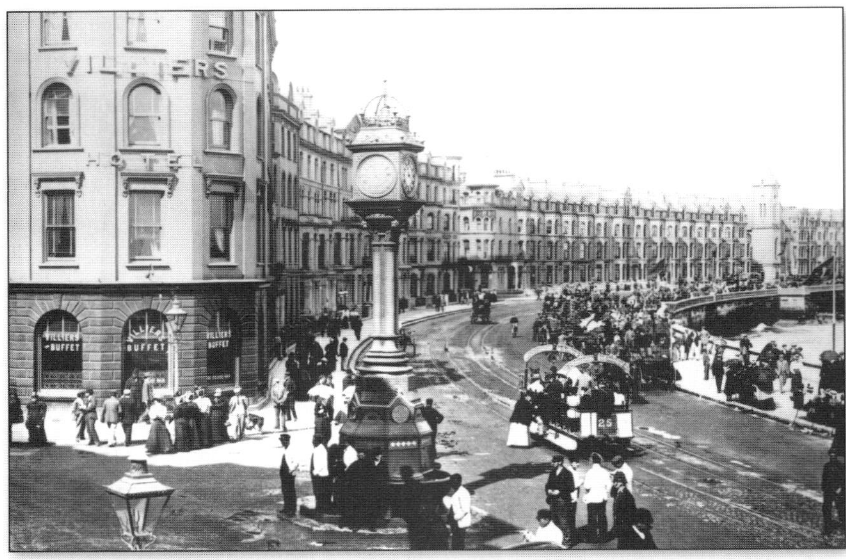

DOUGLAS, THE PROMENADE 1897 39885

The Jubilee Clock at the junction of Victoria Street and Loch Promenade was presented to the people of Douglas by George Dumbell in 1887. Dumbell was a banker, a director of the Laxey mines and a Deemster (justice of the Tynwald), but the failure of his bank on Saturday 3rd February 1900 ('Black Saturday') was one of the greatest financial disasters to hit the island.

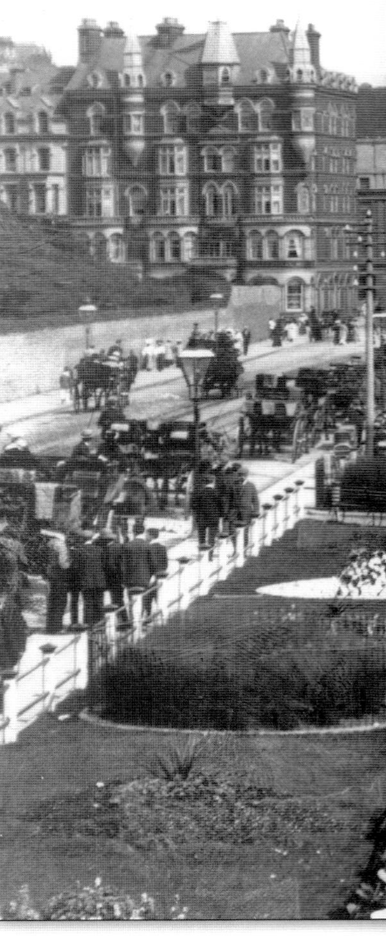

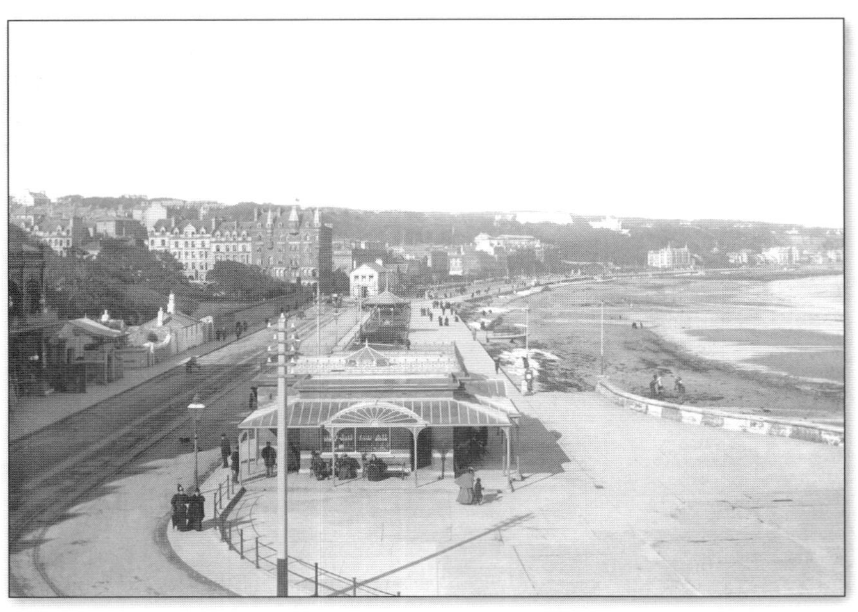

DOUGLAS, THE CENTRAL PROMENADE 1896 38769

The tide is well and truly out in this picture, taken as the shadows lengthen on a summer evening in 1896. Had this picture been taken just a few years earlier it would have featured the Douglas Iron Pier, erected opposite the Central Hotel in 1869; it was dismantled in 1892. Note the white areas on the beach - these are piles of linen from nearby hotels being aired and dried.

DOUGLAS

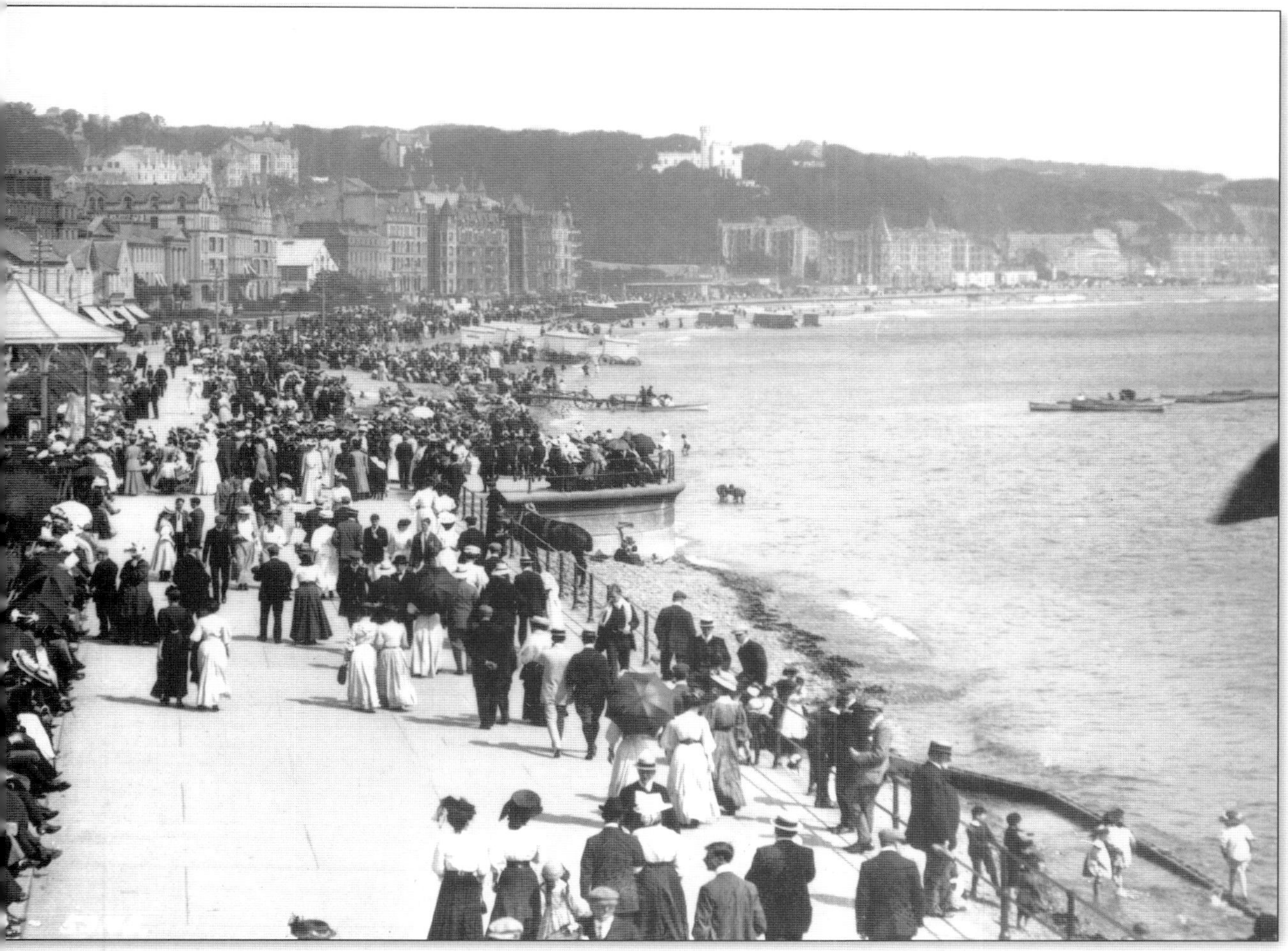

Above: DOUGLAS, HARRIS PROMENADE 1907 59168

Here we see the hustle and bustle of Douglas in high season. The white castle-like structure in the background is the Falcon Cliff Hotel. During the Second World War it was converted to use as a hospital serving the internment camps established at Douglas.

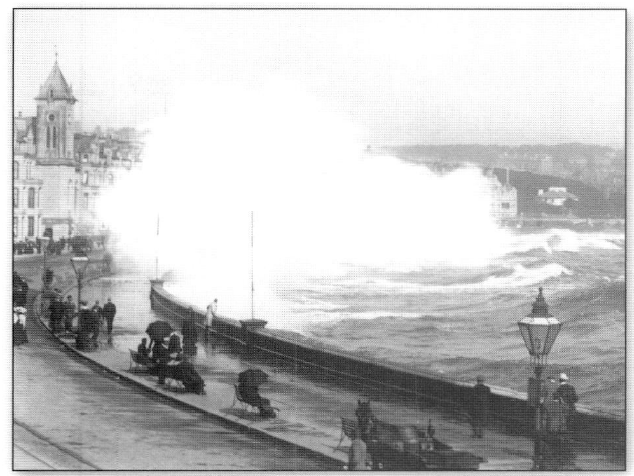

Left: DOUGLAS, A ROUGH SEA 1903 50661

The Irish Sea can be as flat as a mill pond, but when an easterly, south-easterly or north-easterly gale blows up, this is what happens at Douglas. Sir William Hillary, founder of the RNLI, settled in Douglas in 1808. He became so concerned by the loss of seamen in local wrecks that he erected the Tower of Refuge in Douglas Bay.

DOUGLAS

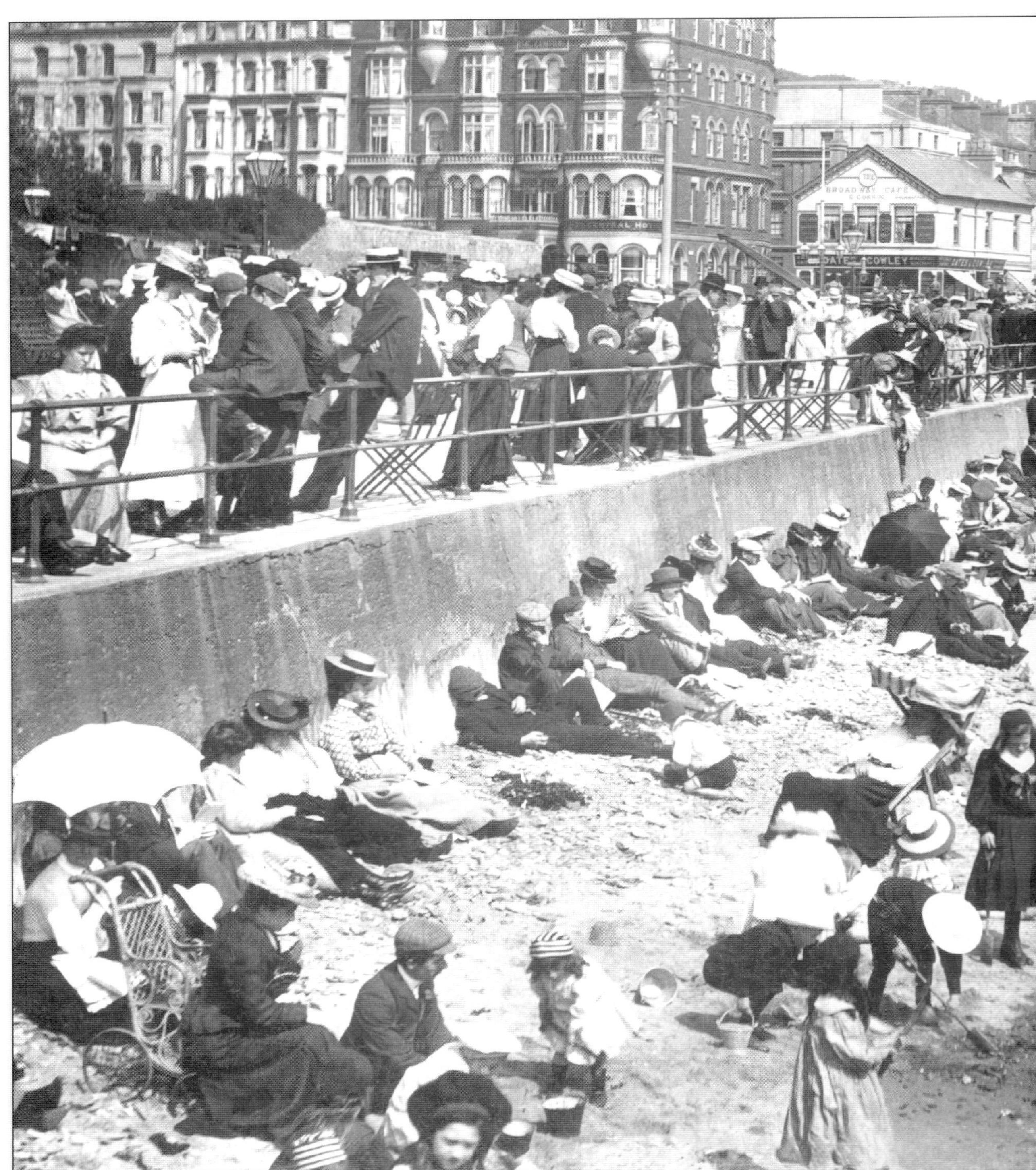

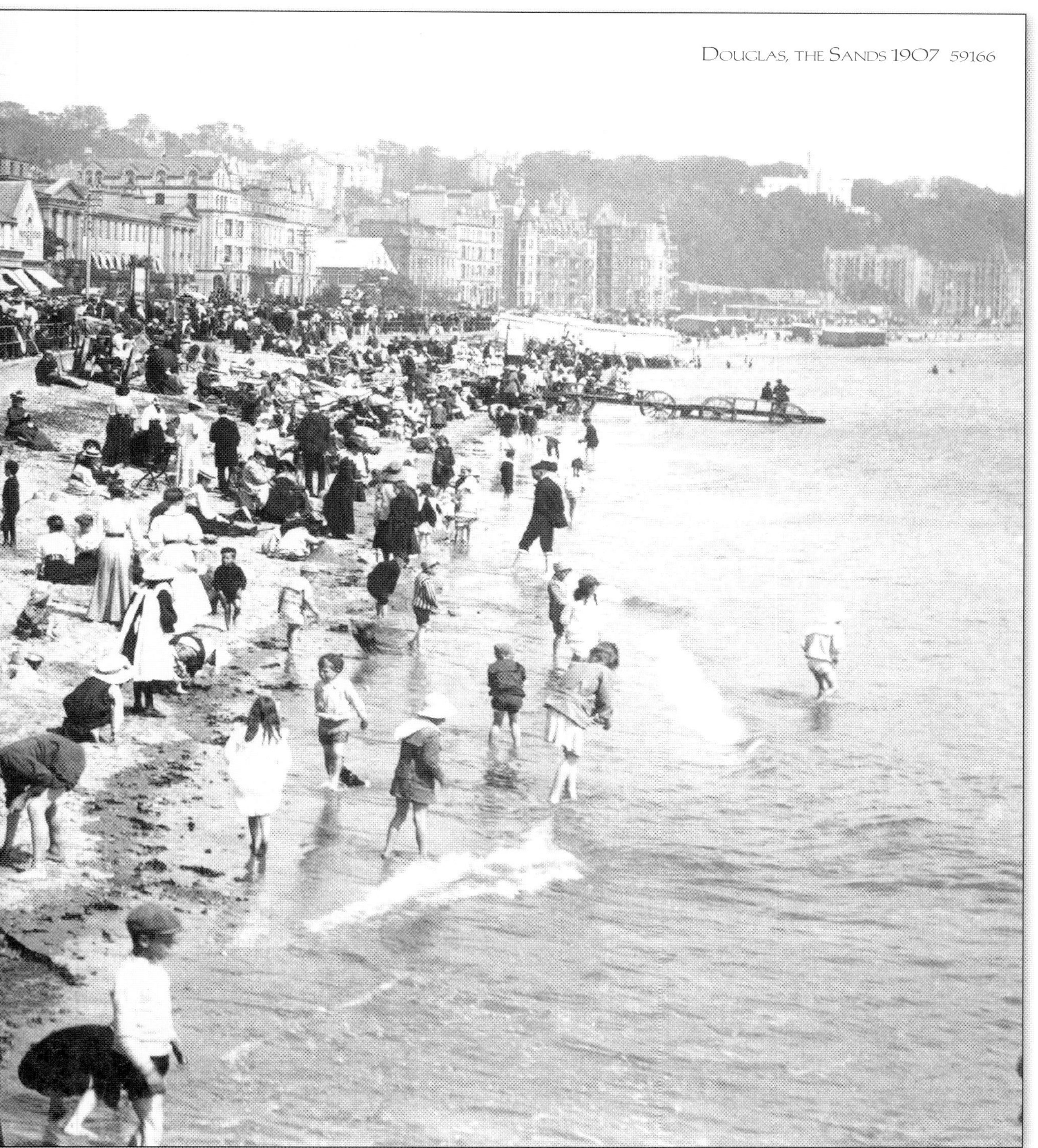

DOUGLAS, THE SANDS 1907 59166

Douglas

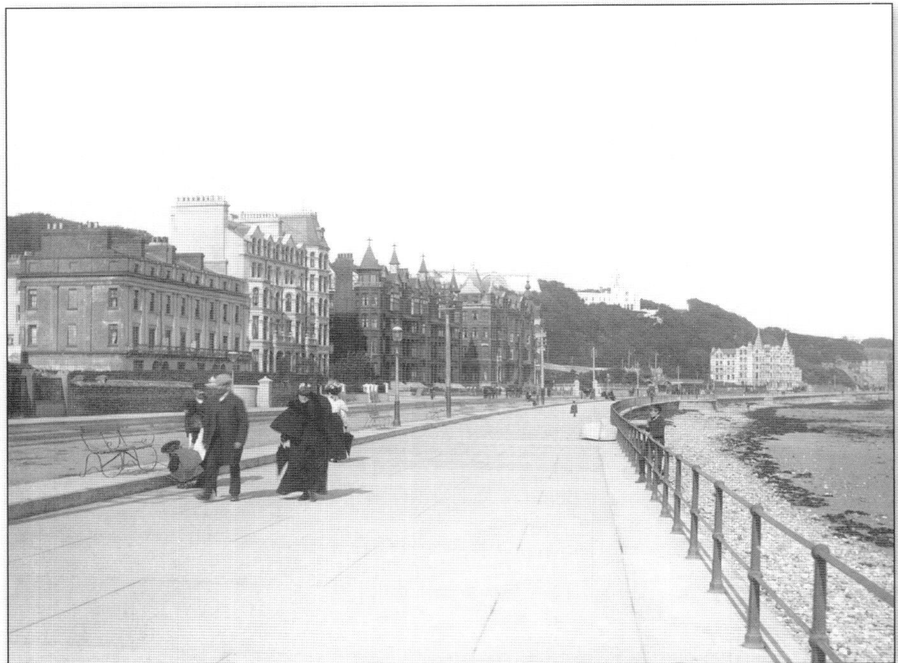

Douglas, The Central Promenade 1896 38770

Prior to the late-Victorian development on this part of the seafront, it would have been possible to see Castle Mona, the residence built in 1804 for Governor James Murray (later Fourth Duke of Atholl) at a cost of £30,000. The residence was converted into a hotel in 1832.

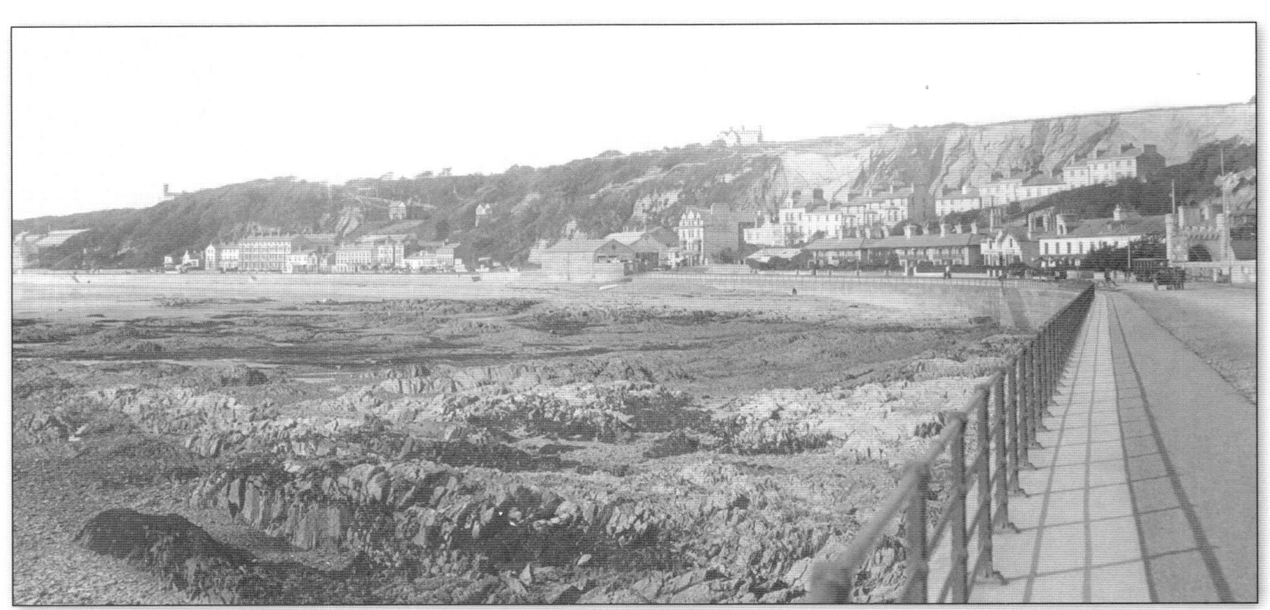

Douglas, The Promenade From Derby Castle 1894 34632

The Falcon Cliff Hotel is little more than a dot on the landscape on the left of the picture. Below that, however, is the imposing bulk of the Palace and New Opera House which opened in 1889 and featured what was then the largest ballroom in Europe.

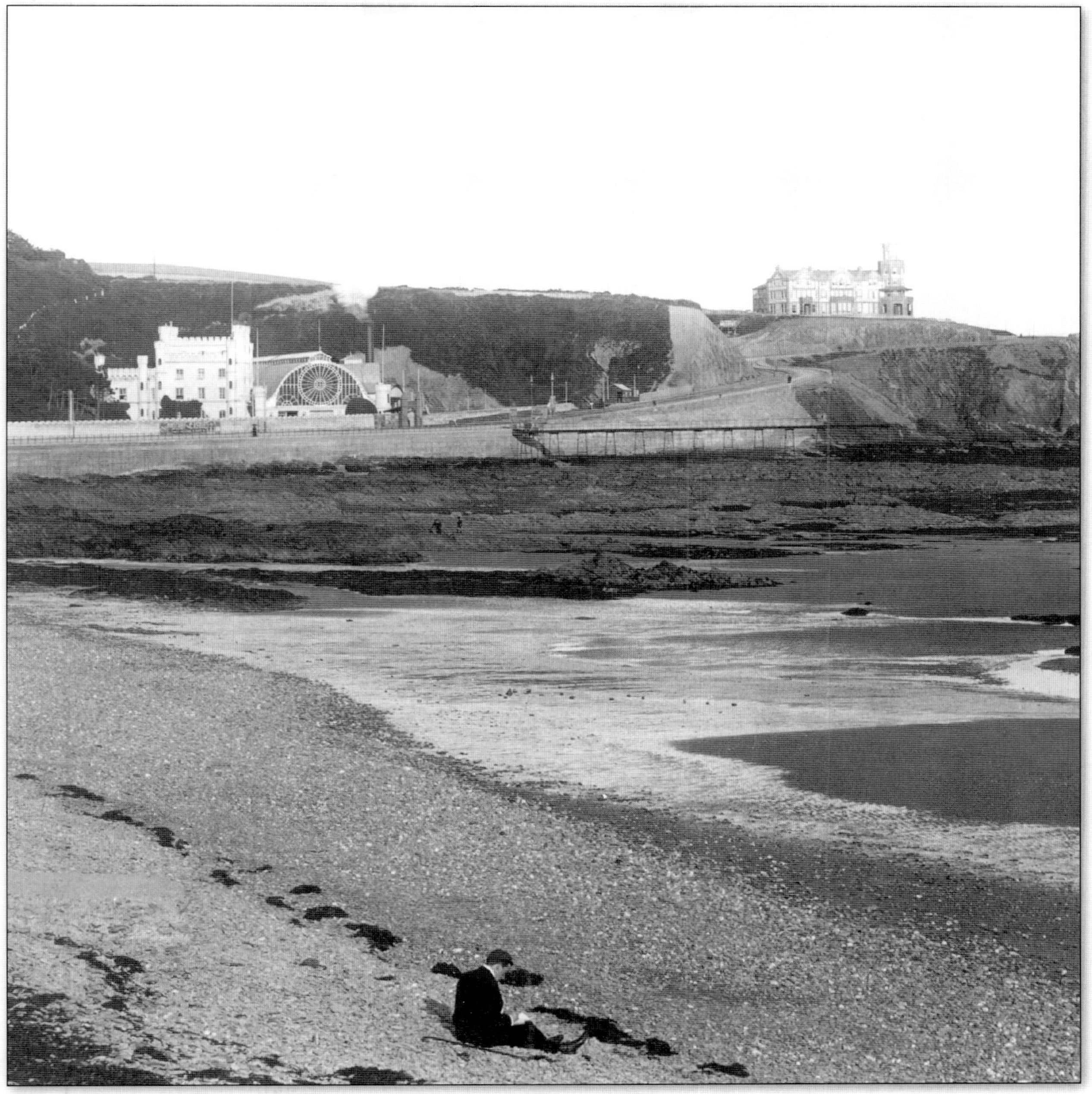

DOUGLAS, DERBY CASTLE AND BAY HOTEL 1894 34634

Built as a private residence in 1834, Derby Castle was converted into an entertainment centre in 1877, featuring variety shows, afternoon concerts and dancing in the ballroom. The site was redeveloped in the early 1970s: the Castle was demolished and replaced by the Summerland complex.

Douglas

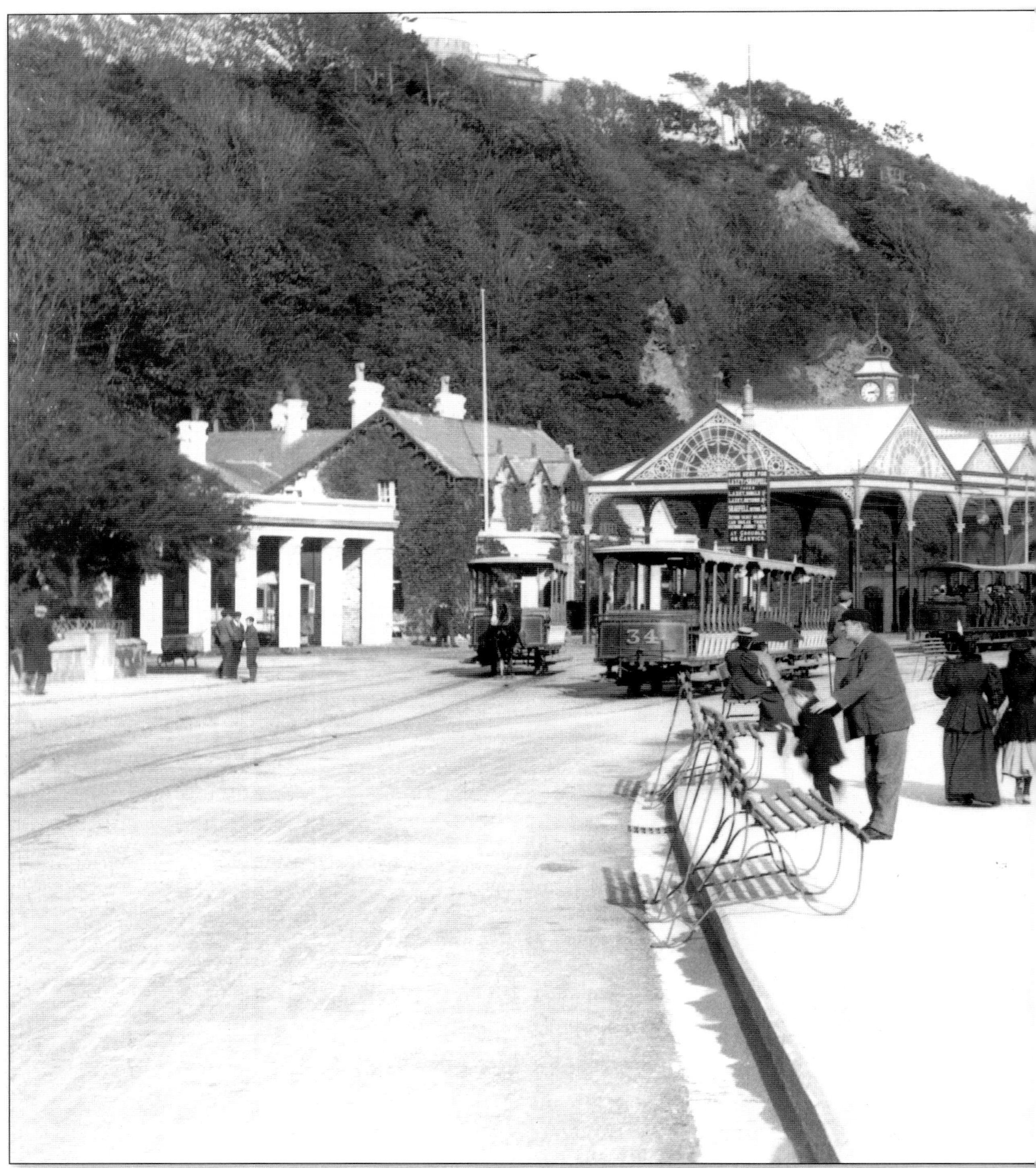

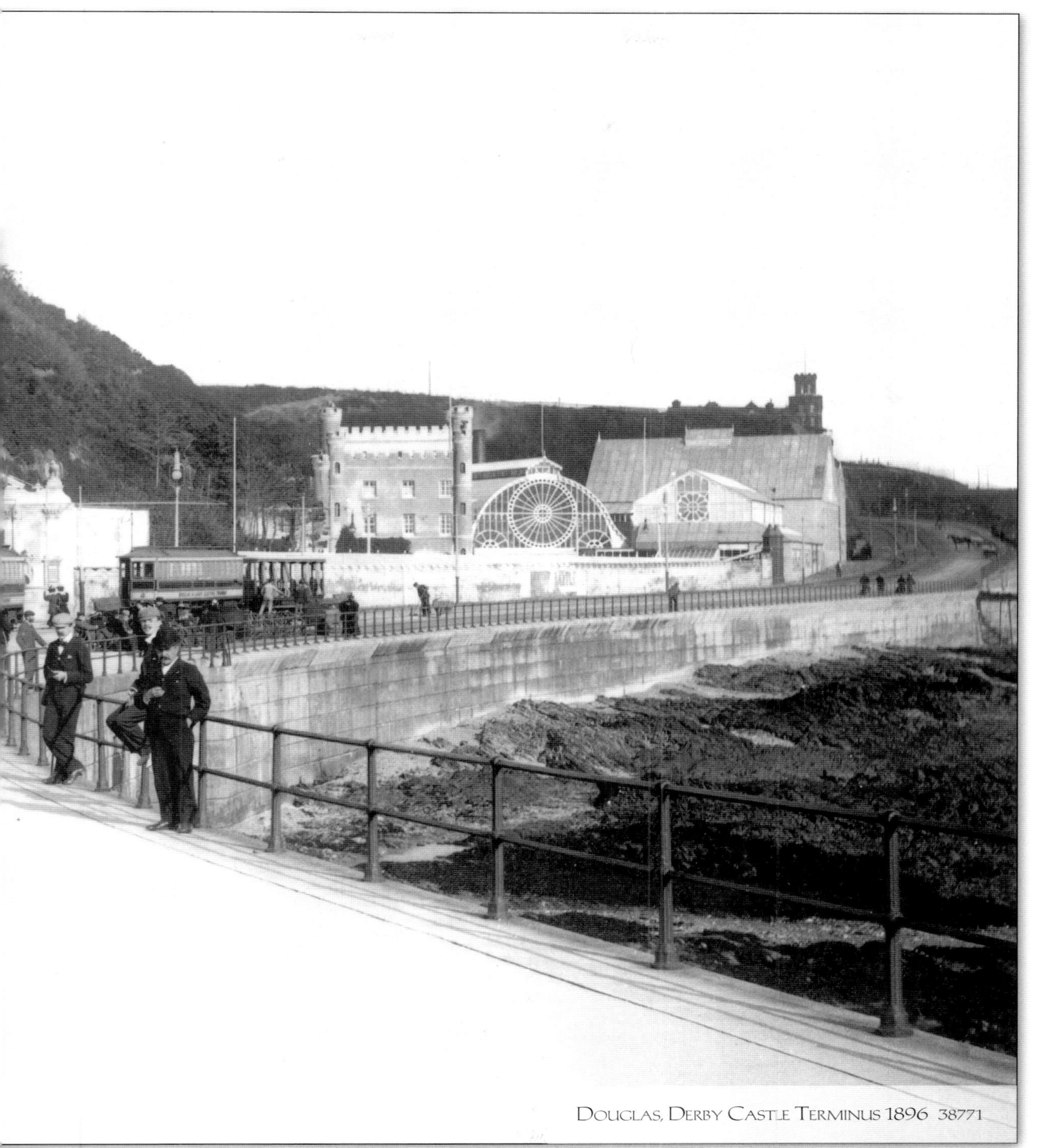

DOUGLAS, DERBY CASTLE TERMINUS 1896 38771

Douglas

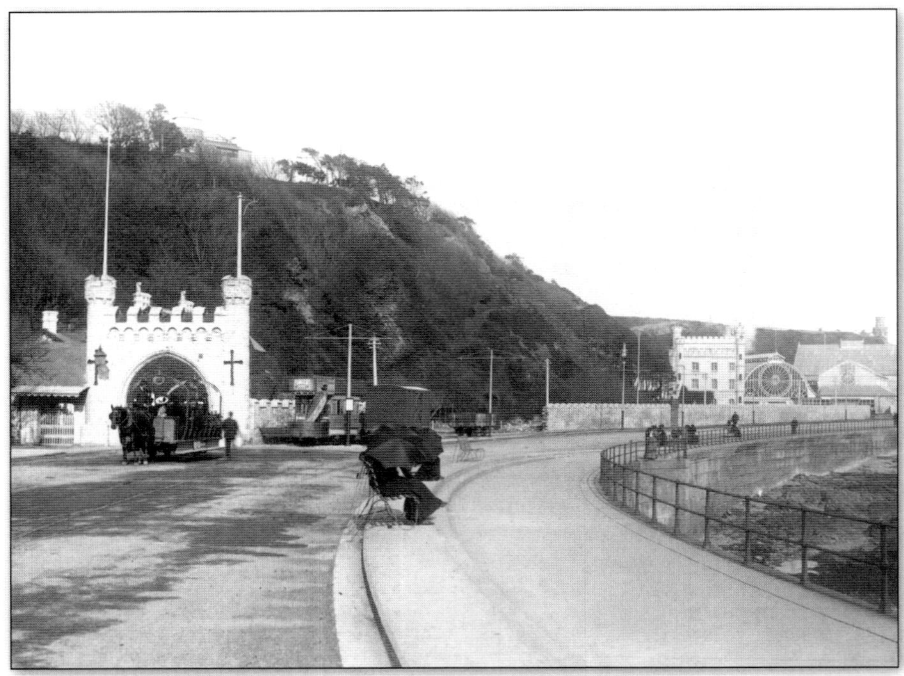

Douglas, Derby Castle 1896 37197

This picture was taken just two years after the horse-trams had been taken over by the operators of the coastal electric tramway. There was talk of converting the horse tramway to electric traction, but nothing ever came of it.

In the picture is a double-deck horse-tram; the last of these were phased out in 1949, though old No 14 survived long enough to be shipped off to Clapham Museum in March 1955.

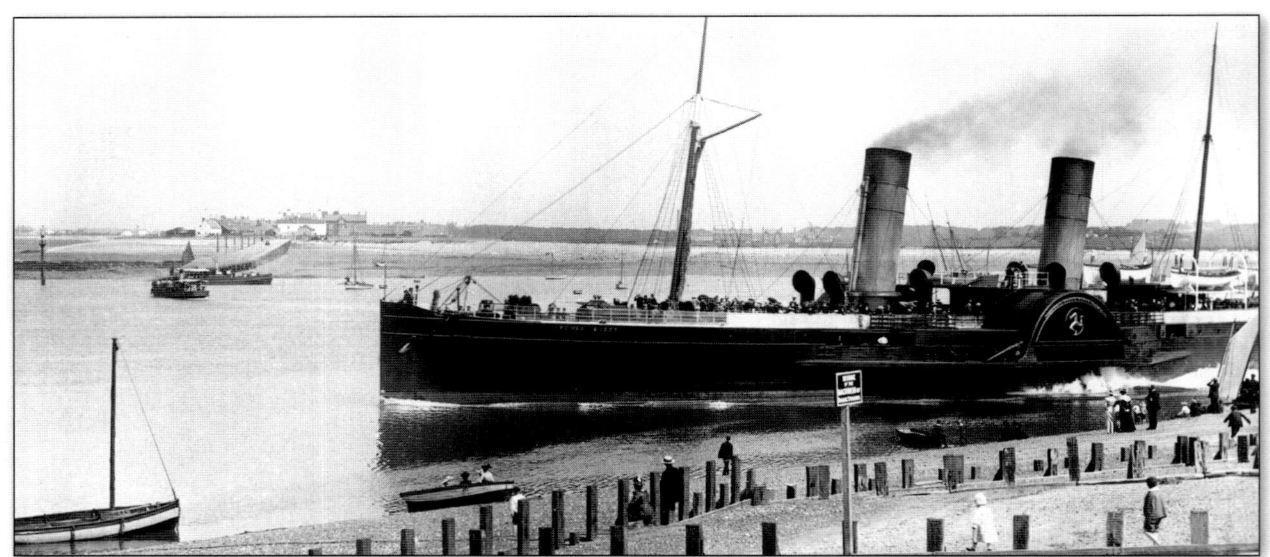

Fleetwood, Mona's Queen 1904 52171

The IOMSPCo's 'Mona's Queen' eases out of Fleetwood on a summer sailing. The crossing to the Isle of Man took about three hours; the daily sailing was scheduled to leave after the arrival of the 2.15pm train. There was also a twice-weekly sailing from Fleetwood to Ramsey via Douglas.

Douglas

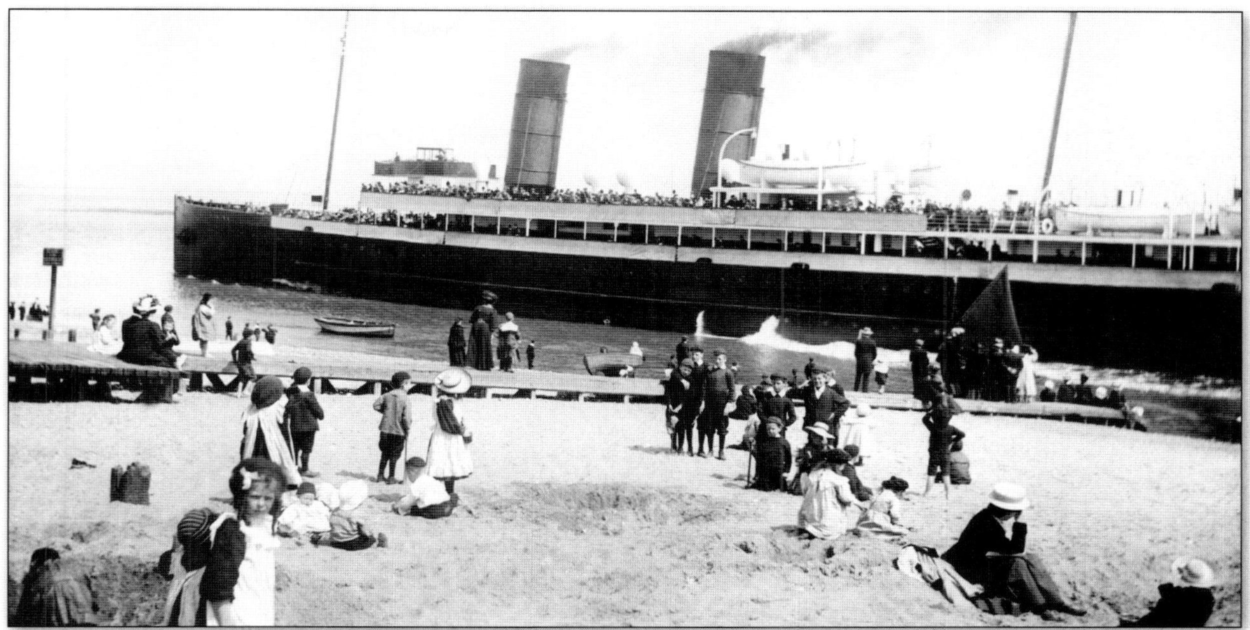

Fleetwood, Viking 1908 59939

The turbine steamer 'Viking' departing for Douglas. When this picture was taken, the turbine steamers were usually assigned to the Liverpool-Douglas and Heysham-Douglas services.

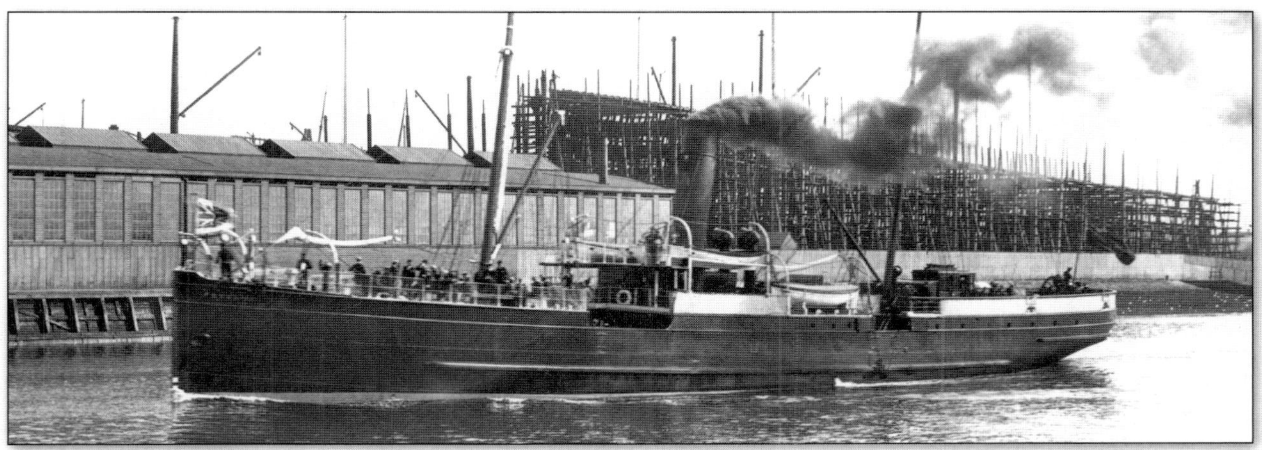

Belfast, The Isle of Man Steamer 'Fenella' 1897 40232

Passengers take an opportunity to experience the sights and sounds of Belfast harbour as the Douglas packet makes her way slowly along. On 3 December 1909 the packet 'Ellan Vannin' was lost with all hands and passengers when she foundered off the entrance to the Mersey, the worst loss in the history of the IOMSPCo.

ISLE OF MAN MAP

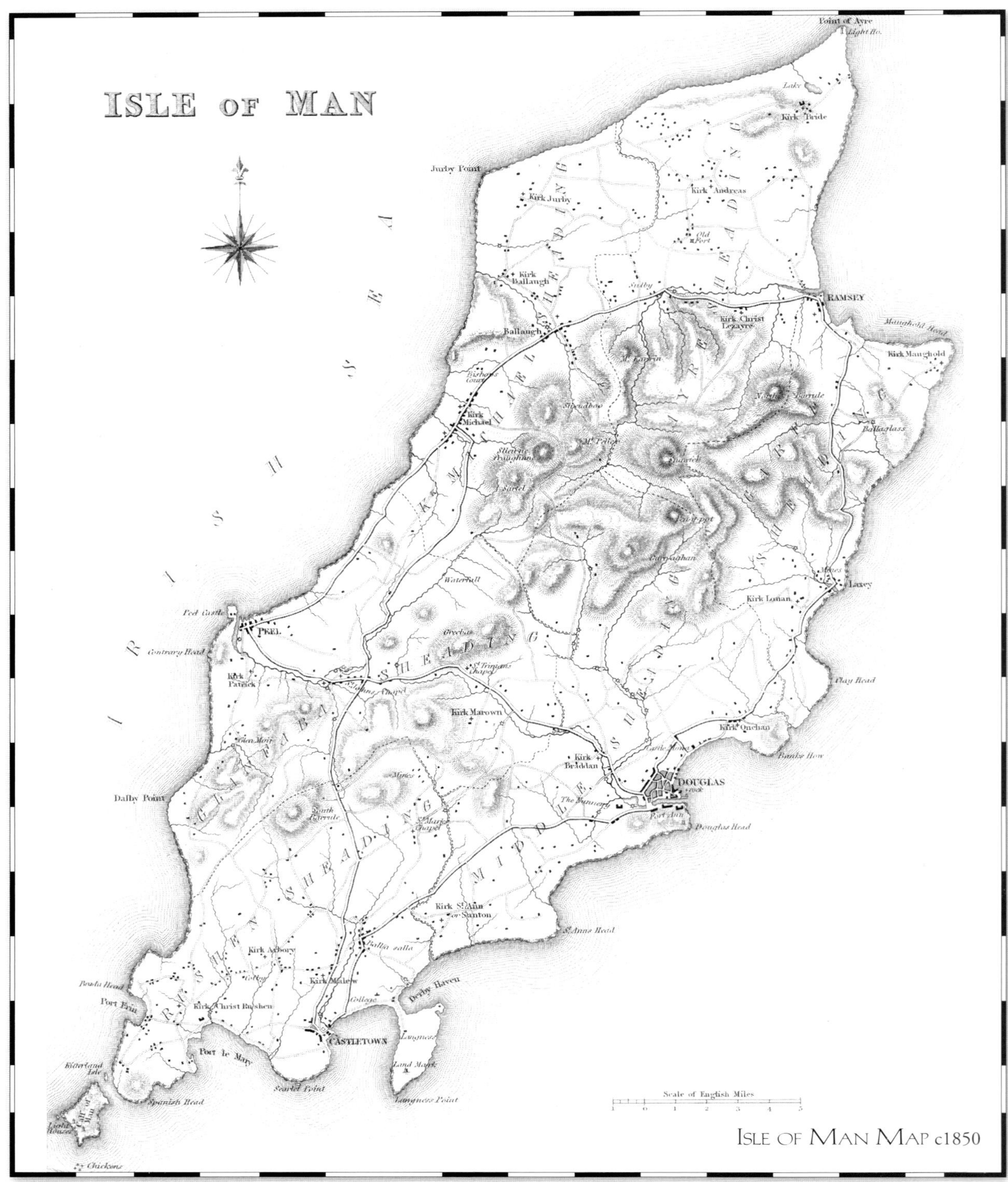

Isle of Man Map c1850

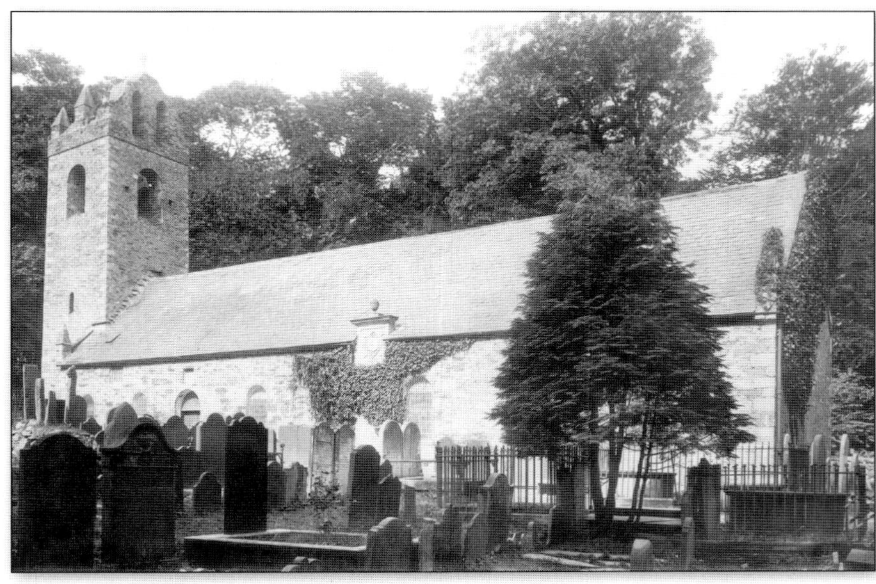

KIRK BRADDAN
THE OLD CHURCH 1893
33018

As well as the old church, Braddan has a newer one built out of local stone in 1869 (at a cost of £4300) to a design by John Loughborough Pearson. A tower and spire were added in the 1880s, though the spire was eventually removed after suffering storm damage. Both before and between the two world wars the Sunday open-air services at Braddan were so popular that the railway used to lay on special trains (see 59172, page 38).

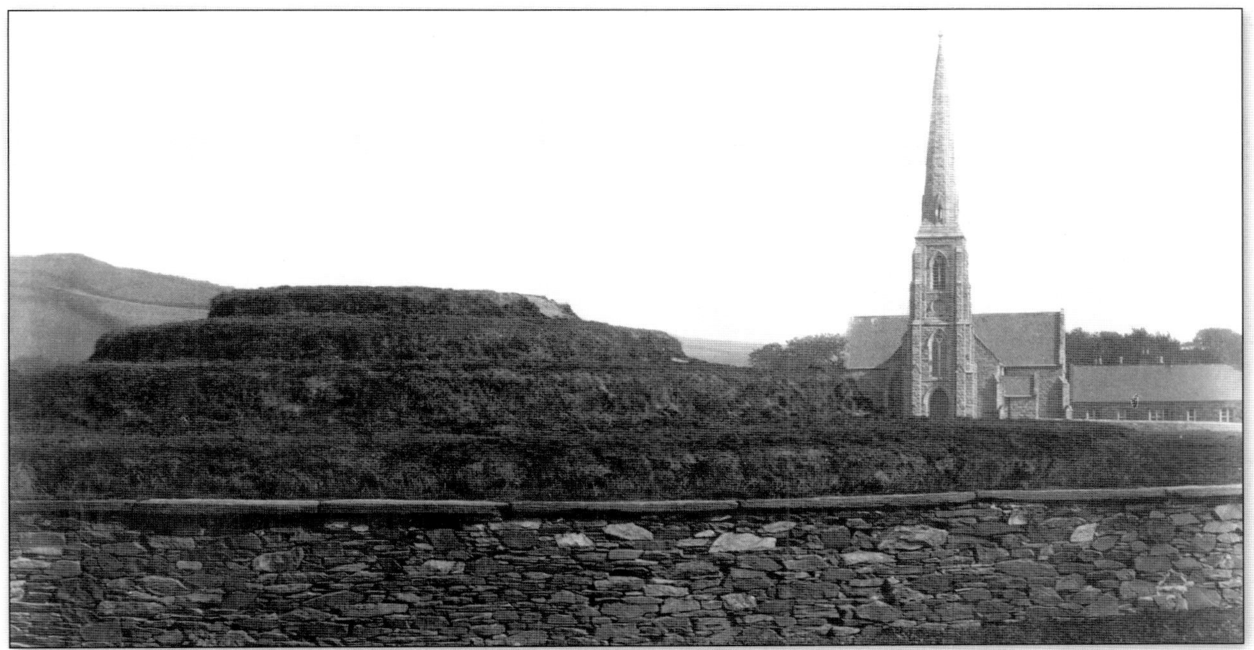

ST JOHN'S, TYNWALD HILL 1903 50668

Around AD 870 Tynwald Hill was selected by the Vikings as a suitable location, or 'vollr' to hold their open-air assembly, the 'Thing', held annually on old Midsummer's Day. Here freemen settled disputes, and laws for the forthcoming year were announced. Tynwald is a derivation of Thingvollr.

Across to Peel

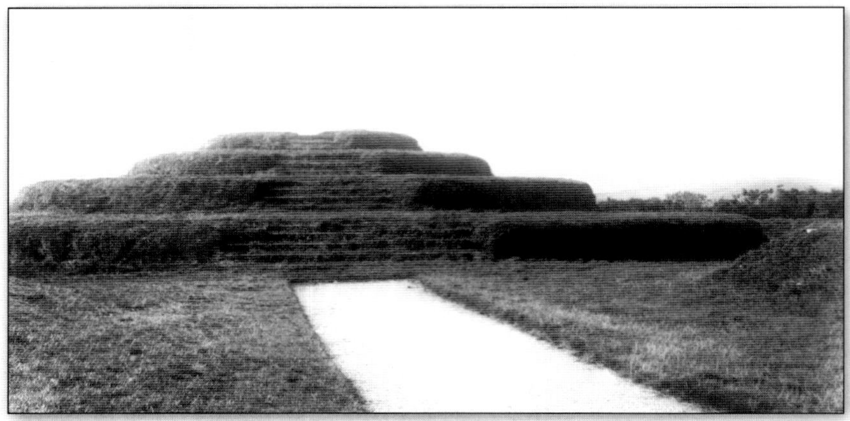

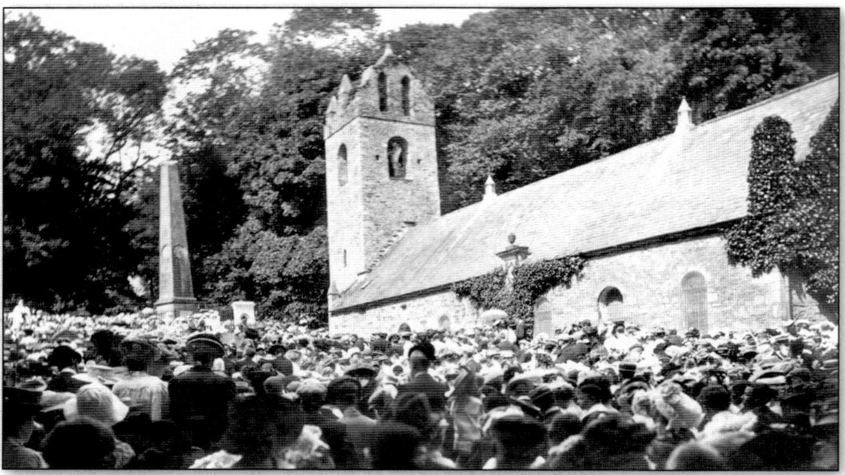

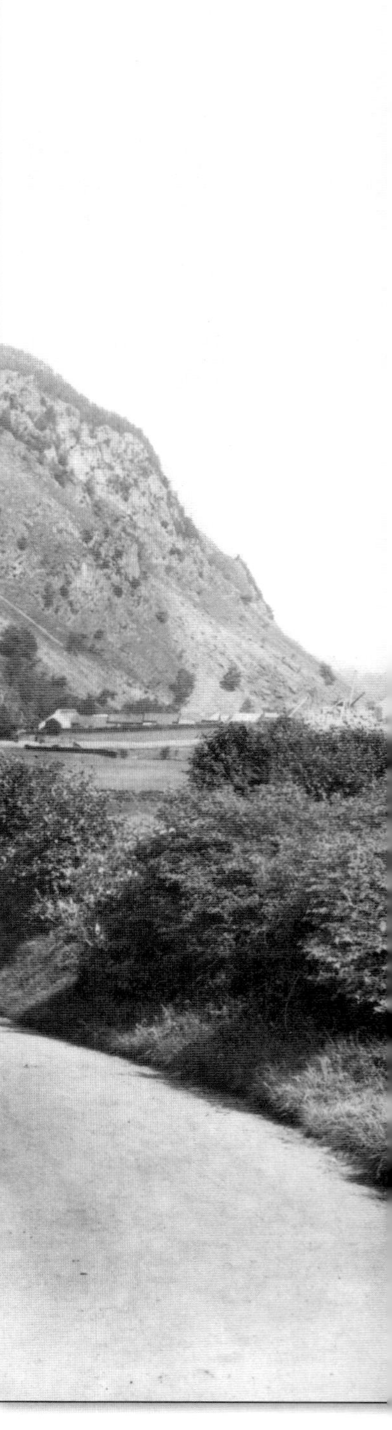

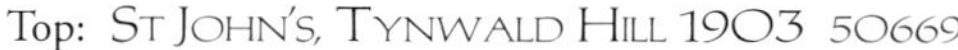

Top: St John's, Tynwald Hill 1903 50669

Tynwald is the oldest unbroken parliament in the world. Godred Crovan created the 'House of Keys', and in his day it included representatives from the Hebrides, but since 1266 it has been comprised solely of Manxmen. The modern Court of Tynwald includes the island's Governor, the ten-member Legislative Council, and the House of Keys.

Above: Douglas, Kirk Braddan, the Old Church 1907 59172

One of the famous open-air services which proved so popular with holidaymakers is in full-swing at old Kirk Braddan, the mother church of Douglas.

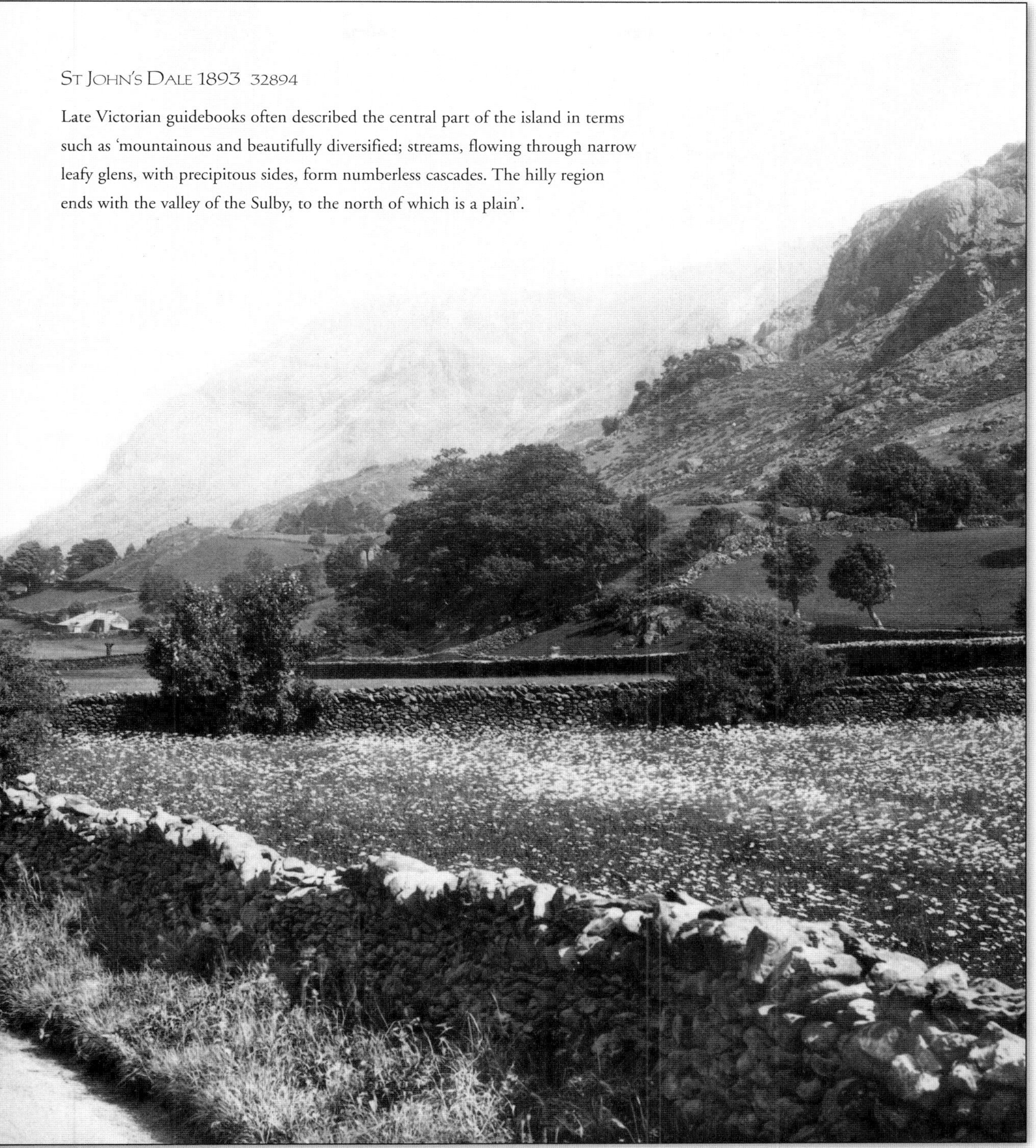

ST JOHN'S DALE 1893 32894

Late Victorian guidebooks often described the central part of the island in terms such as 'mountainous and beautifully diversified; streams, flowing through narrow leafy glens, with precipitous sides, form numberless cascades. The hilly region ends with the valley of the Sulby, to the north of which is a plain'.

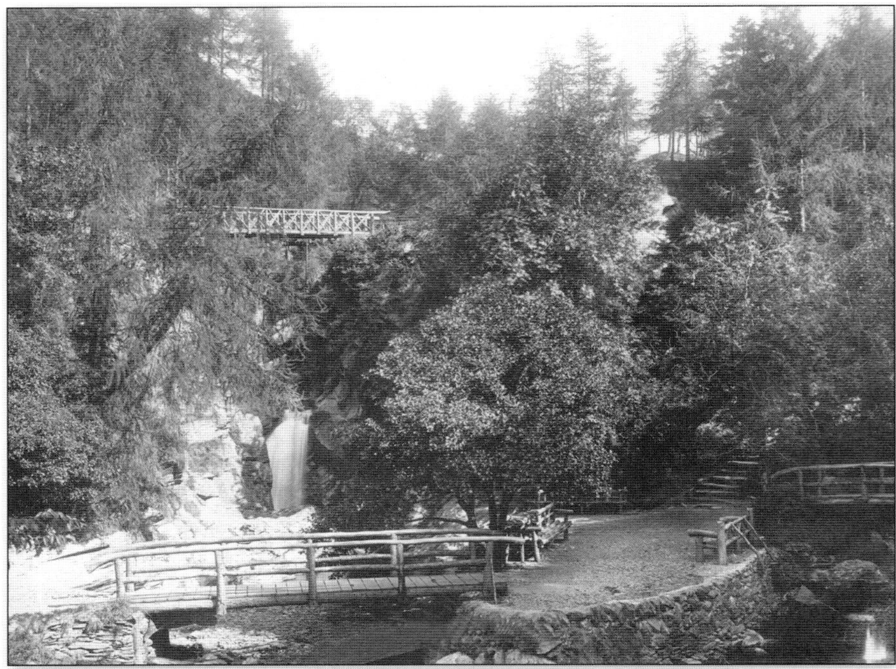

GLEN HELEN
THE WATERFALL 1893
33057

Waterfalls are a feature of Manx glens, and the Rhenass Falls at Glen Helen are probably the finest. Alas, the upper bridge and pathways no longer exist.

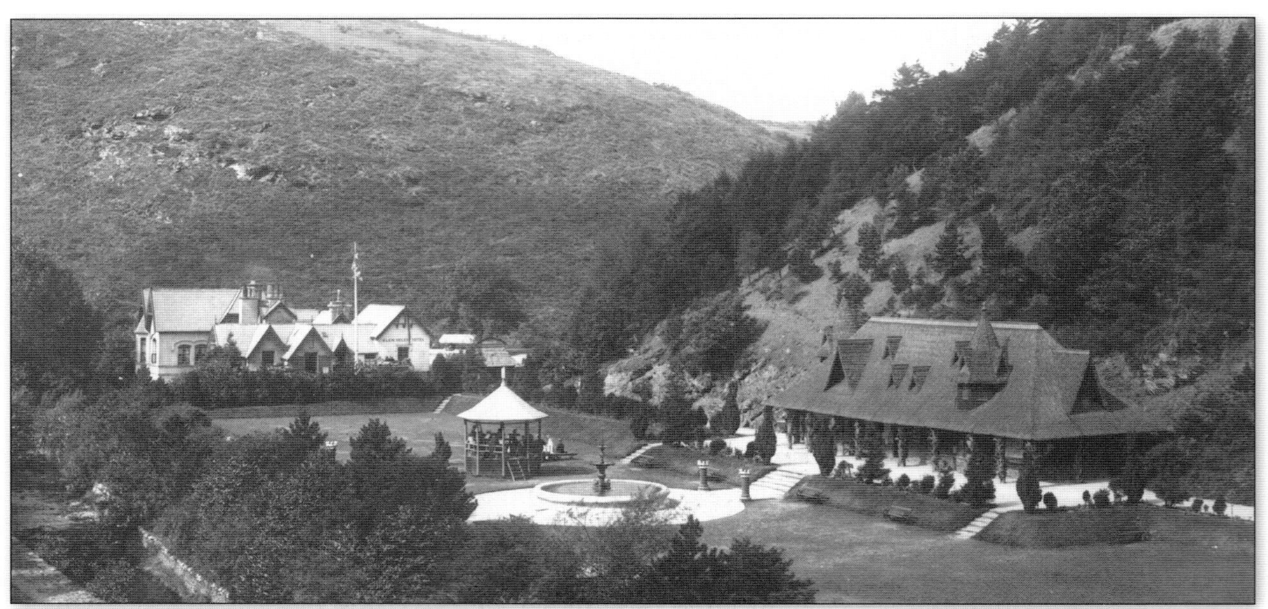

GLEN HELEN, THE SWISS CHALET 1893 33055

By the 1890s Glen Helen was one of the island's favourite beauty spots, offering visitors extensive facilities. An excellent dinner could be had at the Swiss Cottage Hotel for just 1s 6d. Here, despite the lack of an audience, the band plays on.

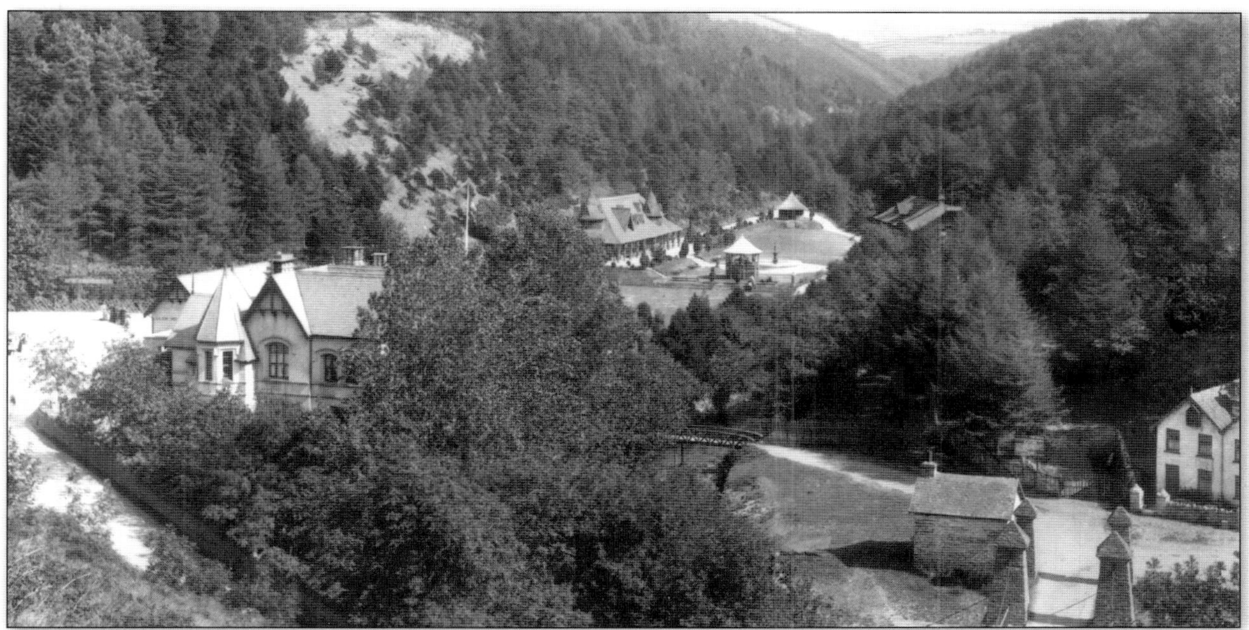

GLEN HELEN, THE HOTEL 1893 33054

Glen Helen is situated about two miles north of St John's, and was developed from 1850 onwards by a Mr Marsden who named the glen after his daughter.

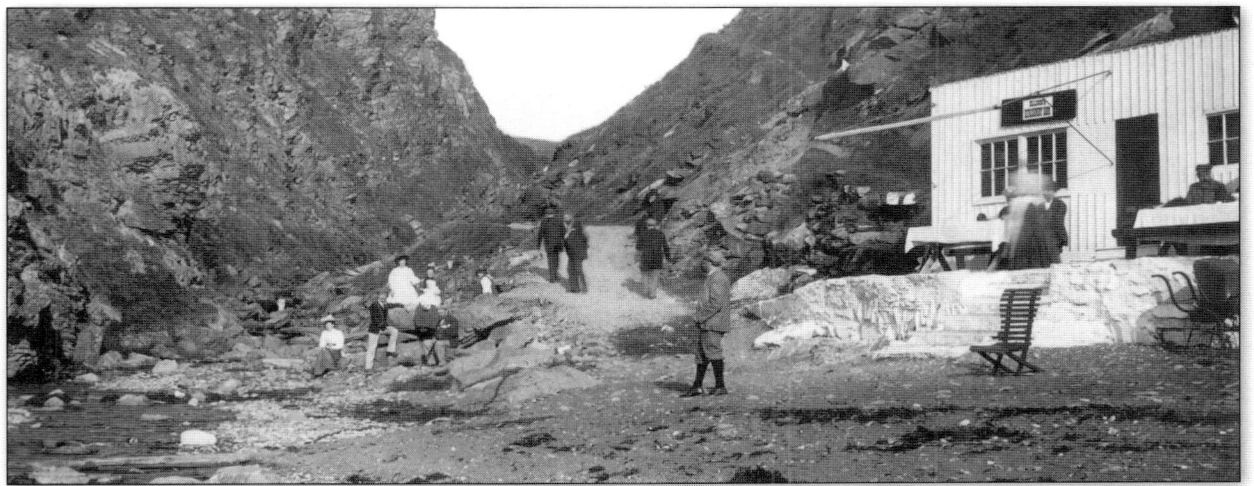

GLEN MAYE 1895 36755

Situated to the south of Peel on what is now the A27 road to Colby via Round Table, Glen Maye opens to the sea. It is a great place for those who like to scramble over rocks and paddle in pools. Those who prefer to sit and wait can do so at Ellison's Refreshment Rooms.

Across to Peel

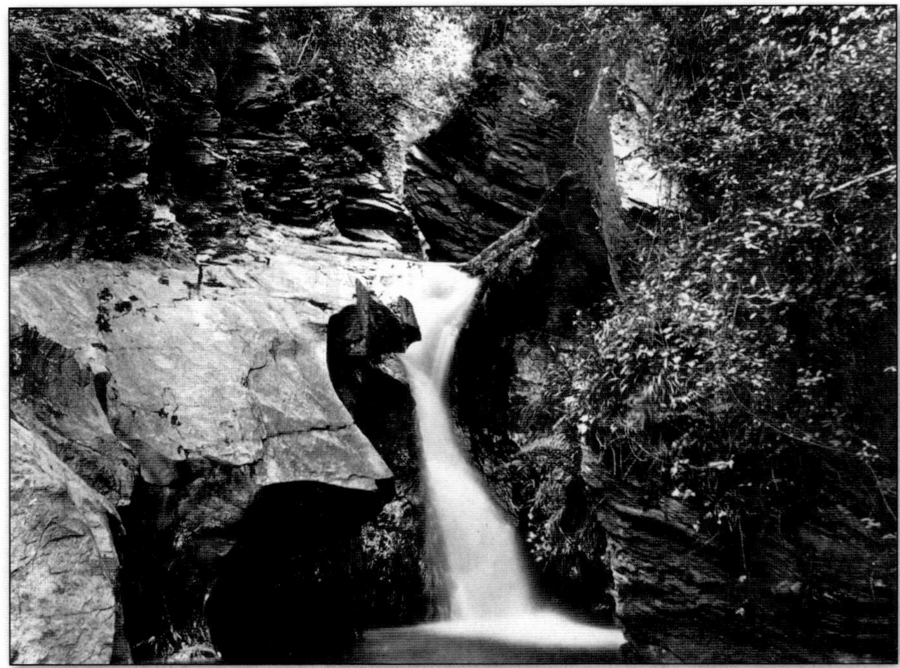

Glen Maye, In The Glen 1895 36756

Some of the water off the surrounding high ground runs through Glen Rushen and Glen Mooar before entering the sea by way of Glen Maye. The admission price to Glen Maye was cheaper than that to nearby Glen Helen.

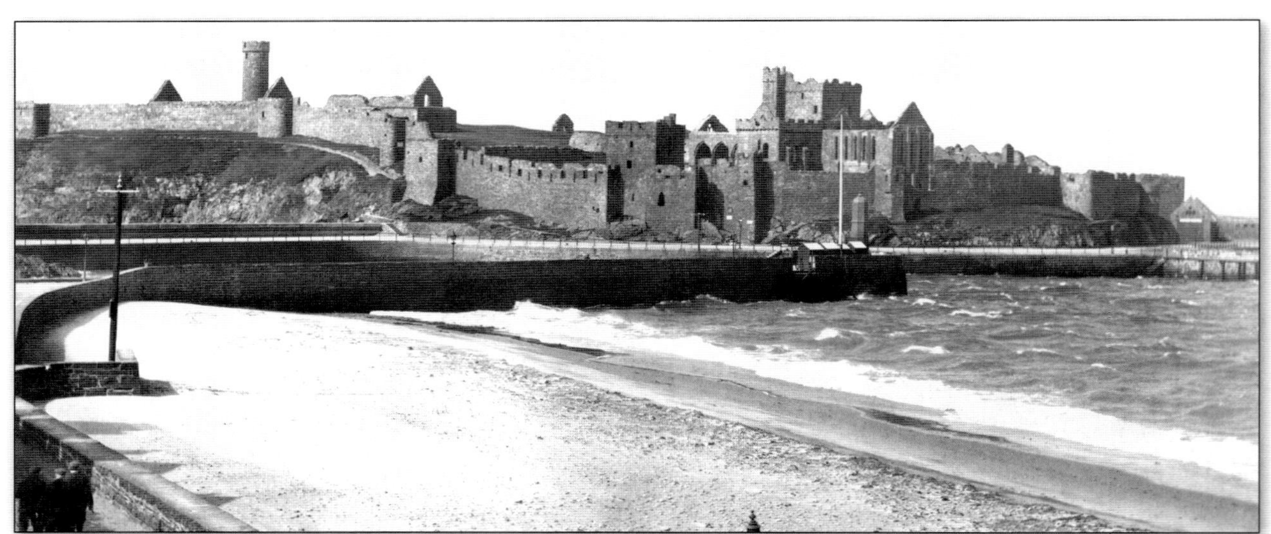

Peel, The Castle and Harbour Entrance 1903 50647

At the height of the season, Peel harbour was often full of fishing boats - Manx, Cornish, Irish and Scottish - as they followed the migrating herring into Scottish waters. In 1881 the Peel herring fleet consisted of 309 boats employing 2163 men and boys; the annual catch was worth around £11,000. By 1891 the local fleet was down to 174 boats employing 860 men and boys with an annual catch valued at just under £3000.

Across to Peel

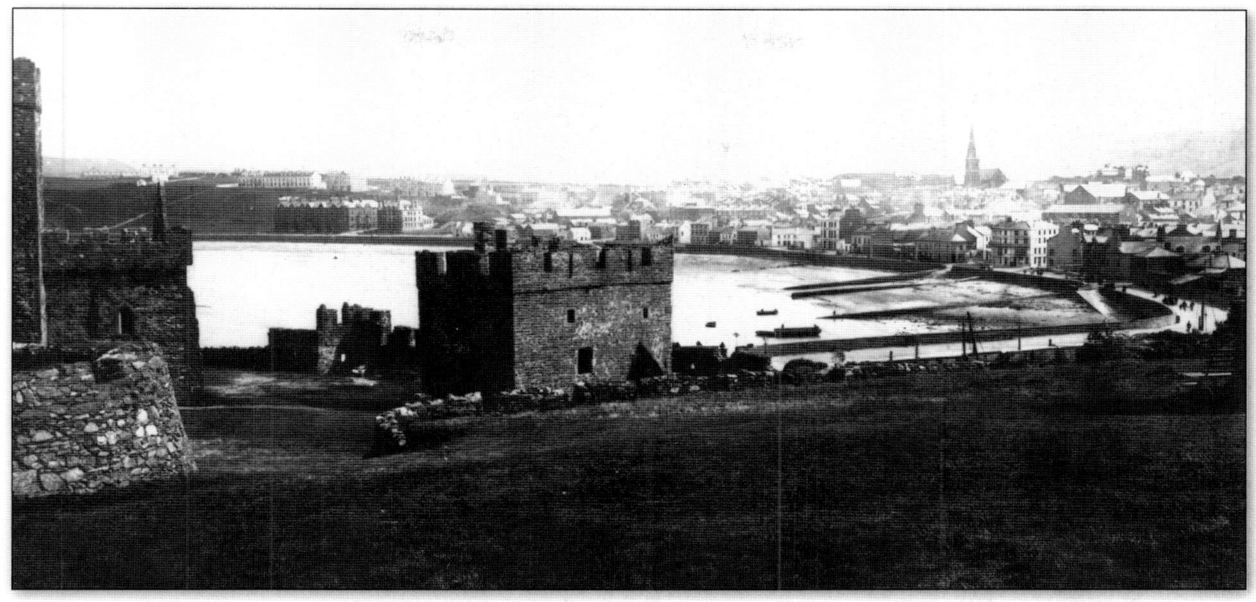

PEEL, THE TOWN FROM THE CASTLE 1893 33045

Magnus Barefoot built a timber fort on St Patrick's Isle between c1098-1103. The bulk of the surviving fortifications date from the time of Thomas, First Earl of Derby, and were constructed between 1460-1504 as a defence against Scottish raiders. The tower in the centre of the picture overlooks the causeway linking the islet with the town, and was probably built by Sir William le Scrope in the 1390s.

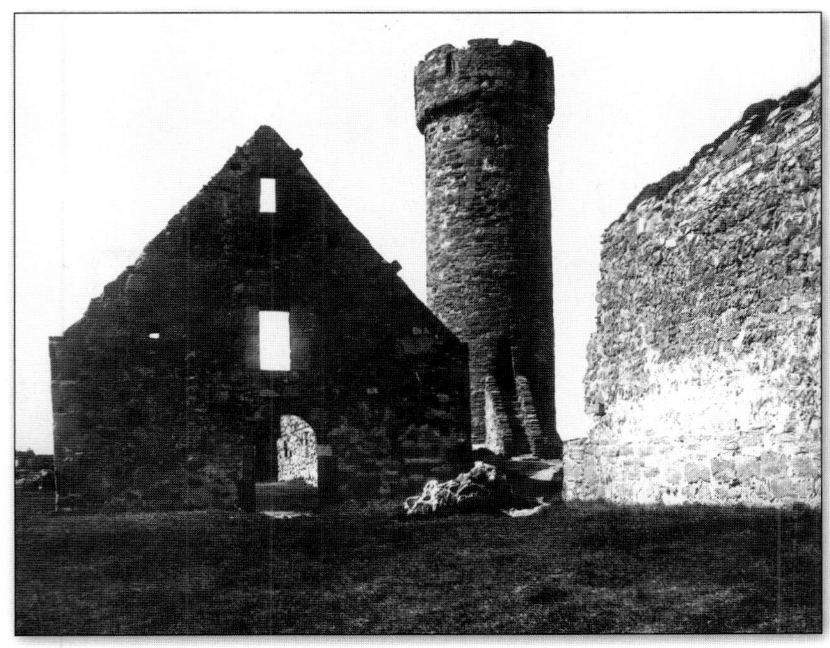

PEEL CASTLE
THE ROUND TOWER 1893 33052

Built in the Irish style, the round tower dates from the 10th or 11th centuries and would have been used by the monks as a place of refuge during raids by pirates or Vikings. It is built from local red sandstone and stands 50 ft high. Originally it would have had a conical stone roof, but this was replaced by the crenellated top many centuries ago.

Across to Peel

Peel, St German's Cathedral 1893 33050

St German's was begun by Bishop Symon of Argyll in c1230 as the cathedral church of the Sudreys, built on the site of the old parish church of Kirk German. Symon built the chancel, tower and transepts, and his successor Bishop Richard added the nave. The central tower is 68 ft high and has a bell turret rising above it.

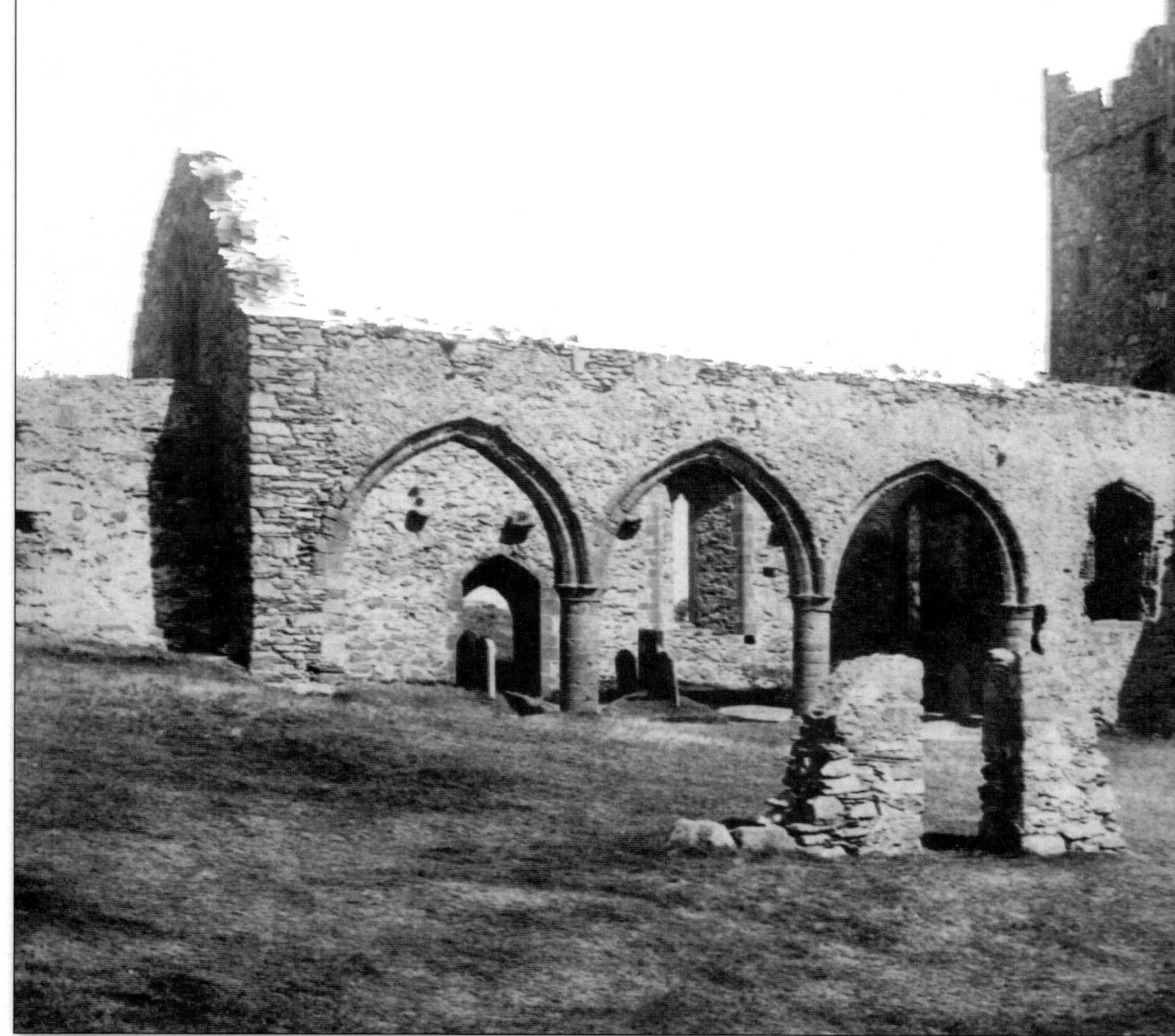

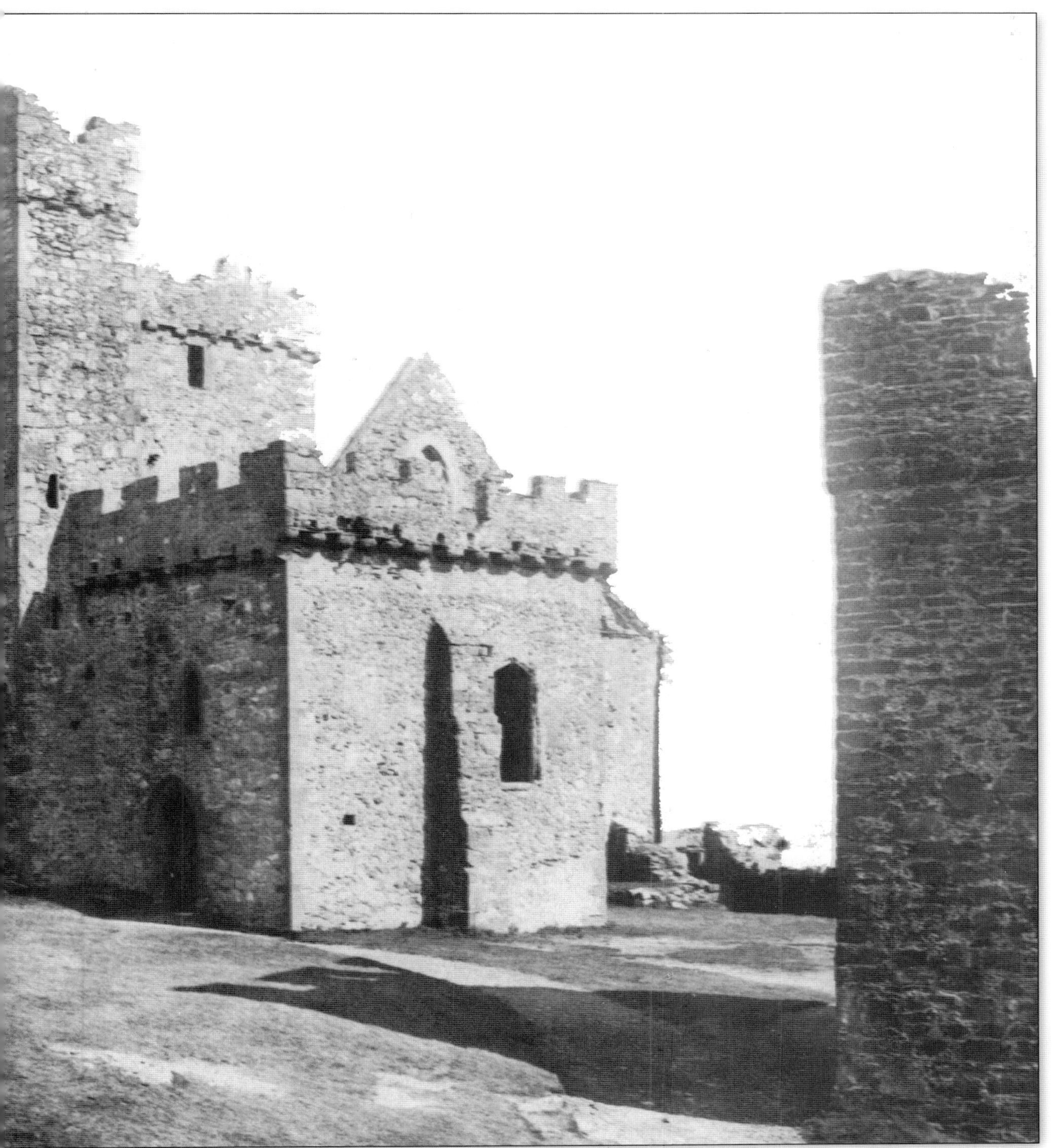

Across to Peel

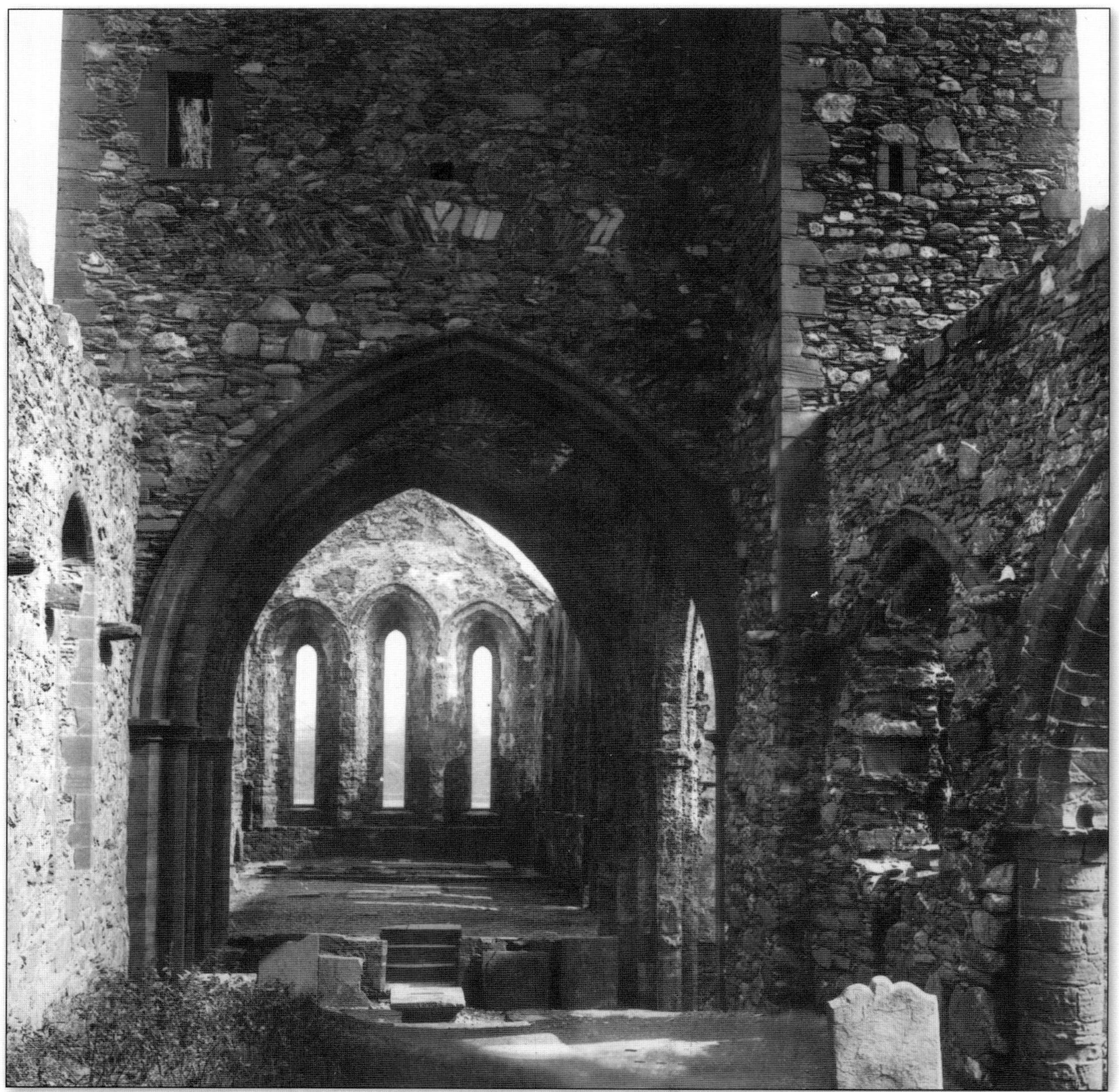

PEEL, ST GERMAN'S CATHEDRAL 1893 33051

The crypt of St German's used to house the bishop's prison, where those found guilty by the ecclesiastical court were imprisoned. The bishop's prison was last used in 1780. Inmates were usually those found guilty of adultery, fornication, cursing, or for being drunk and disorderly. The power of the court was undermined in the 1720s when the Governor allowed those sentenced by the church to appeal to a civil court.

Across to Peel

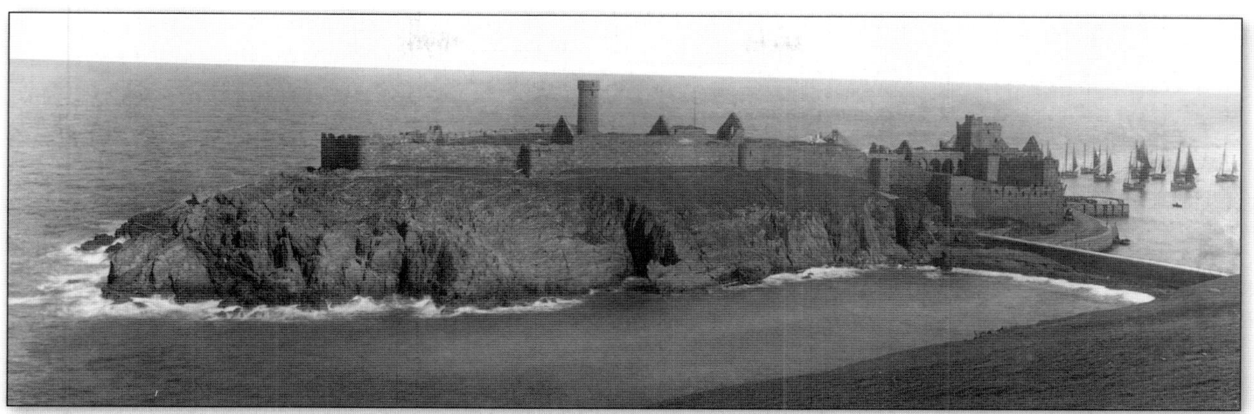

Peel, The Castle 1893 33044

19th-century visitors wishing to get a good view of the town and castle were advised to climb the tower, known as Corrin's folly, on Corrin's Hill (485 ft). It was built by a wealthy nonconformist eccentric to the memory of his wife and family, who were buried nearby. Mr Corrin also wanted to be buried on the hill, but he finished up in the local churchyard. However, he had arranged with some of his friends that if this happened they were to dig him up and bury him near his family. This they did.

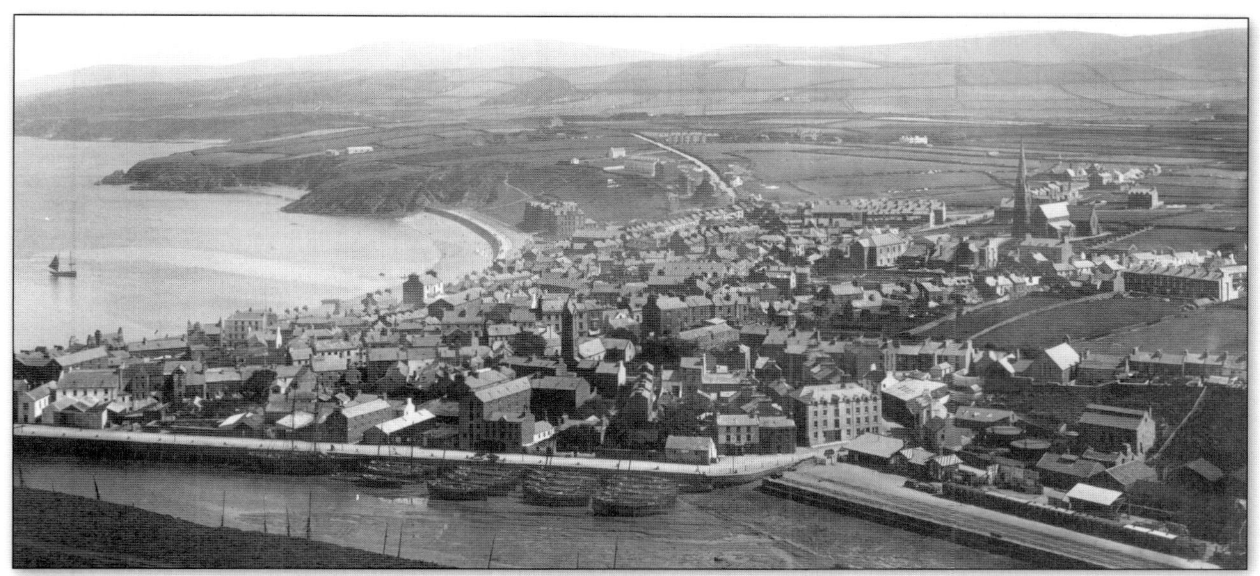

Peel, The Town and Bay 1895 36758

In the centre foreground of the picture stands St Peter's church, intact at this time, built out of locally quarried Triassic red sandstone and identified by its unusual helm-roof tower. Following a disastrous fire in 1950, only the tower and west window now survive. Also in the picture is the original railway station, the main building of which was replaced in the early years of the 20th century by one designed by Armitage Rigby.

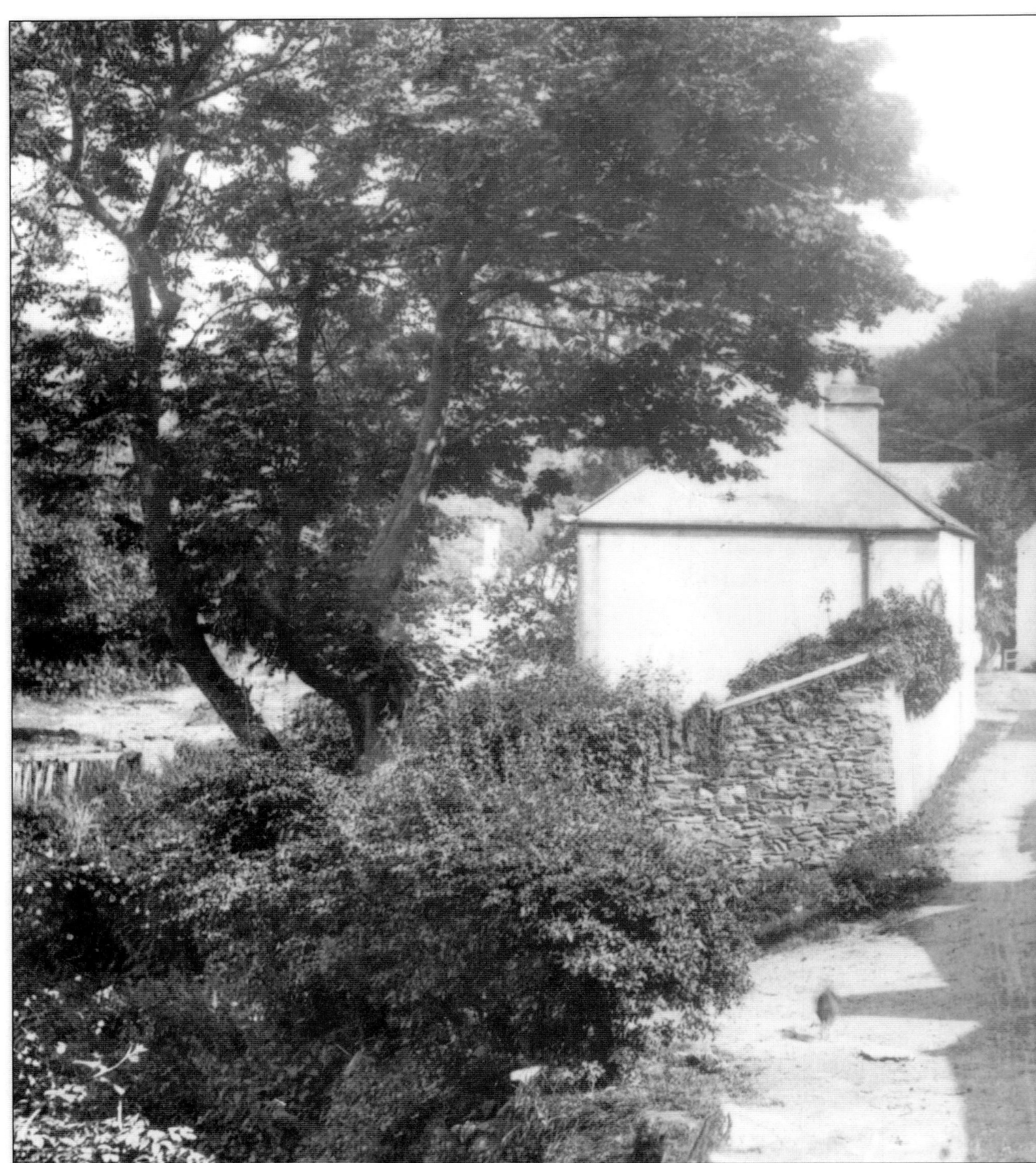

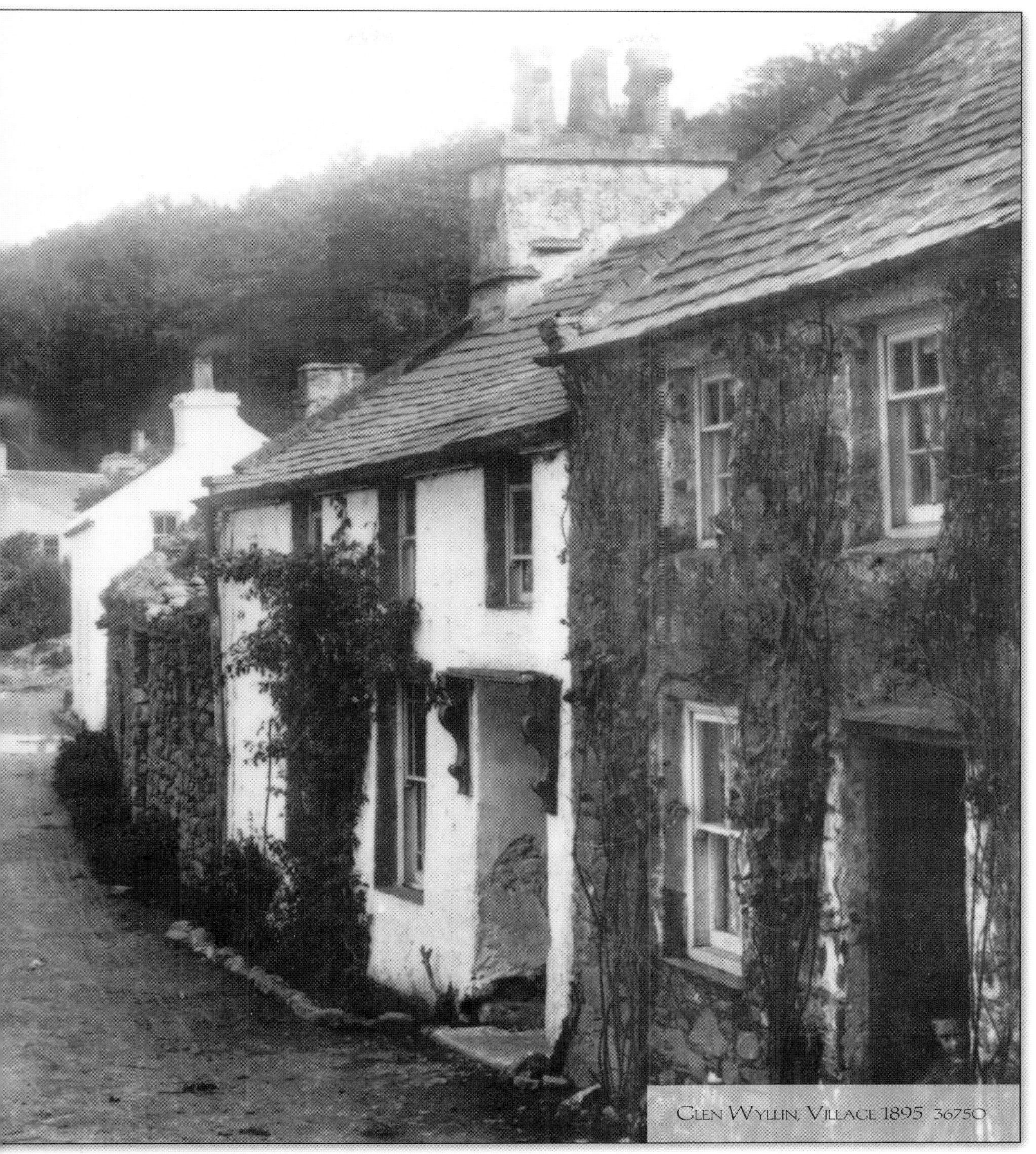

GLEN WYLLIN, VILLAGE 1895 36750

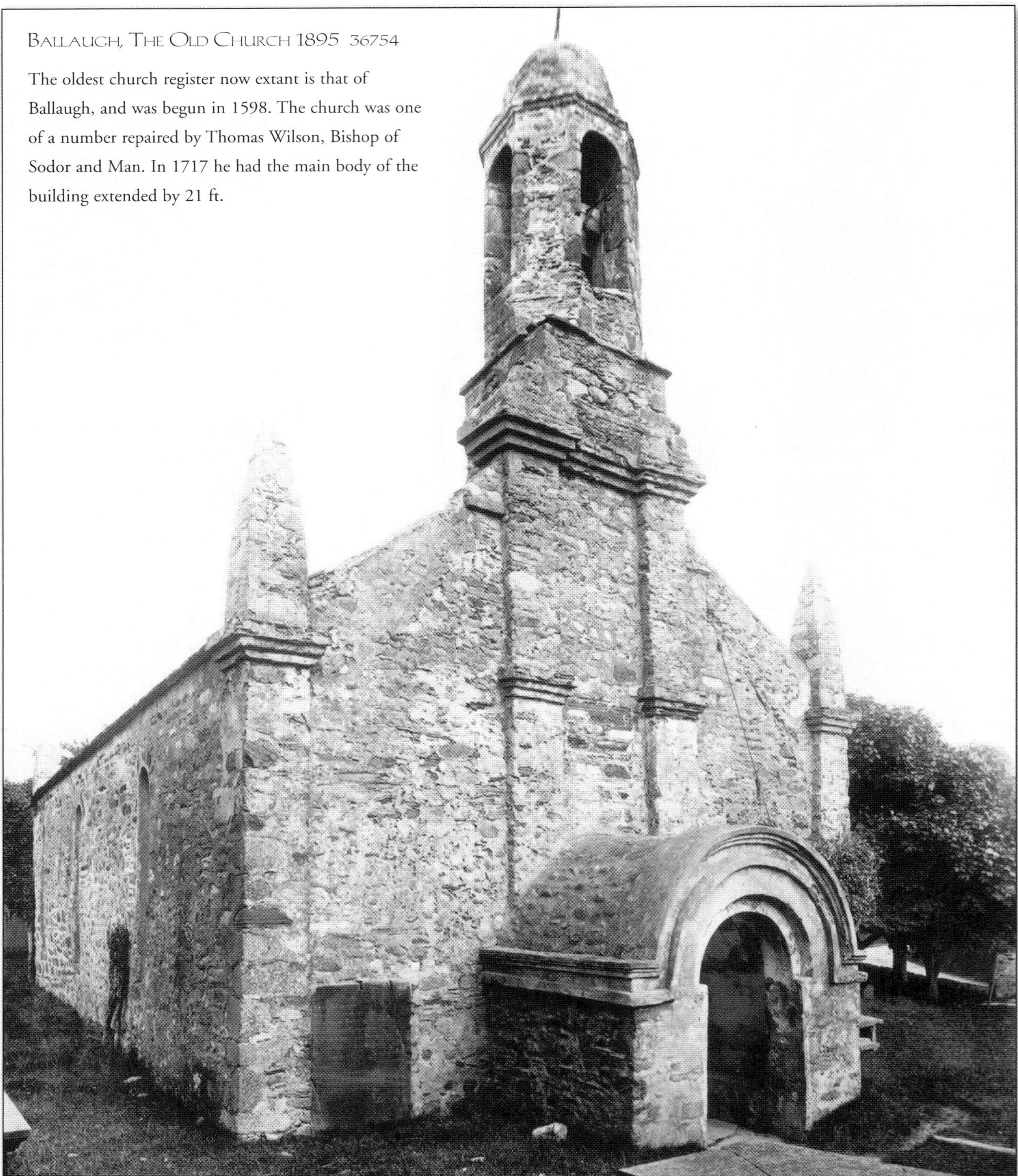

Ballaugh, The Old Church 1895 36754

The oldest church register now extant is that of Ballaugh, and was begun in 1598. The church was one of a number repaired by Thomas Wilson, Bishop of Sodor and Man. In 1717 he had the main body of the building extended by 21 ft.

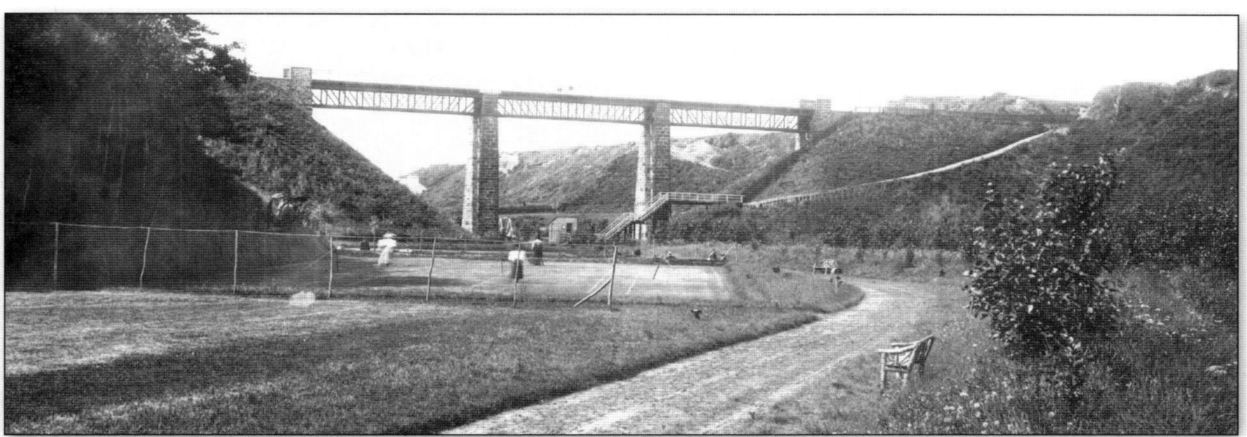

GLEN WYLLIN, THE VIADUCT 1895 36749

This was one of two viaducts on the Manx Northern line between St John's and Ramsey. The other was at Glen Mooar. Glen Wyllin was only a few minutes walk from Kirkmichael station, and in summer special excursions were run to it from Douglas and Ramsey. The glen was purchased by the IOMR in the 1930s, who added a boating lake, bowling greens and children's play area.

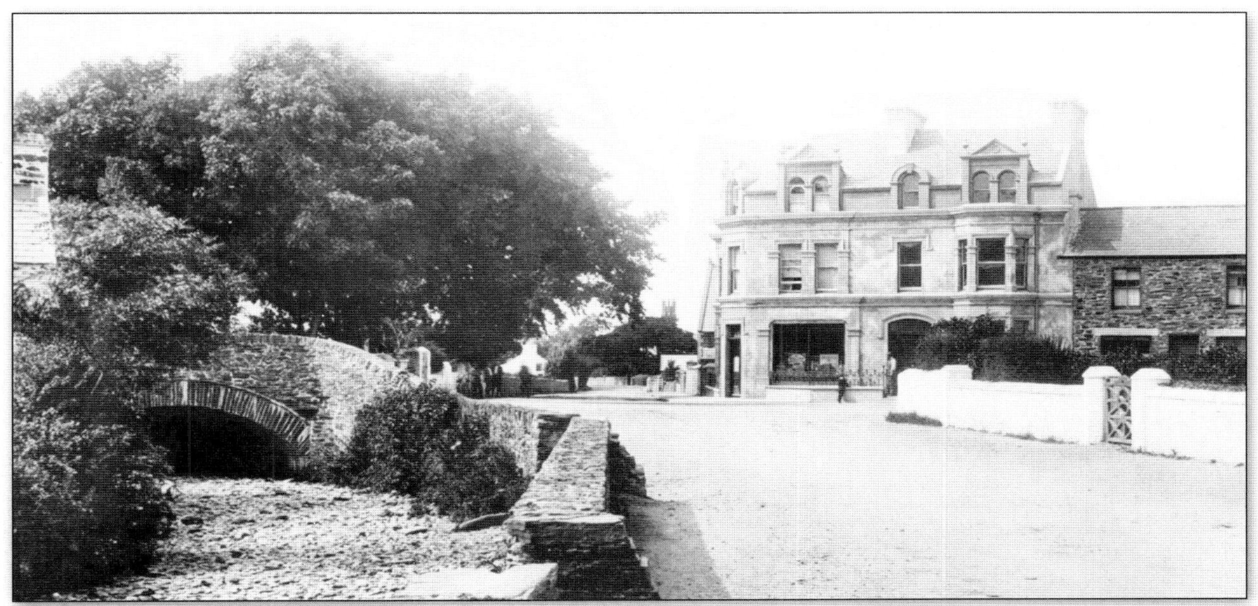

BALLAUGH, THE VILLAGE 1895 36752

Ballaugh is in the Sheading of Michael. The precise meaning of the word is unclear, but one possibility is that it is derived from 'skeid-thing', a Norse word for a local assembly of the freemen, who, when required, served in the king's longships for the defence of the island. Each of the island's six 'skeid-things' provided crews for four ships, thereby providing the king with sufficient crews for 24 warships.

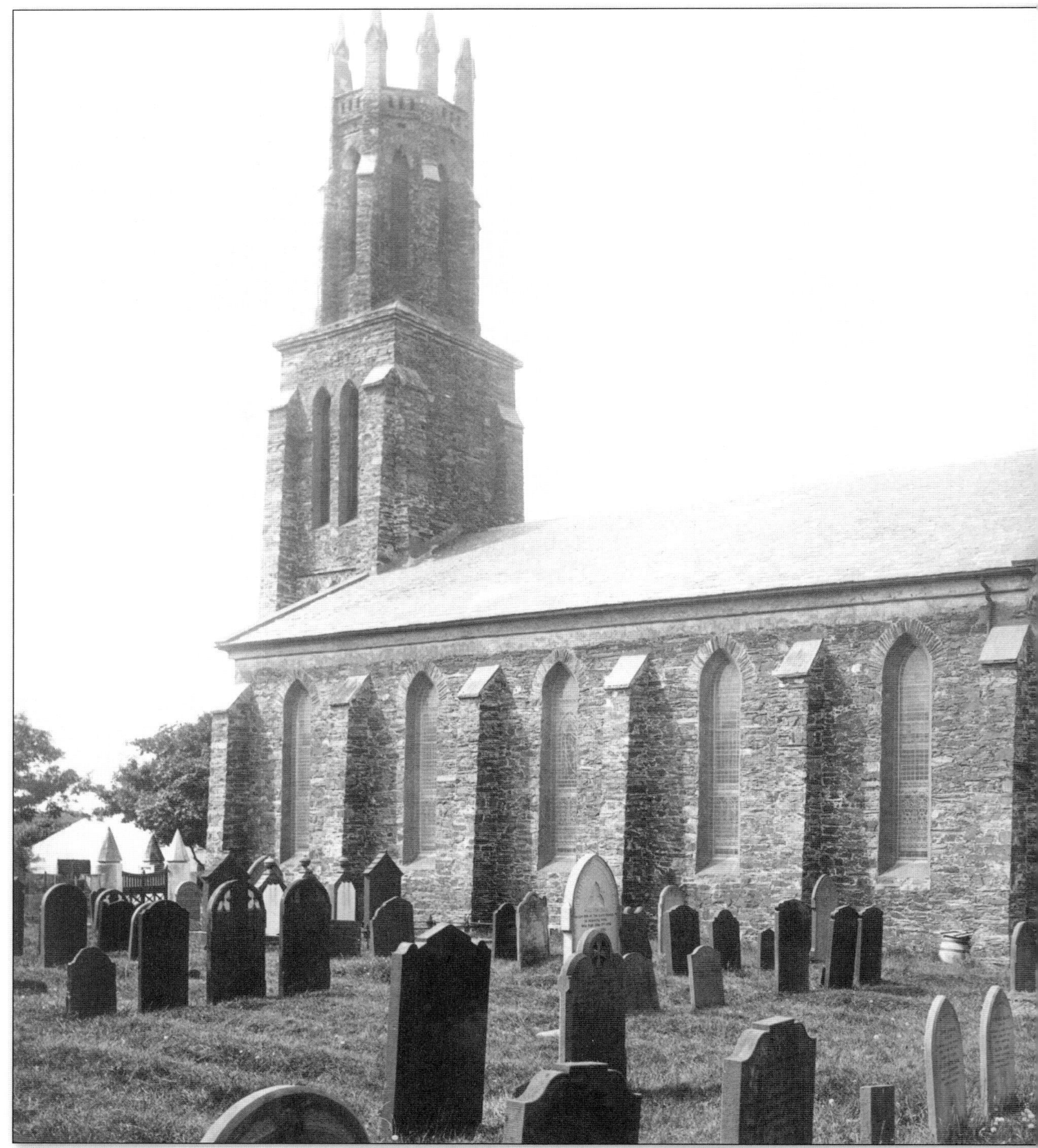

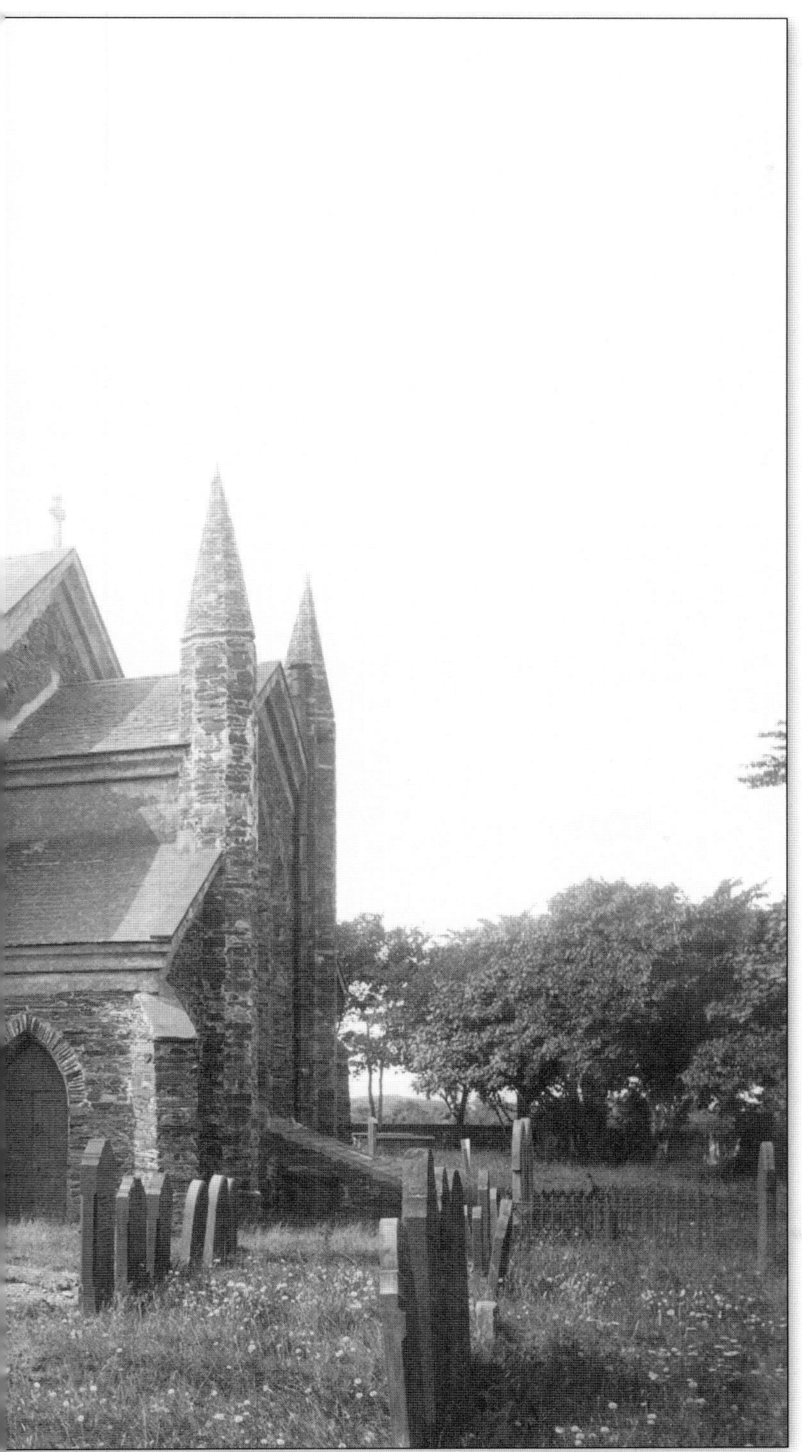

BALLAUGH
THE NEW CHURCH 1895 36753

Designed by John Welch and built in the 1830s, the new Ballaugh church was one of a number built or rebuilt in the early decades of the 19th century. Others include St Patrick's, Jurby (rebuilt 1813); Kirk Michael (rebuilt 1835); St Paul's, Ramsey (erected in 1822); and St Bridget's Roman Catholic Church, Douglas (opened in 1814, the first modern Catholic place of worship to be built on Man).

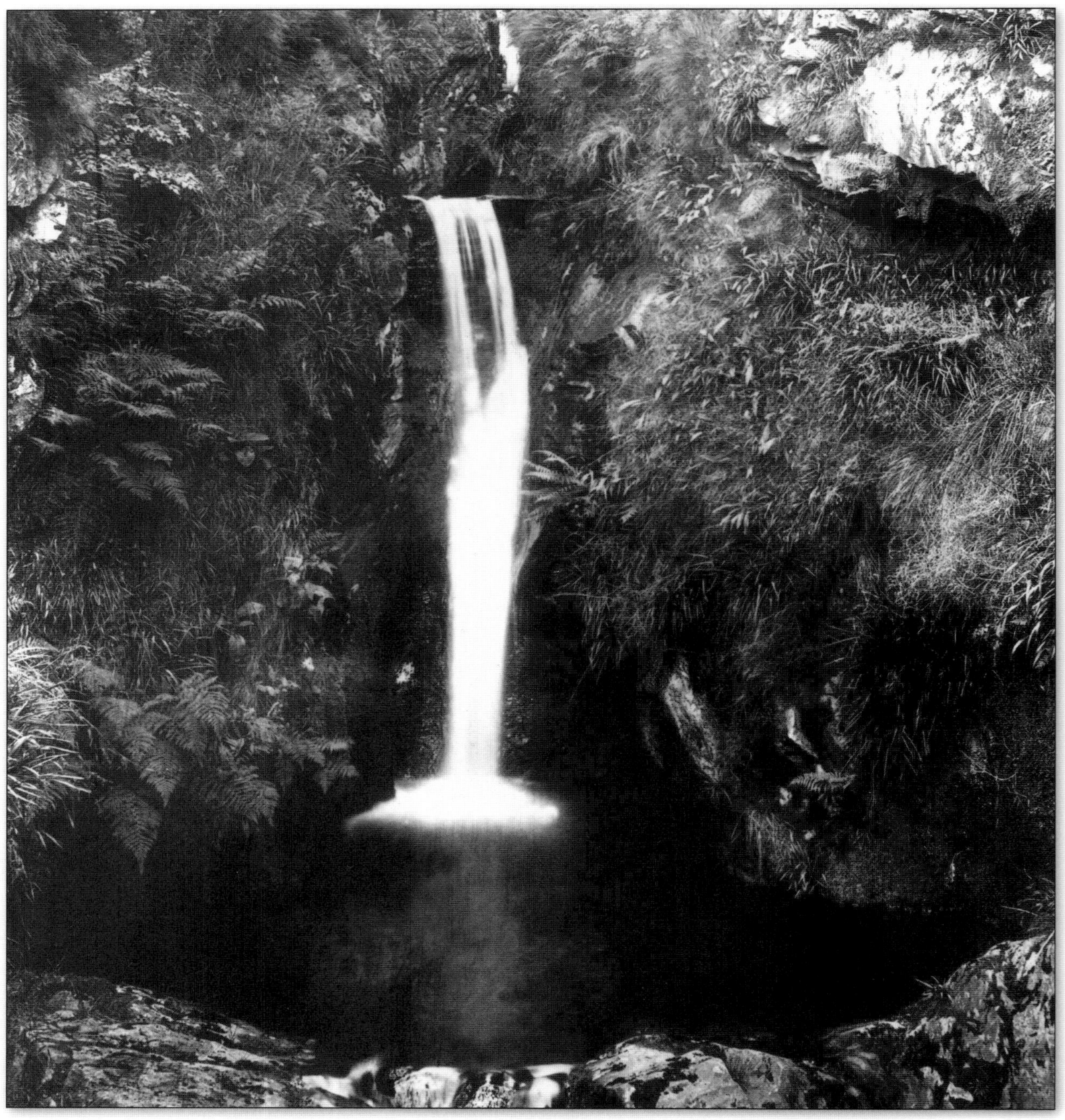

Sulby, The Waterfall 1894 34661

The entrance to Sulby Glen is at the Tholt-e-Will Hotel, and in 1894 admission was only a few pence. The glen features two waterfalls, the Alt and the Tholt-e-Will, of which the former is the more impressive.

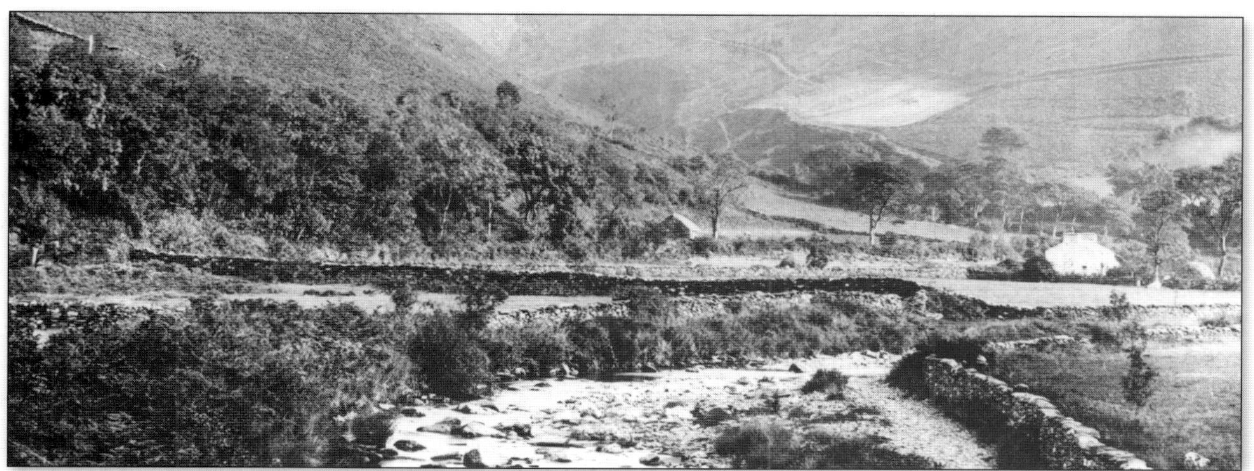

SULBY GLEN 1894 34659

Lying between Mount Karrin and Slieav Managh, Sulby Glen was often referred to by the Victorians as 'the Manx Switzerland', though the compilers of the Baedecker Guides thought the place more reminiscent of the Scottish Highlands.

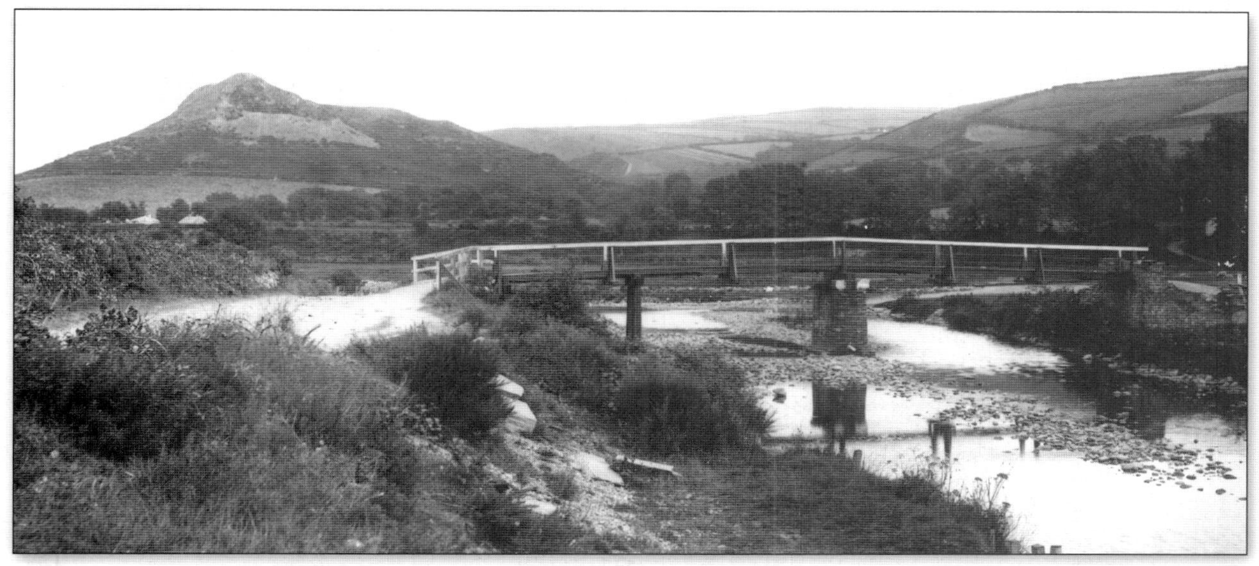

SULBY, THE FOOTBRIDGE AND PRIMROSE HILL 1894 34655

The Manx Electric Railway was quick to capitalise on the popularity of Sulby Glen by offering personally conducted tours. For an all-in price, tourists travelled from Derby Castle to Laxey, where they boarded a Snaefell Mountain Railway car to the Bungalow. From the Bungalow they were taken by charabanc to Sulby Glen, where they were free to explore the area before making the return journey. The price included lunch at the Tholt-e-Will Hotel and admission to the glen.

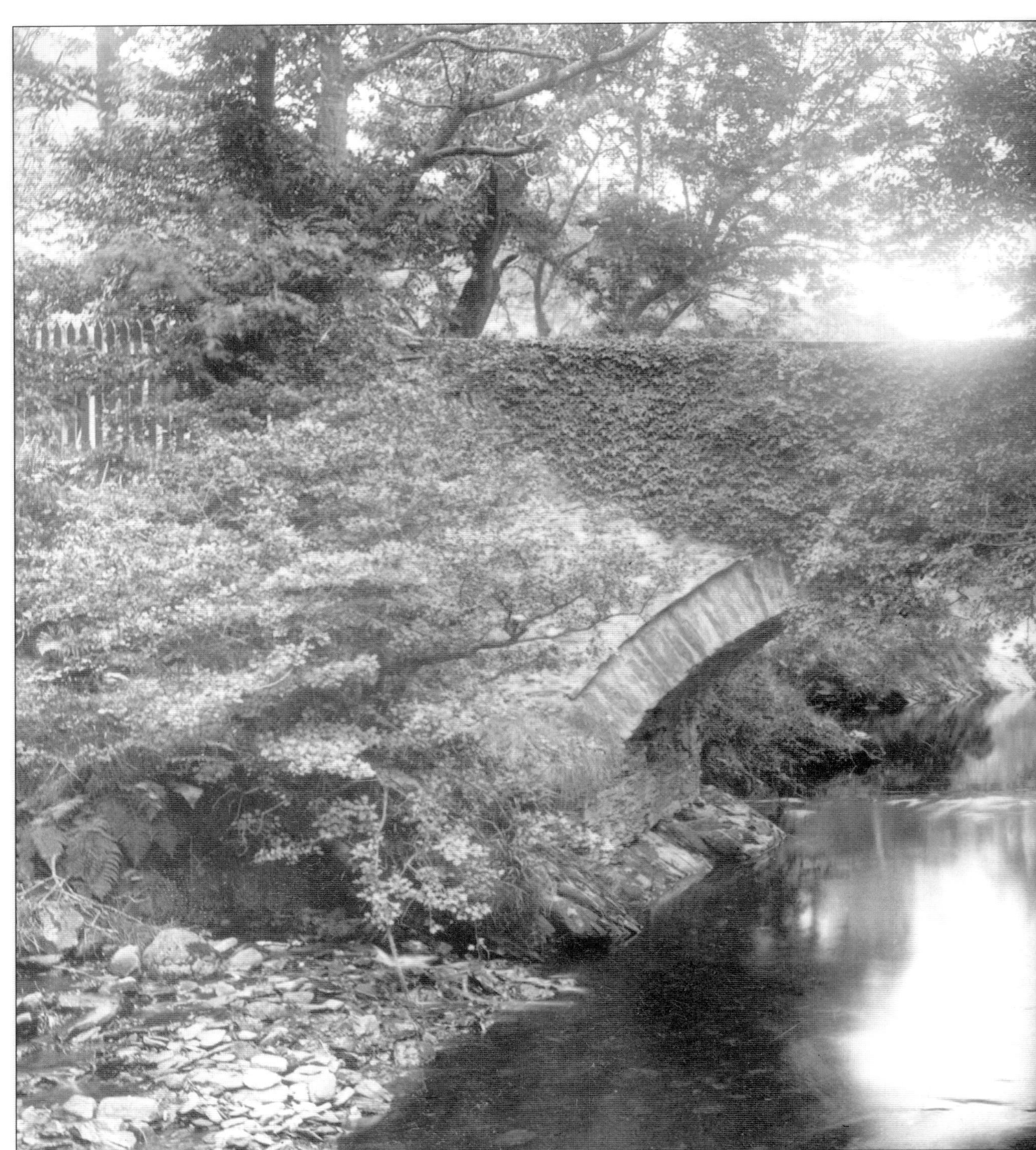

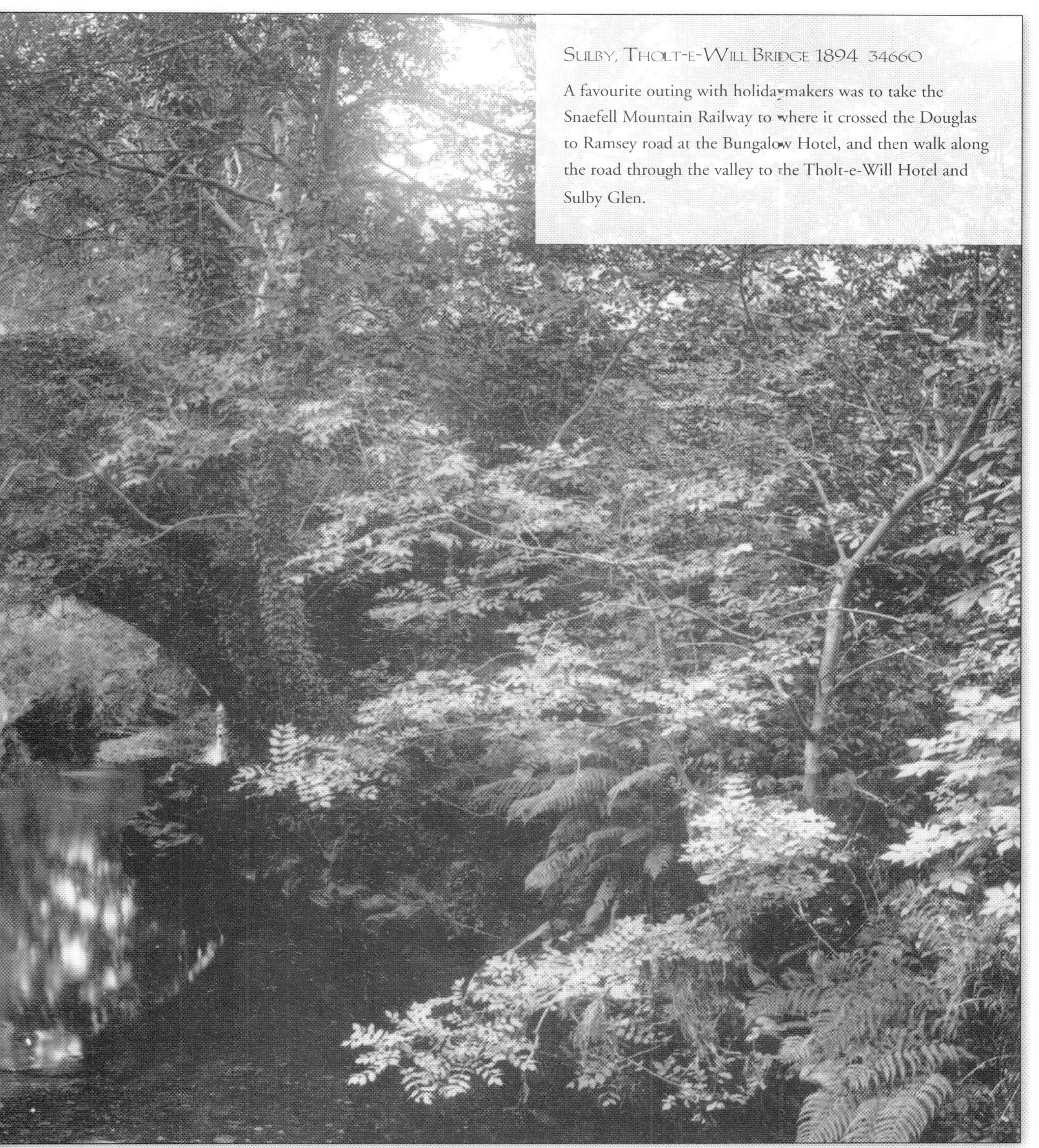

Sulby, Tholt-e-Will Bridge 1894 34660

A favourite outing with holidaymakers was to take the Snaefell Mountain Railway to where it crossed the Douglas to Ramsey road at the Bungalow Hotel, and then walk along the road through the valley to the Tholt-e-Will Hotel and Sulby Glen.

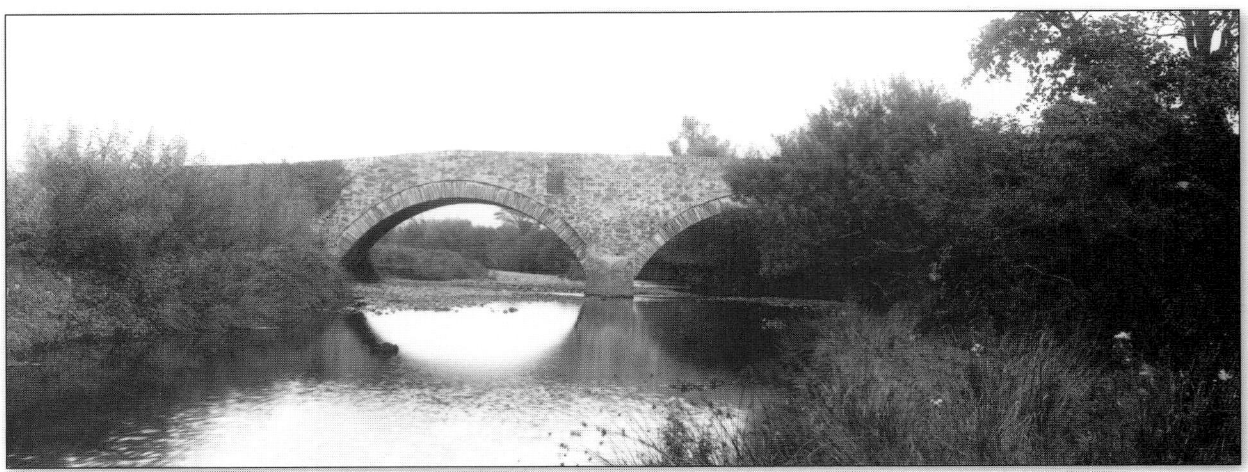

Sulby, The Bridge 1894 34654

Sulby not only gives its name to the island's longest river but also to (probably) its tallest inhabitant. Arthur Caley, the eleventh of twelve children and known as the Sulby Giant, was 7 ft 6 ins tall, and weighed in at 44 stone. Arthur's height landed him a job with Barnum & Bailey's circus.

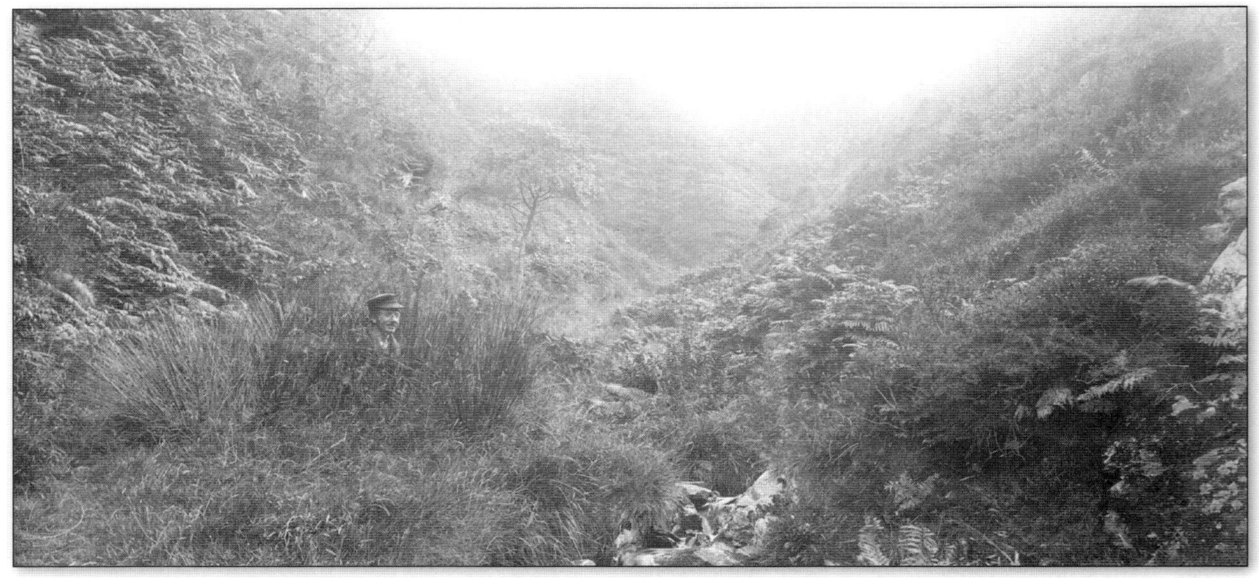

Glen Auldyn, A Hideaway 1894 34651

The 1906 Baedecker Guide states that 'in July and August especially, Douglas and its neighbourhood are practically the playground for the operatives of Lancashire and Yorkshire, but at other seasons and in the smaller town and country districts the 'tripper' element is not conspicuous'. It looks as though our man is on his own.

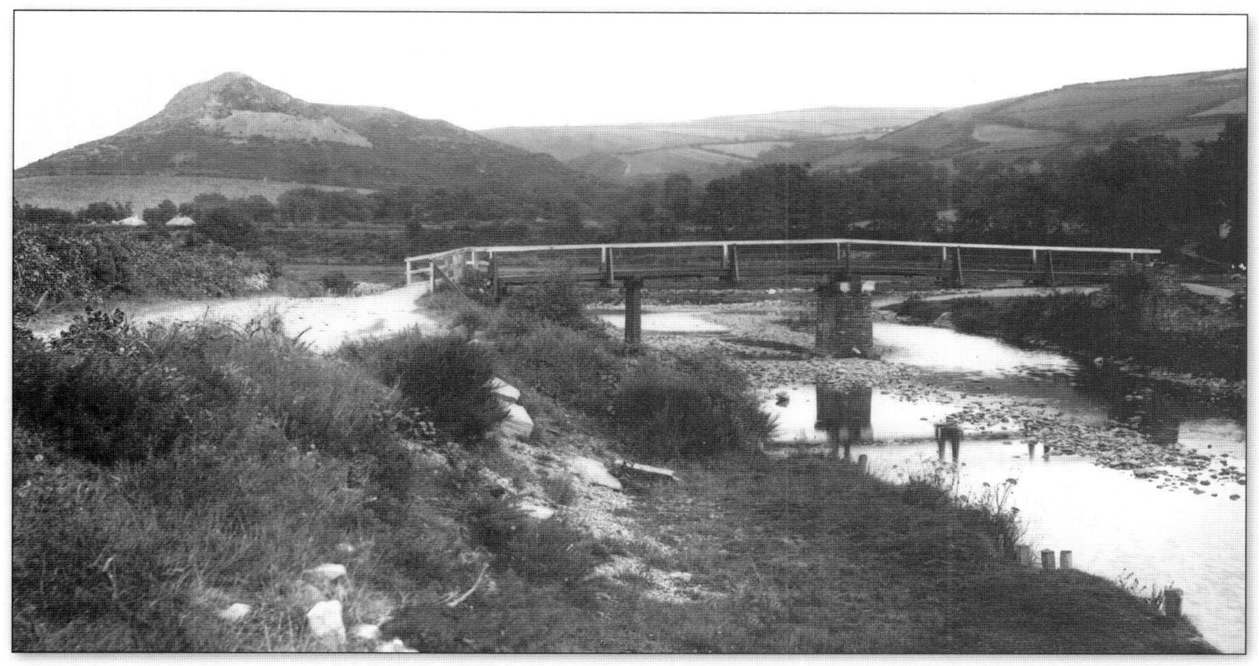

SULBY, THE FOOTBRIDGE AND PRIMROSE HILL 1894 34655

The Manx Electric Railway was quick to capitalise on the popularity of Sulby Glen by offering personally conducted tours. For an all-in price, tourists travelled from Derby Castle to Laxey, where they boarded a Snaefell Mountain Railway car to the Bungalow. From the Bungalow they were taken by charabanc to Sulby Glen, where they were free to explore the area before making the return journey. The price included lunch at the Tholt-e-Will Hotel and admission to the glen.

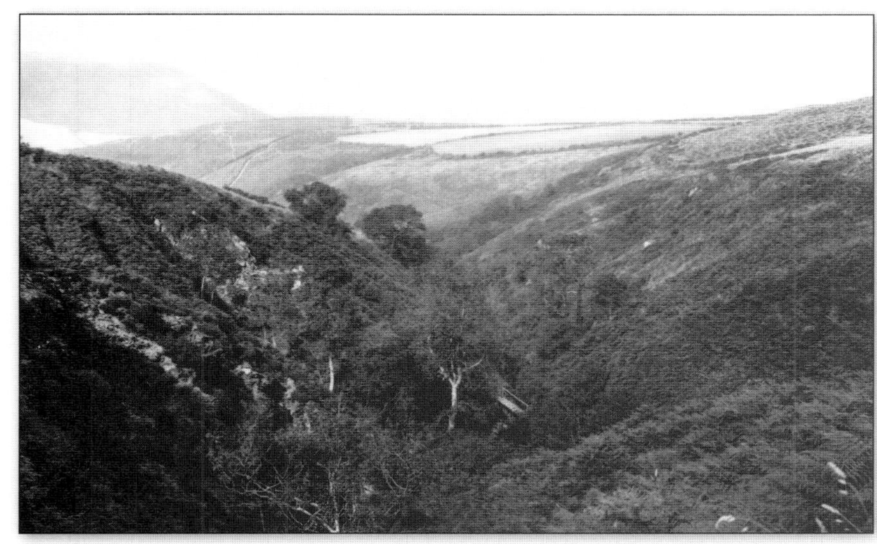

GLEN AULDYN, GENERAL VIEW 1894 34653

This beautiful glen is situated to the north east of Snaefell with steep slopes on either side.

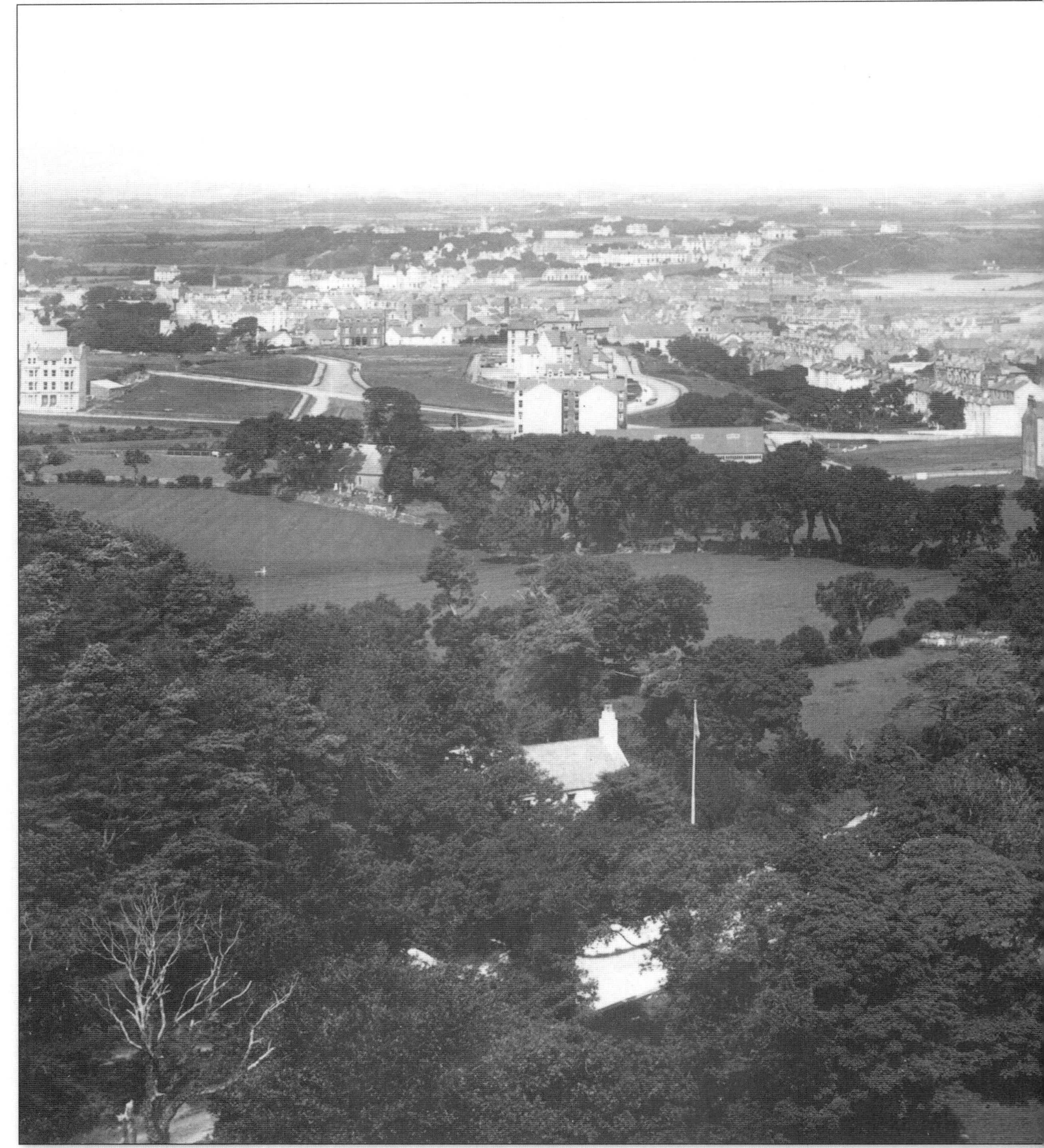

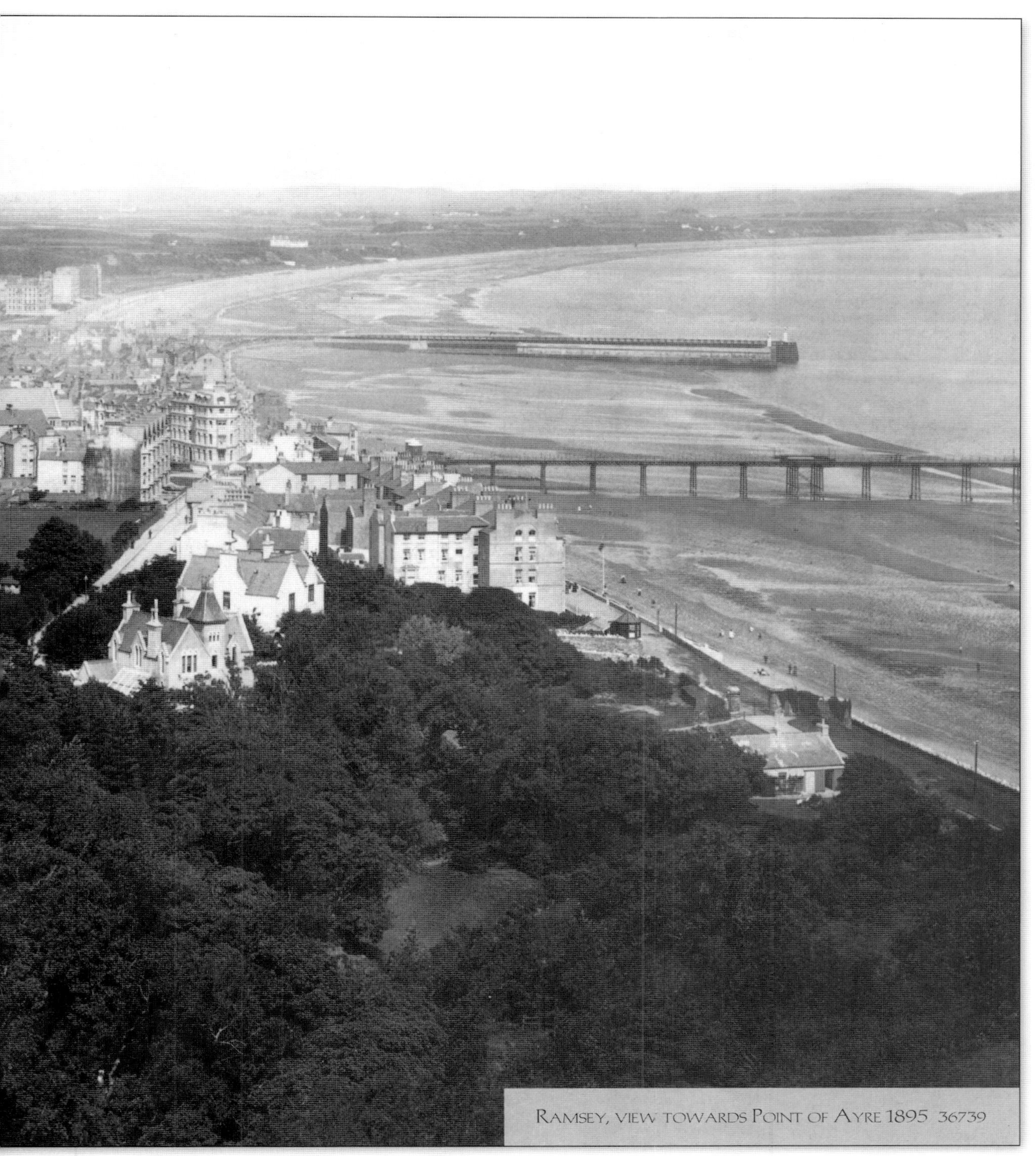

RAMSEY, VIEW TOWARDS POINT OF AYRE 1895 36739

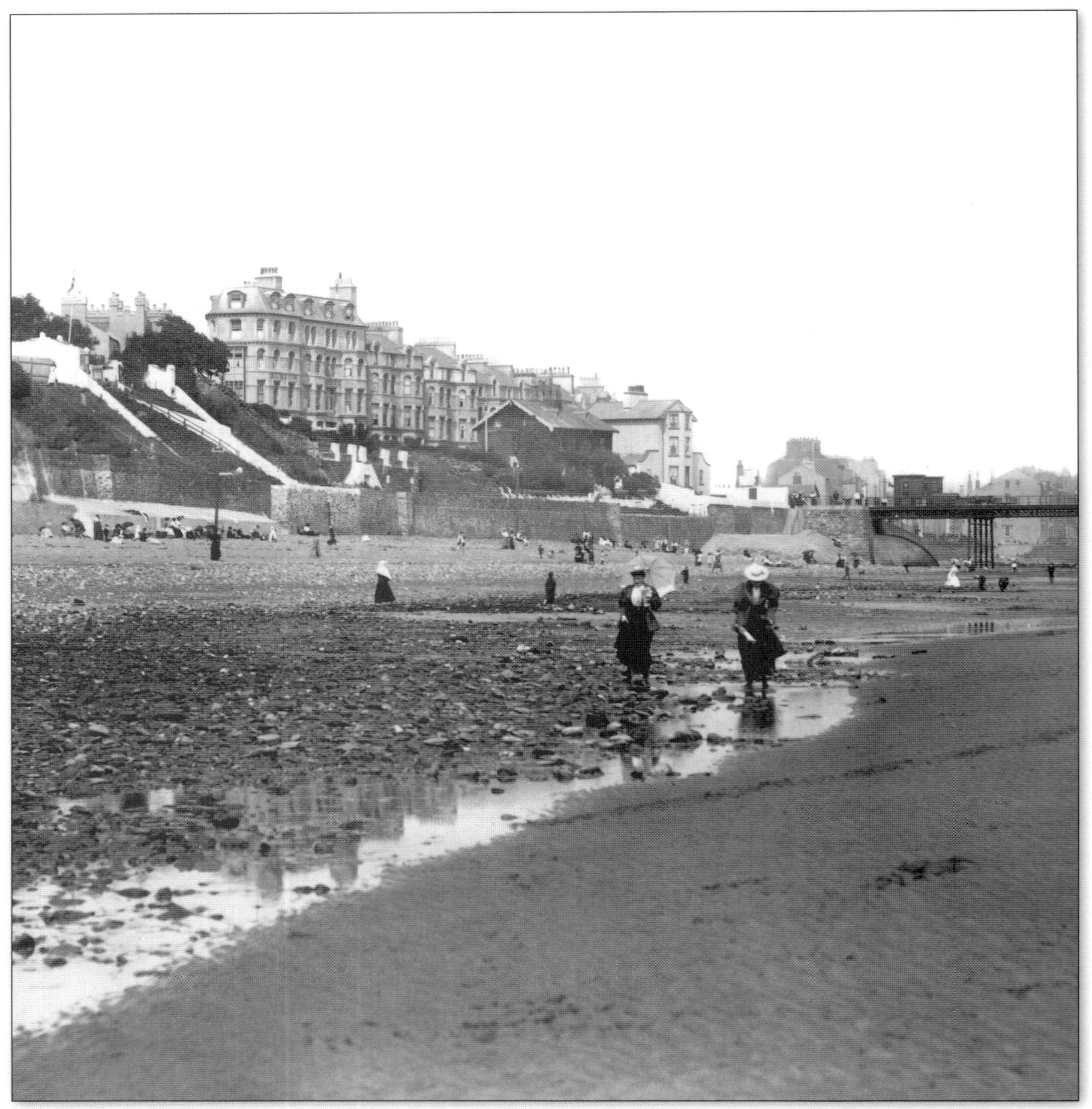

Ramsey, On The Sands 1895 36744

Though the shore to the south of Ramsey is rocky, a stroll along it at low tide was a popular Victorian way of taking some gentle exercise. Following a visit by Edward VII in 1902, the town styled itself 'Royal Ramsey', and why not? After all, Queen Victoria and Prince Albert had also visited the town back in 1847.

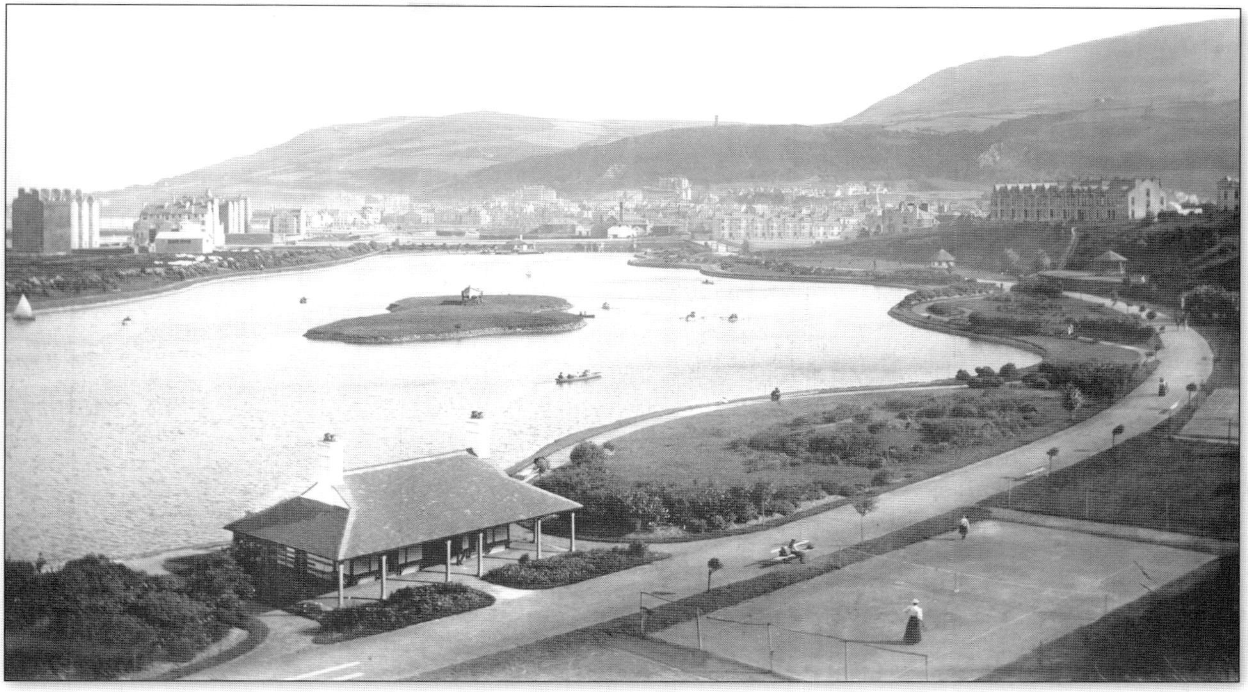

RAMSEY, THE PARK 1895 36741

The Mooragh Park, Lake, and Golf Links were part of a major development begun in 1887 that also included Mooragh Promenade with its fine late-Victorian terraced properties. For those of you who know Mooragh Promenade, the gaps between the terraces are not due to demolition; the houses were never built.

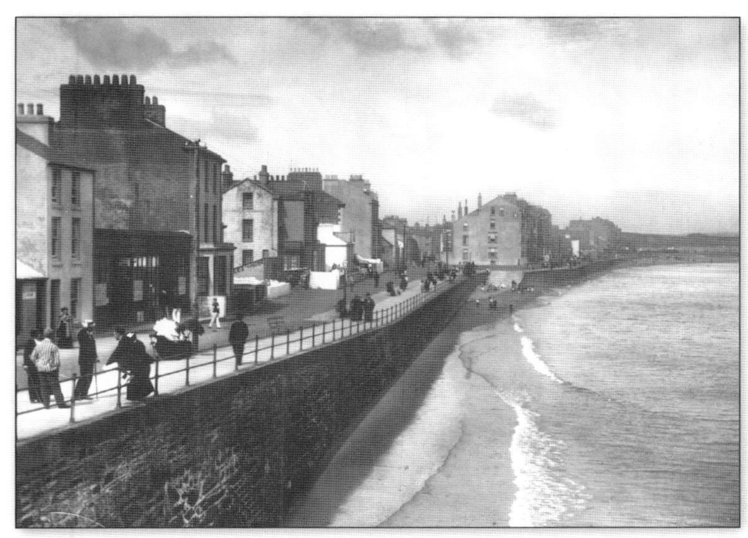

RAMSEY
THE SOUTH PROMENADE 1894 33059

At the height of the season the South Promenade would often be crowded with holidaymakers. The more energetic and adventurous could make their way to the small wooden shed with the sloping roof, where they could hire cycles by the day, week, or longer. This area of the town was redeveloped in the 1970s with the building of the multi-storey Queen's and King's Courts.

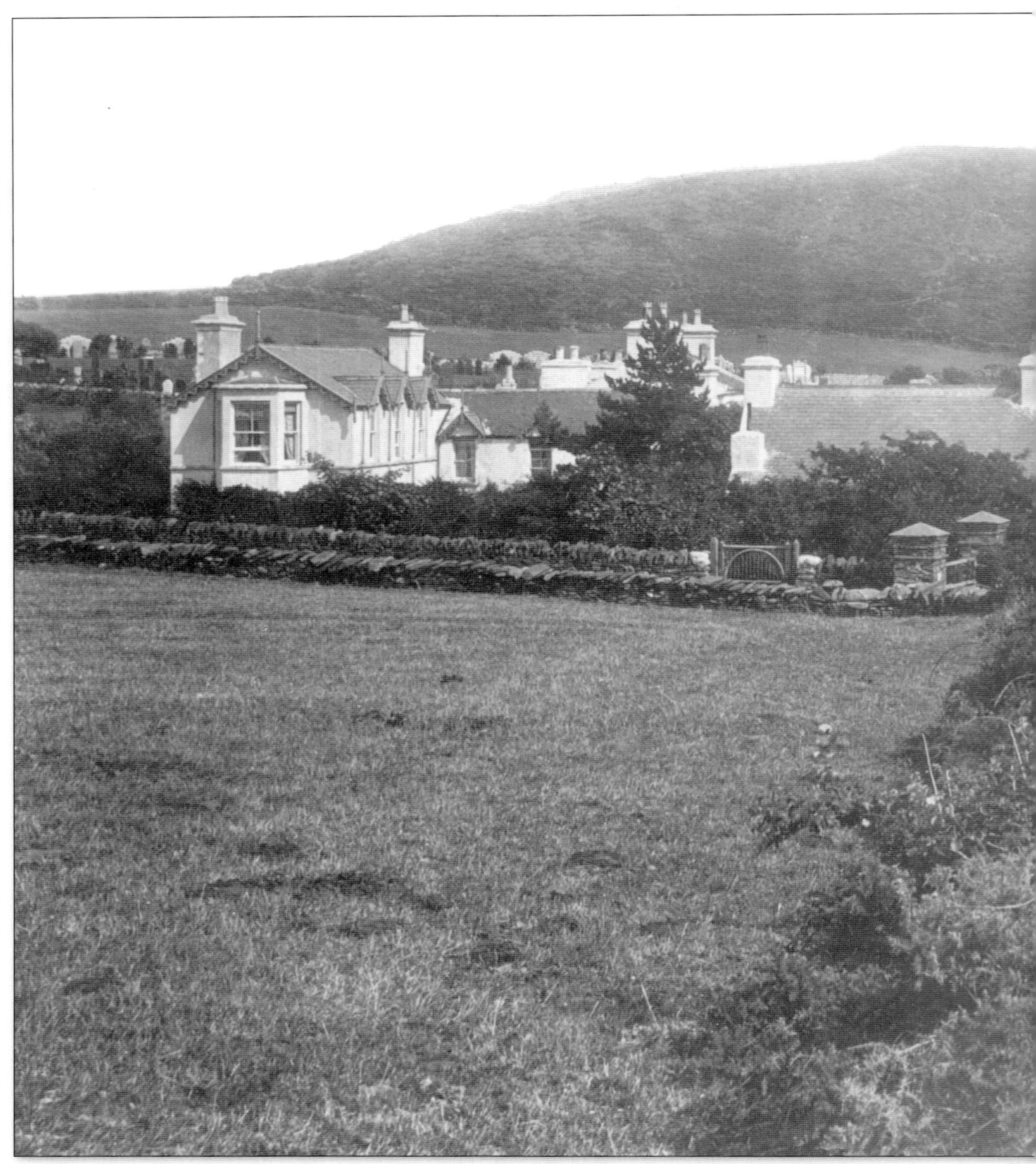

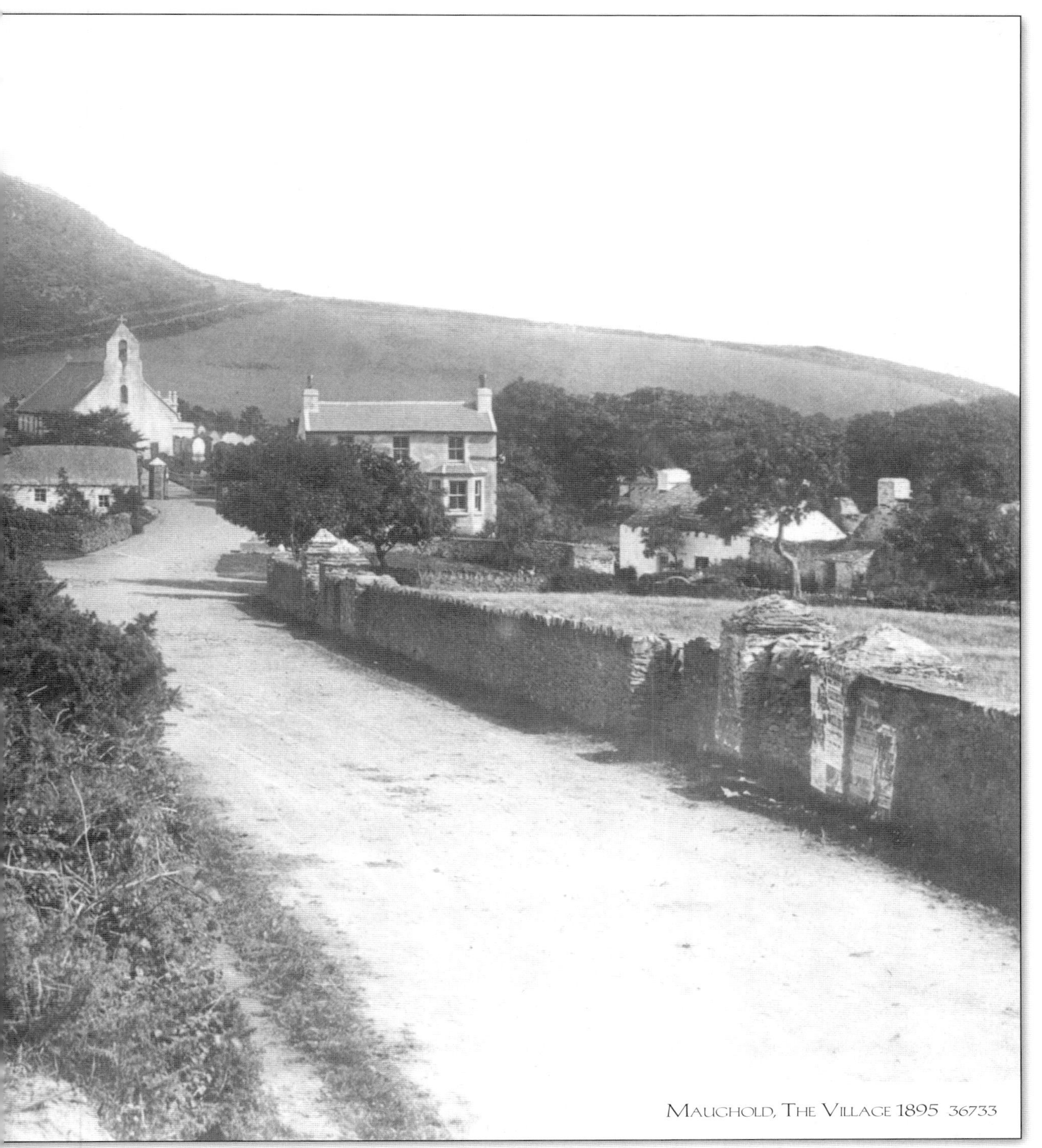

MAUGHOLD, THE VILLAGE 1895 36733

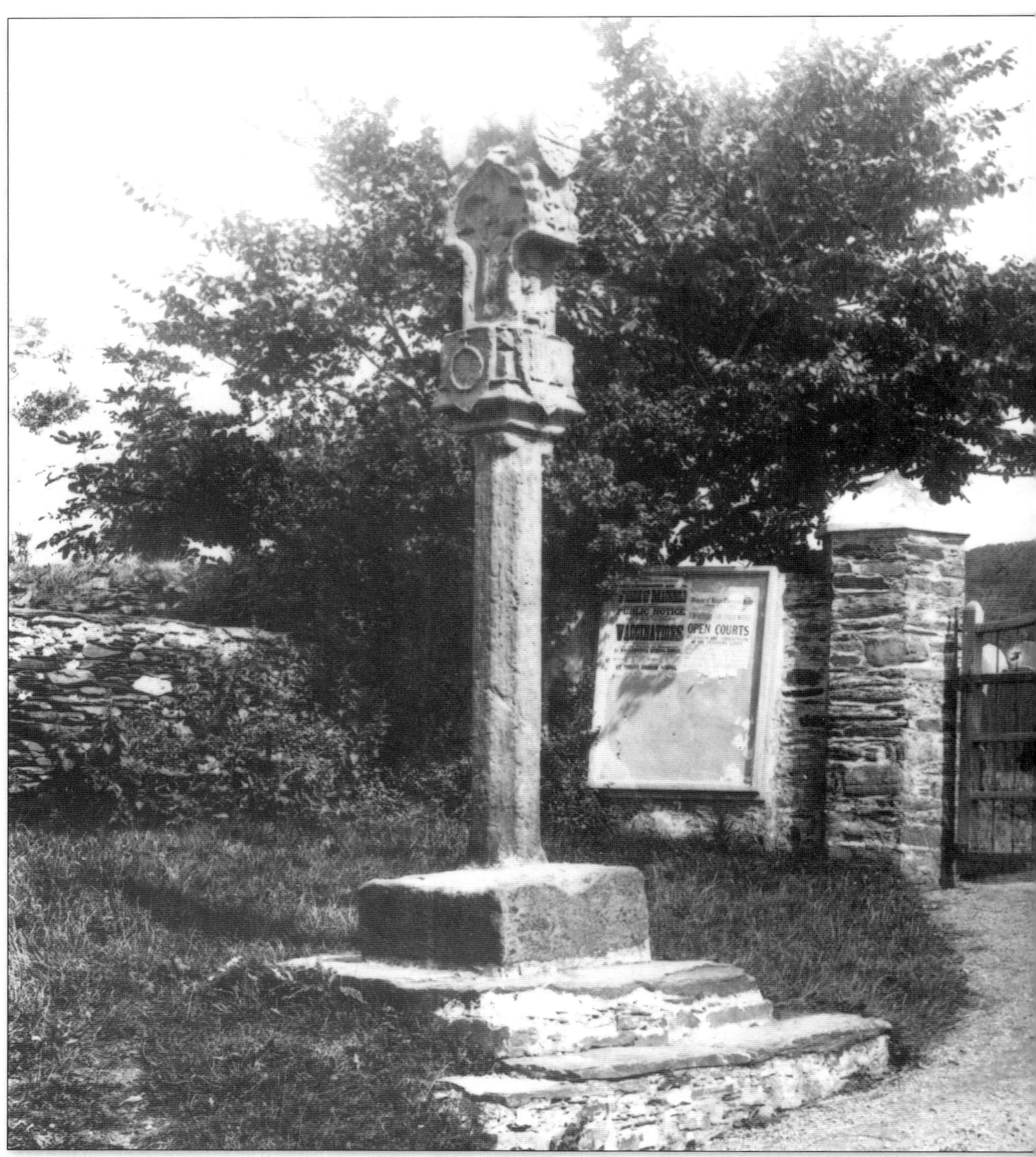
OPEN COURTS

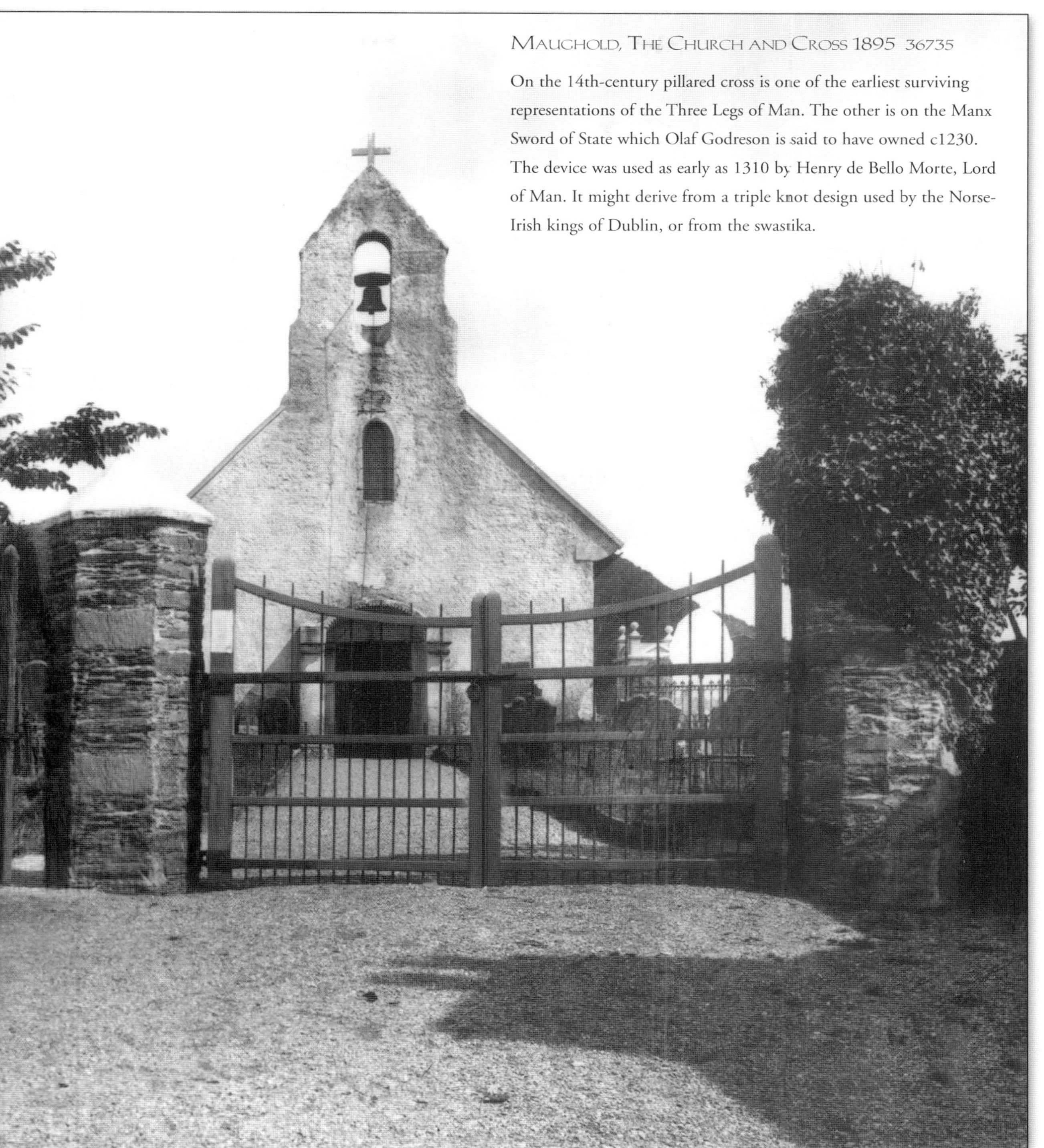

MAUGHOLD, THE CHURCH AND CROSS 1895 36735

On the 14th-century pillared cross is one of the earliest surviving representations of the Three Legs of Man. The other is on the Manx Sword of State which Olaf Godreson is said to have owned c1230. The device was used as early as 1310 by Henry de Bello Morte, Lord of Man. It might derive from a triple knot design used by the Norse-Irish kings of Dublin, or from the swastika.

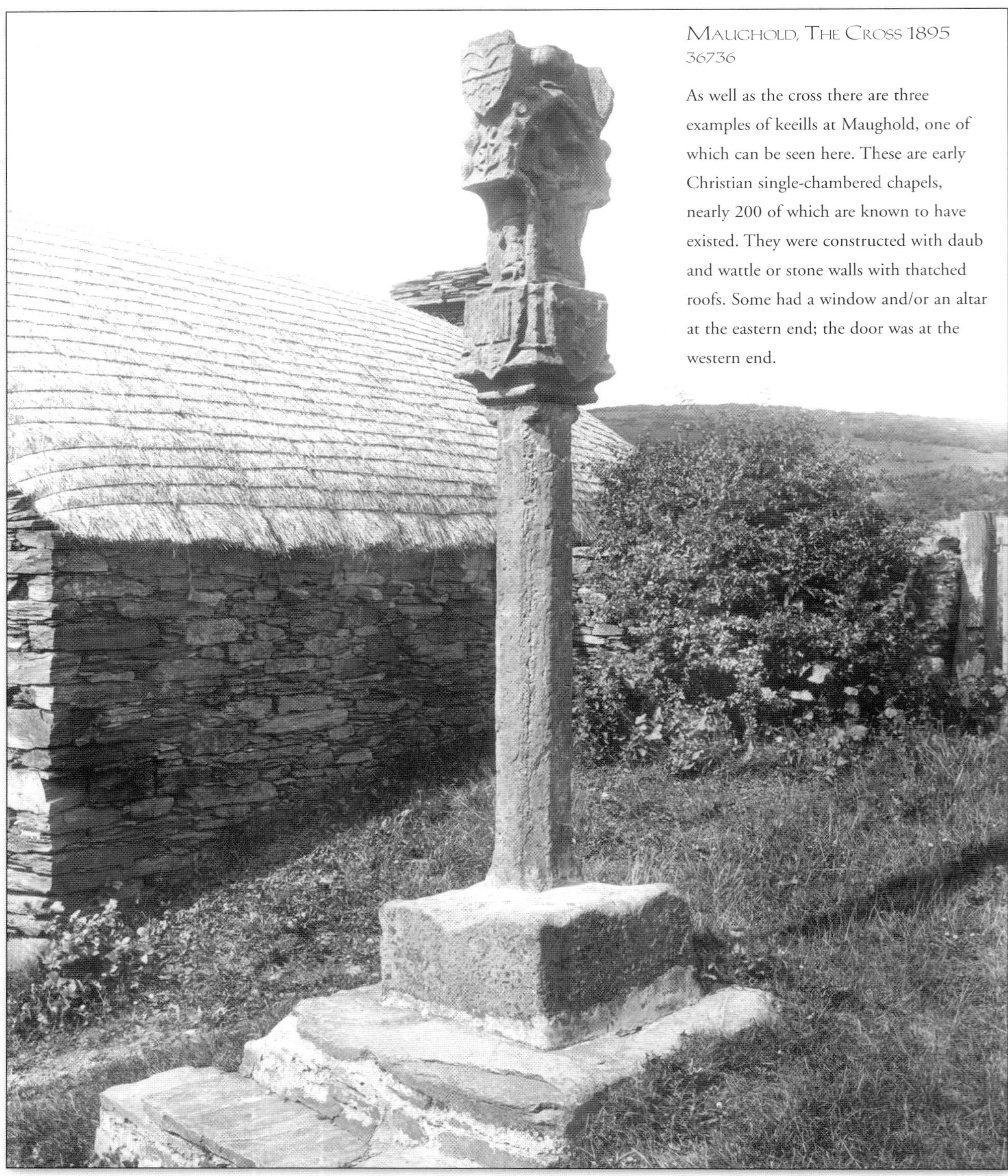

Maughold, The Cross 1895
36736

As well as the cross there are three examples of keeills at Maughold, one of which can be seen here. These are early Christian single-chambered chapels, nearly 200 of which are known to have existed. They were constructed with daub and wattle or stone walls with thatched roofs. Some had a window and/or an altar at the eastern end; the door was at the western end.

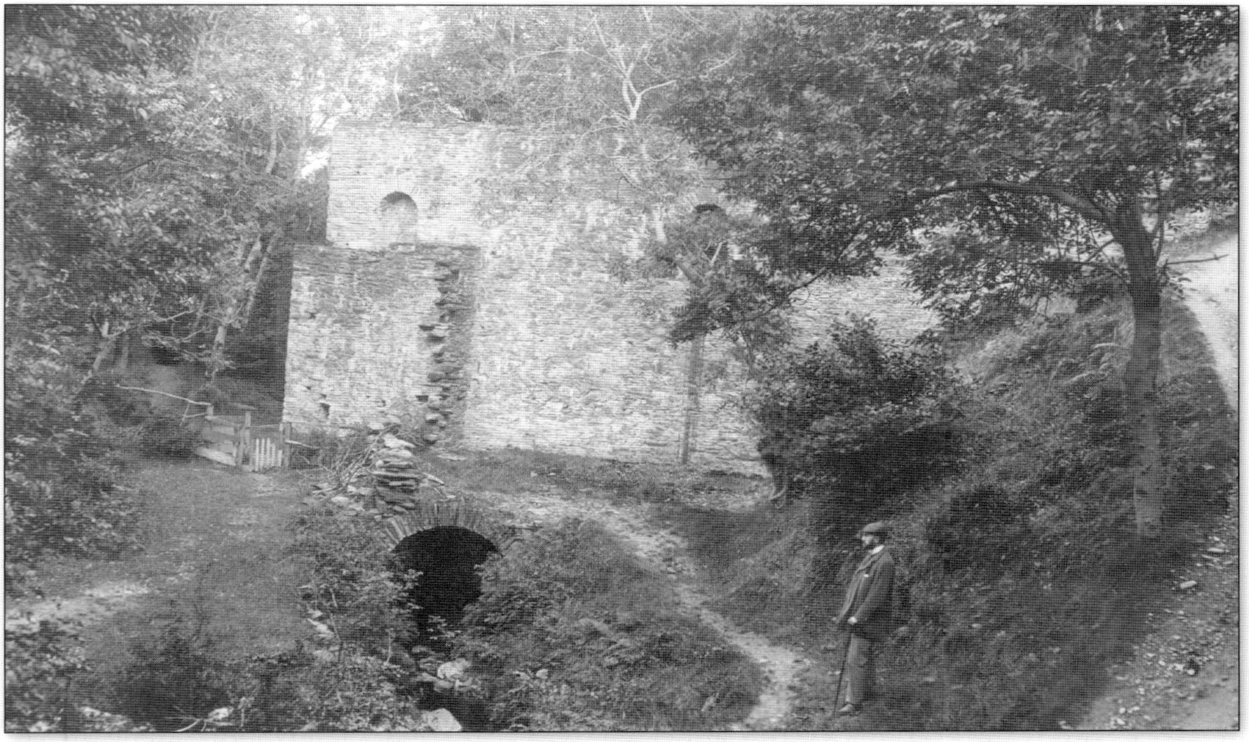

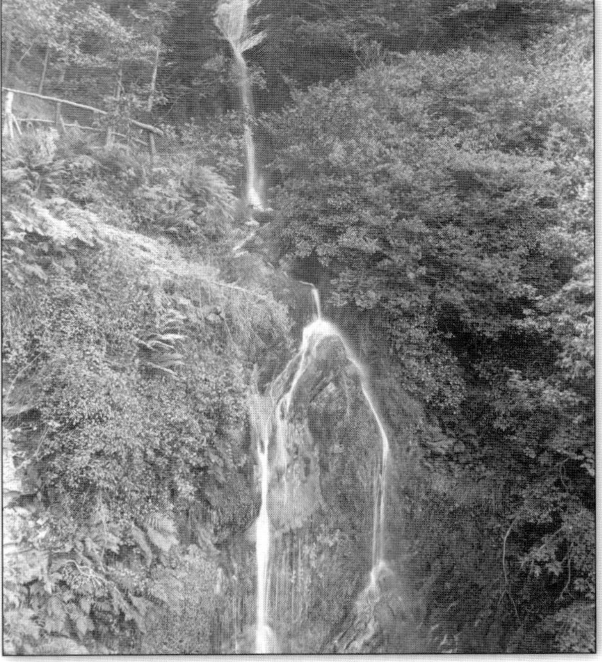

Above: DHOON GLEN 1894 34646

In Manx, 'Dhoon' means fort, though this structure is the nearest to a fortification. As with other glens, Dhoon also had its hotel, a wooden affair at the entrance which burnt down in 1932 and was never rebuilt.

Left: DHOON GLEN
THE WATERFALL 1894 34644

Dhoon Glen is now a Manx National Heritage site of special ecological importance, as there are plants here which are not found anywhere else on the island, and others that are rare in Man. It is also a site of geological interest.

RAMSEY TO DOUGLAS

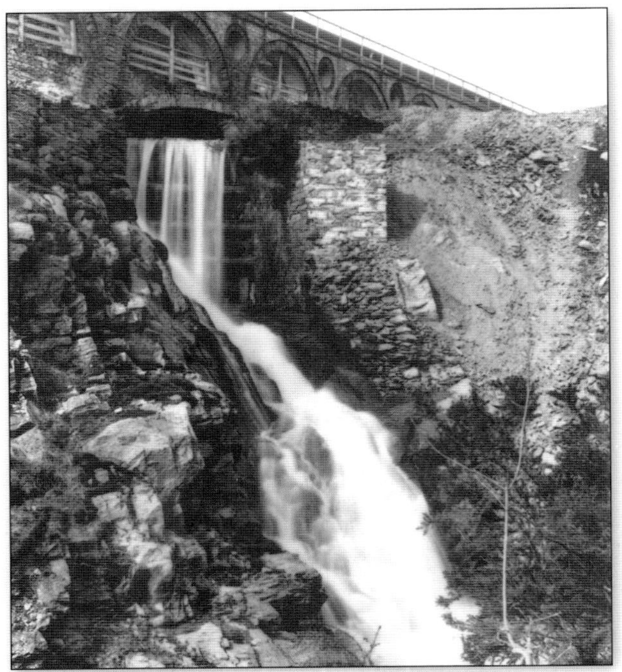

Left: LAXEY, THE WATERFALL 1896 37208

This photographs shows the waterfall, and above that the T-rocker viaduct of the Lady Isabella. In 1930 a flash flood swept down Laxey Valley with sufficient force to destroy the central section of the T-rocker, though it was later restored.

Below: LAXEY, THE WHEEL 1896 37206

Designed by Manxman Robert Casement and commissioned in September 1854 to pump water from the Laxey mines, the wheel was in regular use until 1920. It is named Lady Isabella in honour of Lady Isabella Hope, wife of Governor Hope. When this picture was taken, the mining company charged visitors 3d each to use the observation platform. In 1854, Laxey Mining's £80 paid shares were trading at £1,200 each.

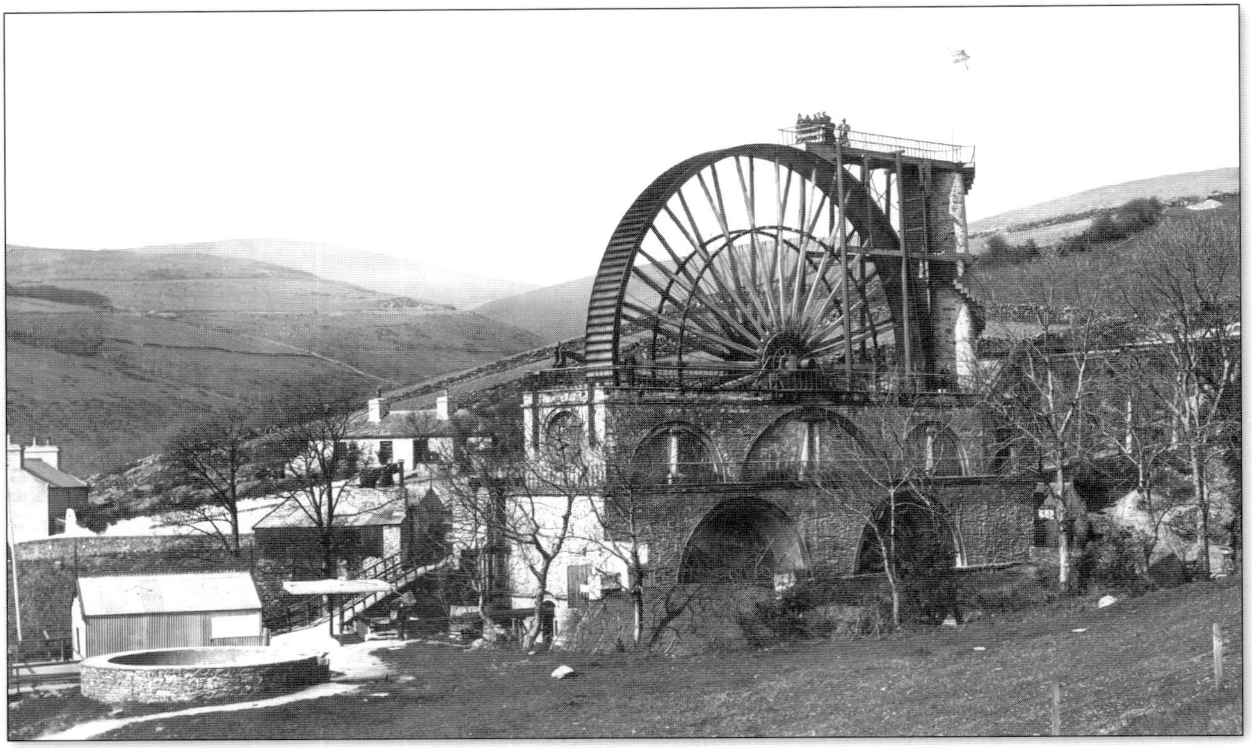

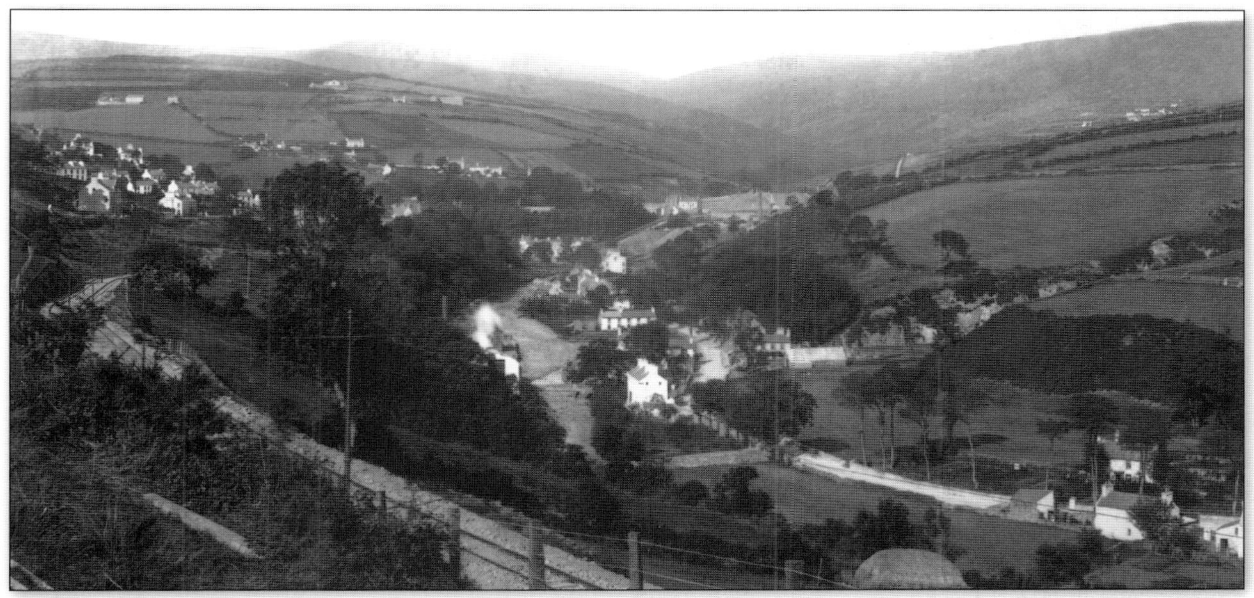

LAXEY, GENERAL VIEW 1894 34641

A number of cottages in Laxey were built by George William Dumbell, chairman of the Laxey Mining Co, for his miners and their families. He also donated land for a chapel. Dumbell's Row still stands, as do other links with Laxey's mining past; the Station Hotel was once the Mine Captain's house.

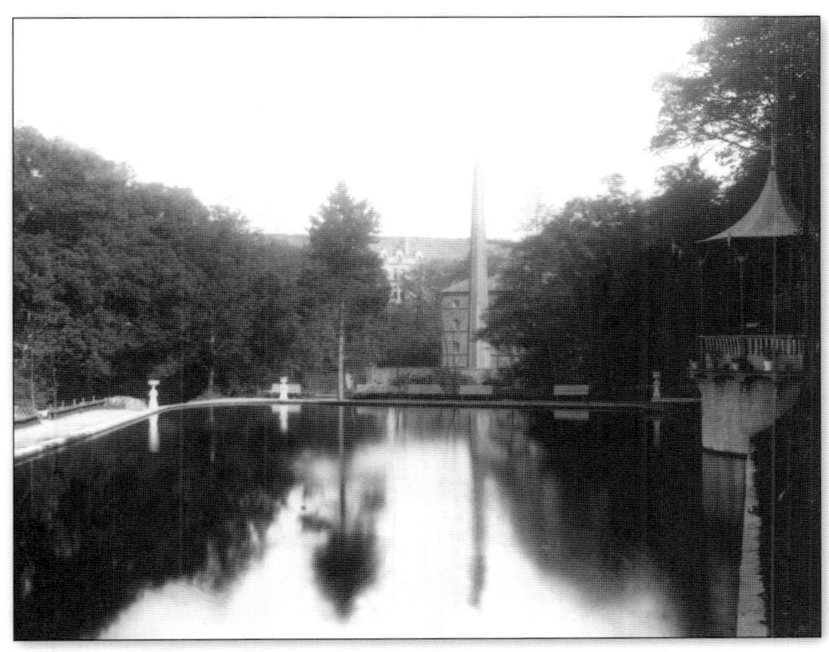

LAXEY, VIEW OF THE GARDENS 1894 34643

Laxey's popularity with holidaymakers grew after the opening of the coast electric tramway. The operators of Laxey Glen Gardens were among the pioneers of today's leisure and theme parks. Visitors paid an entrance fee, the entertainments were free: tennis, quoits, bowling, croquet, hobby horses, swings, and brass band concerts.

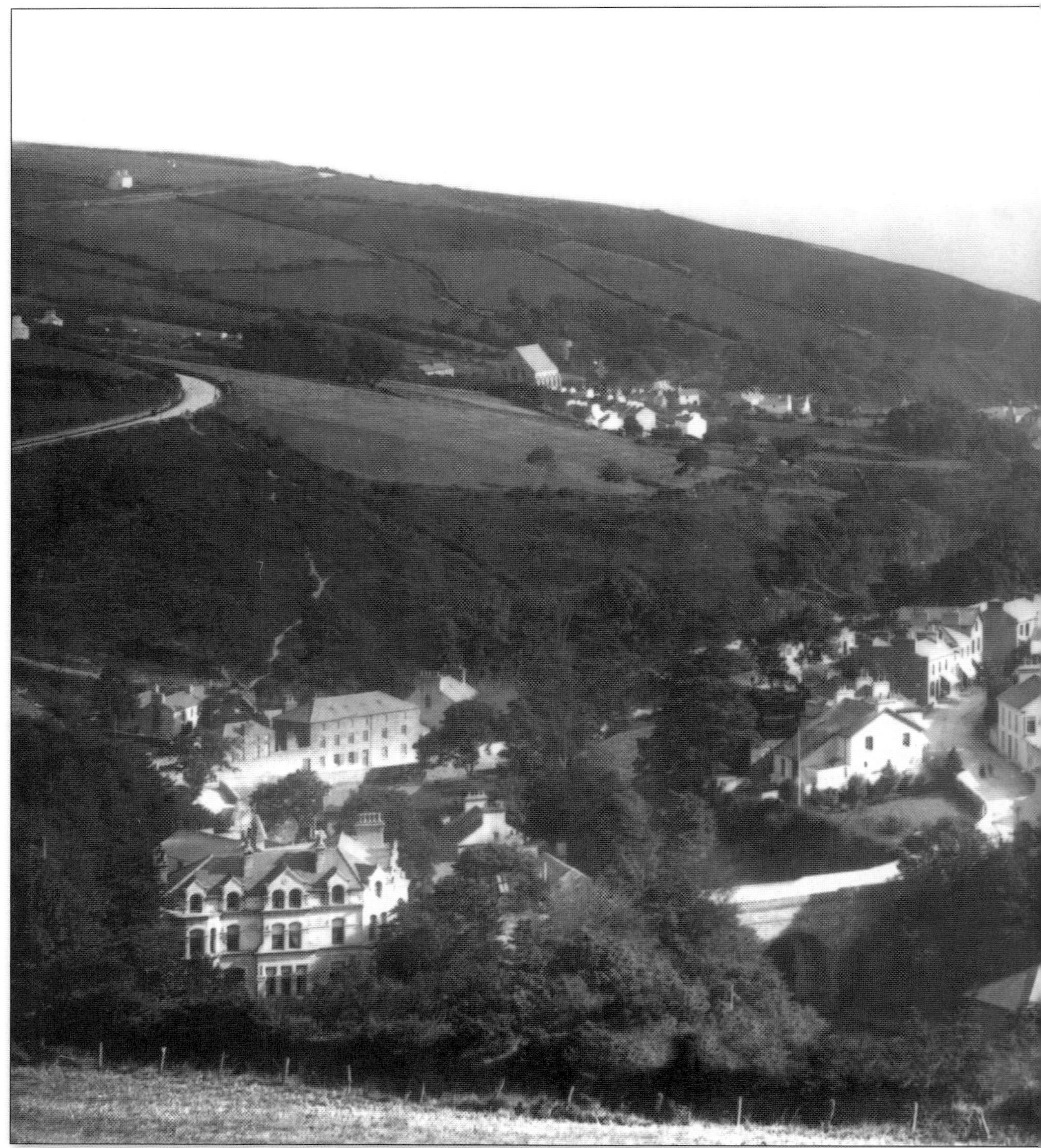

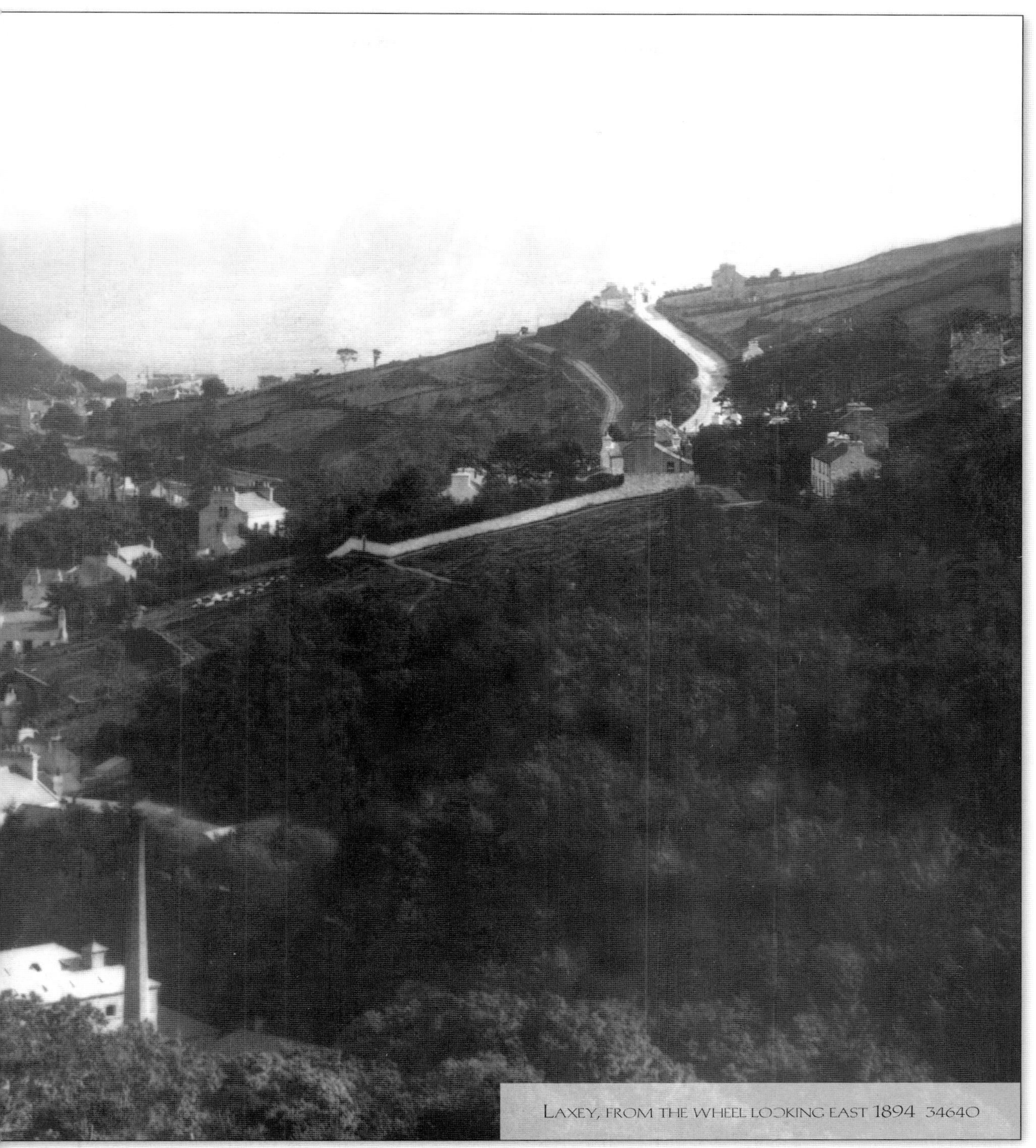

LAXEY, FROM THE WHEEL LOOKING EAST 1894 34640

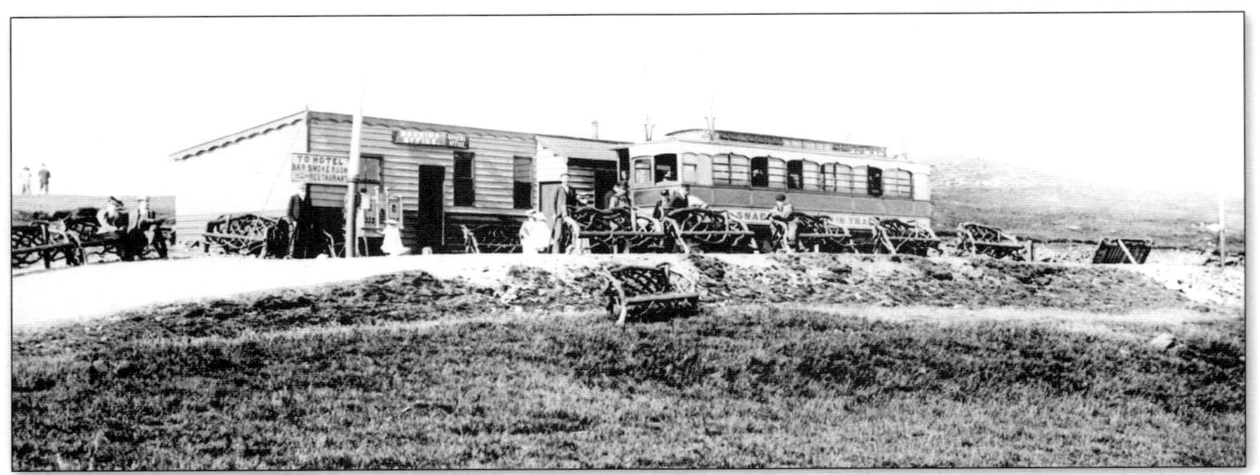

SNAEFELL, SUMMIT STATION 1897 39890

The Snaefell Mountain Railway opened for traffic in August 1895. It operates on the Fell system, whereby a third rail is laid in the centre of the track. This is gripped by wheels that ensure the car stays on the rails, and by brake shoes that provide additional braking on the line's severe gradients. In 1897 a return trip up Snaefell from Laxey cost 2s return.

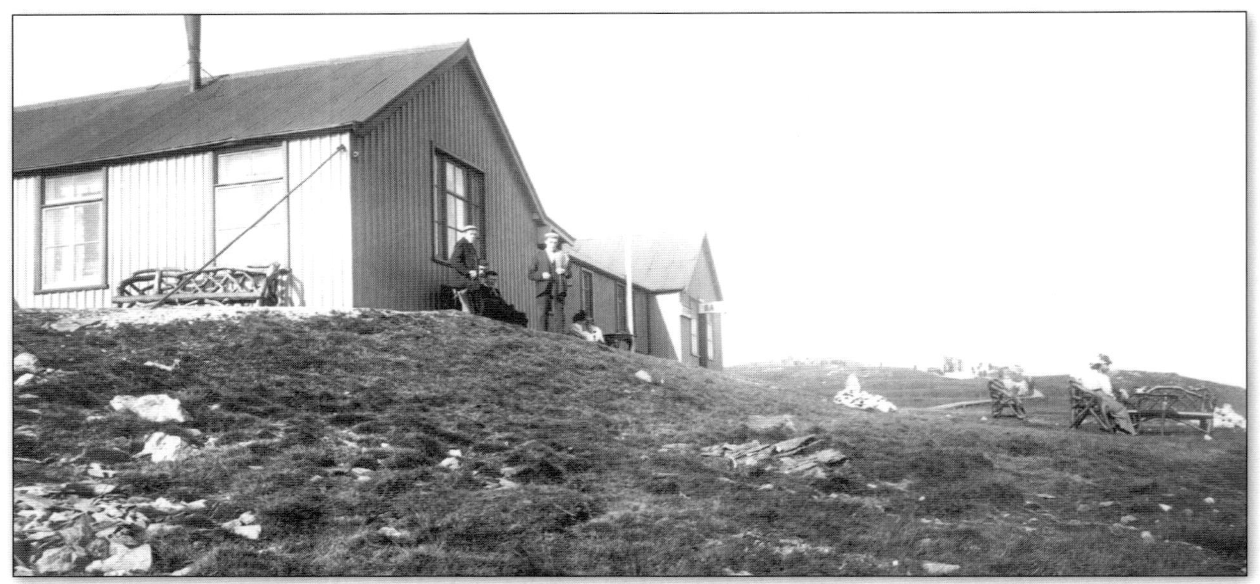

SNAEFELL, THE SUMMIT 1897 39888

On sunny days, Snaefell summit (2034 ft) offers the visitor superb views of England, Ireland and Scotland. In 1906 the Summit Hotel was rebuilt in the castellated style complete with turrets. Unfortunately, it was badly damaged by fire in 1982 and restoration work has left a much plainer building.

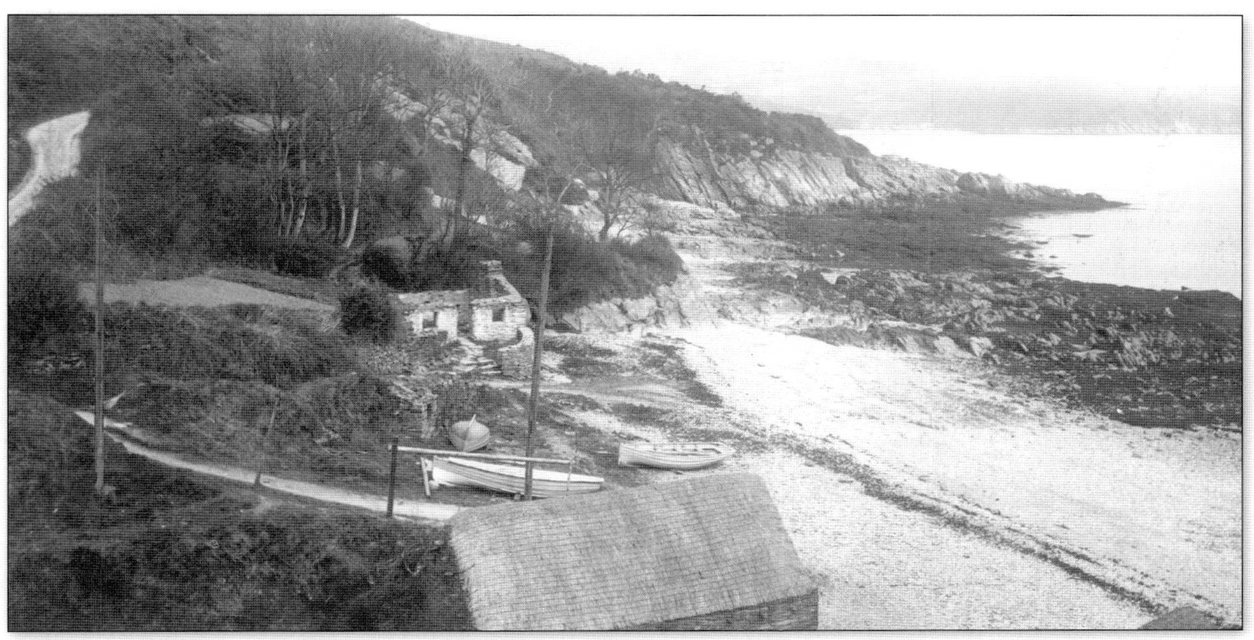

GARWICK, THE BEACH AND GLEN 1896 37203

Situated between Groudle Glen and Laxey, Garwick was just twenty minutes away from Douglas on the Manx Electric Tramway, but it looks as though our intrepid cameraman had the place all to himself. The view is towards Laxey Bay and Gob y Rheynn.

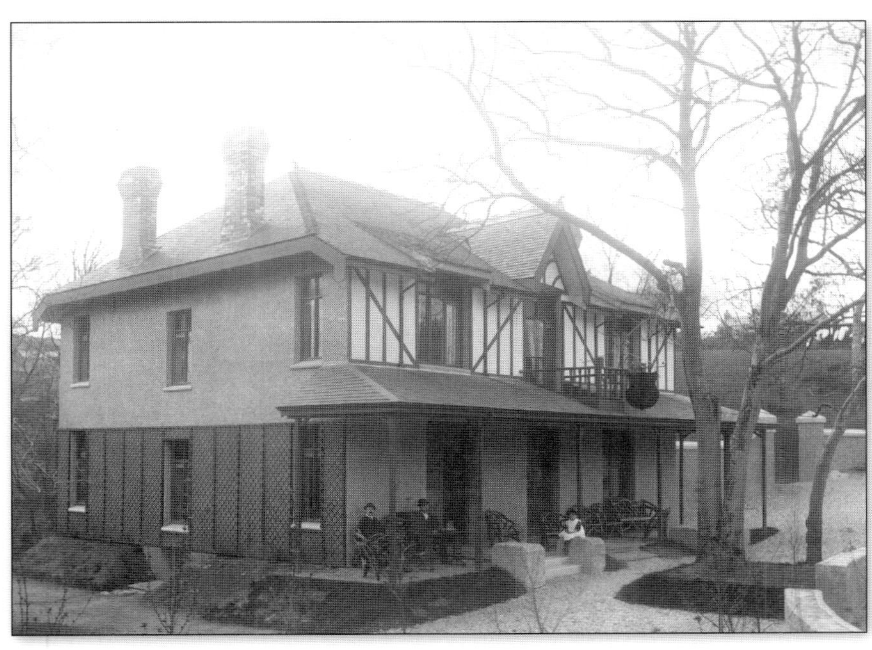

GARWICK, THE HOTEL 1896 37205

There were hotels at or near most of the glens. Prices for a pension (room, meals and service) at the glen hotels were on a par with those charged by some of the Peel and Port St Mary hotels for similar arrangements.

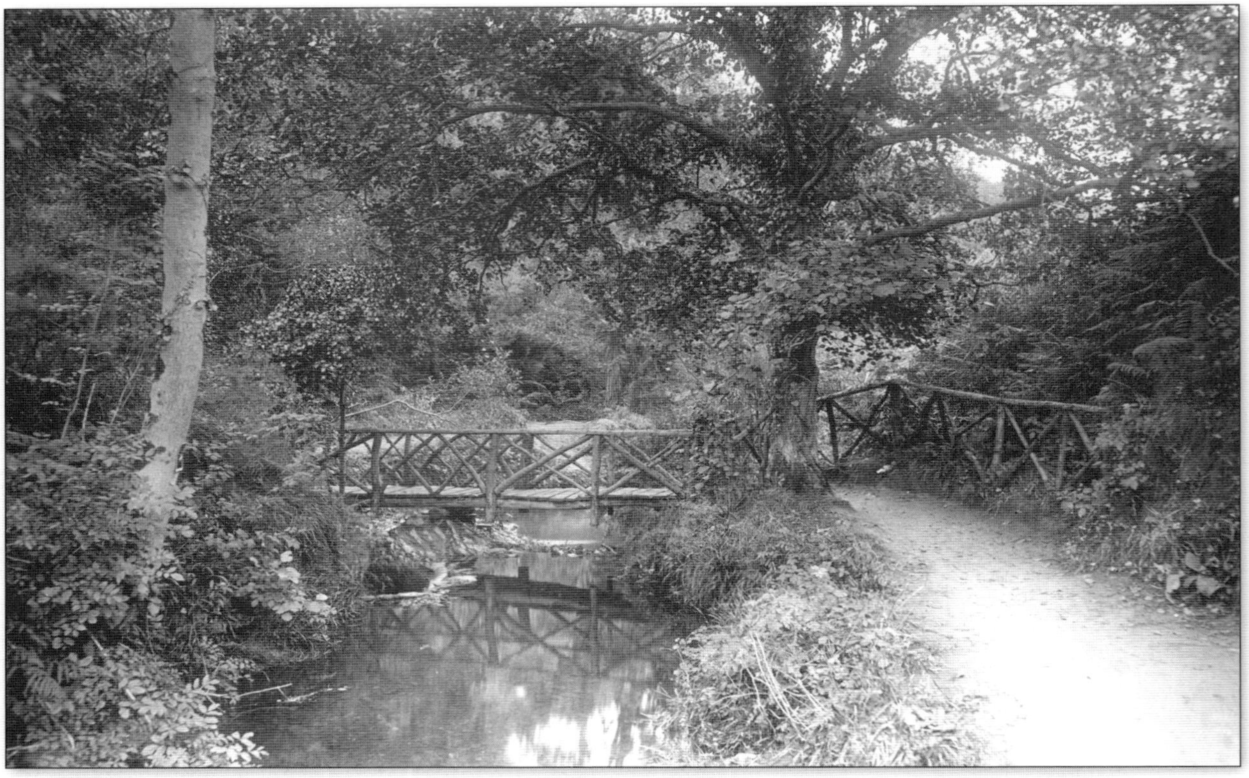

Ramsey to Douglas

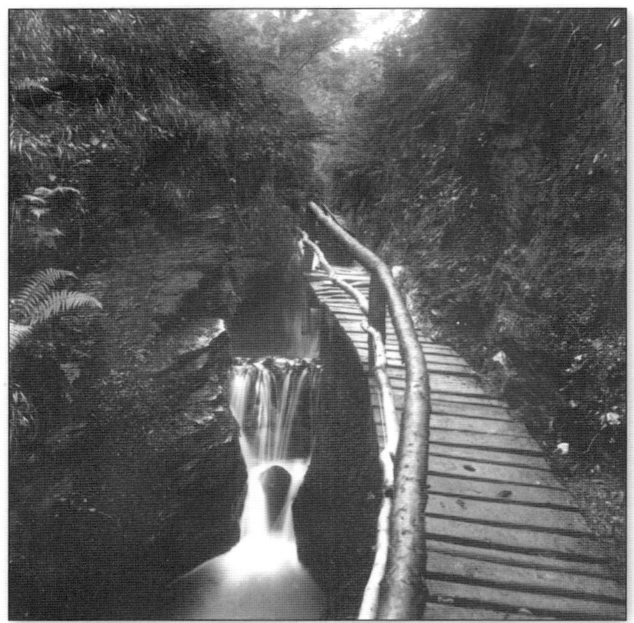

Above: Groudle Glen 1894 34635

The vast majority of day visitors to the island rarely strayed beyond Douglas and Onchan, but the opening of the first section of the Manx Electric Railway in September 1893 brought Groudle Glen within easy reach. Situated just two and a half miles from Douglas, the Glen is known as 'the Fern Land of Mona'.

Left: Groudle Glen, Lhen Coan 1894 34637

In 1896 Groudle Glen opened its own railway from Lhen Coan station to a terminus at Sea Lion Cove, and at less than one mile in length it was one of the shortest passenger-carrying railways in the world. Not only were the passengers treated to some wonderful natural scenery, there were also enclosures for both polar bears and sea lions. Lhen Coan translates as 'lovely Glen'.

Right: GROUDLE GLEN, THE WATERWHEEL 1907 59178

The Groudle Glen waterwheel is somewhat smaller than the Lady Isabella. It was built neither to grind corn, drive machinery, nor pump out a mine. It was of no practical use, having been built purely as an attraction for Edwardian visitors.

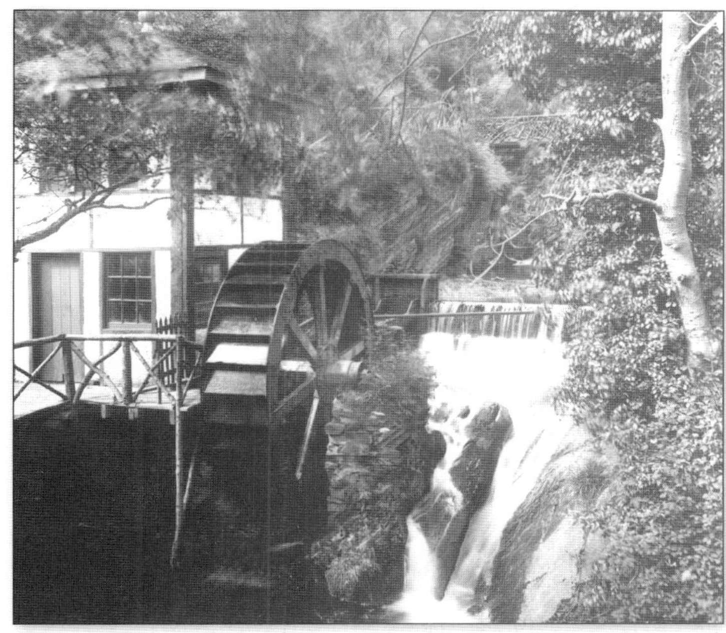

Below: GROUDLE GLEN, THE RUSTIC PATH 1894 34636

Only a year earlier Mr R M Broadbent had opened the Groudle Glen Hotel as part of a continuing series of improvements to attract visitors. The natural beauty of the glen could be experienced by taking the rustic walkways to the rocky and often breezy headland with its deep inlets.

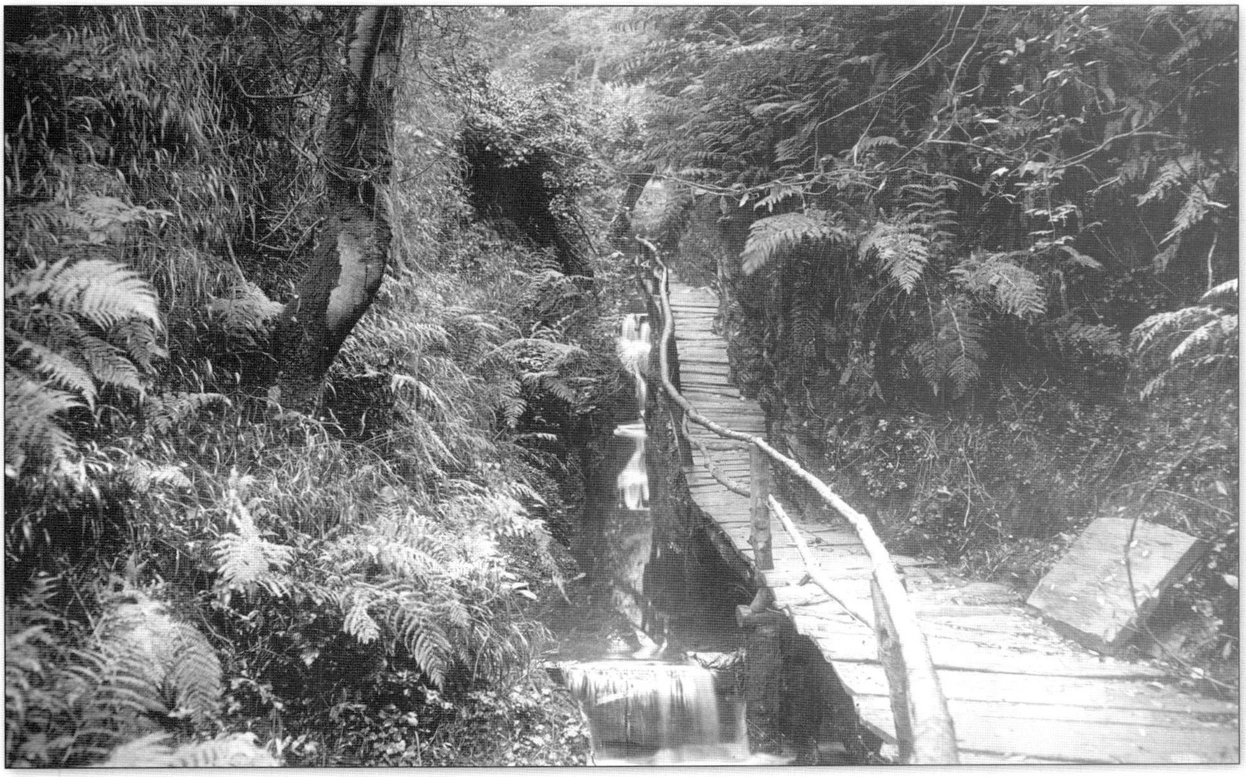

Douglas to Port Erin

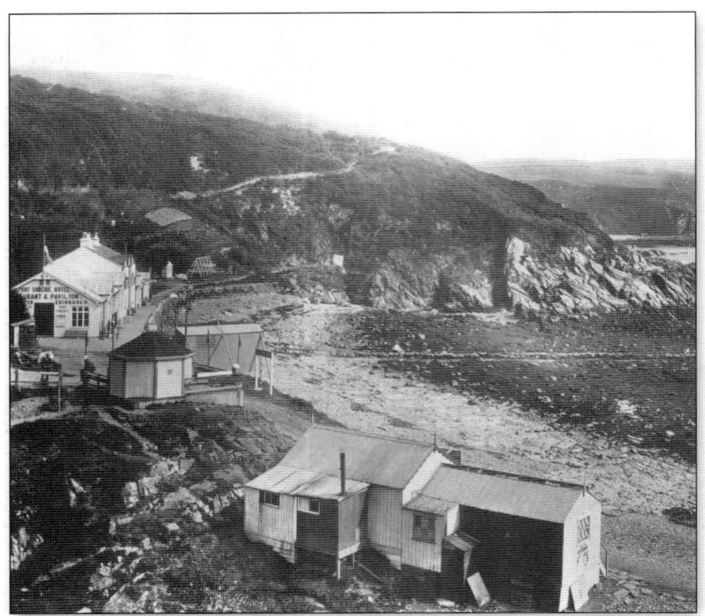

Left: Port Soderick, The Beach 1893 33026

Port Soderick was developed in the 1890s by the Forrester family, and was one of the first attractions created for the tourist industry. It was close enough to Douglas to entice day trippers to pay a visit.

Below: Port Soderick, The Hotel 1893 33028

On the left of the picture is a poster advertising a sacred concert at the Bijou Theatre, one of a number of ways in which Victorian holidaymakers could celebrate their Christian faith. During the season, open-air services were held at Douglas Head, and of course there were the tremendously popular services at Kirk Braddan, some of which are said to have attracted congregations approaching 20,000 people.

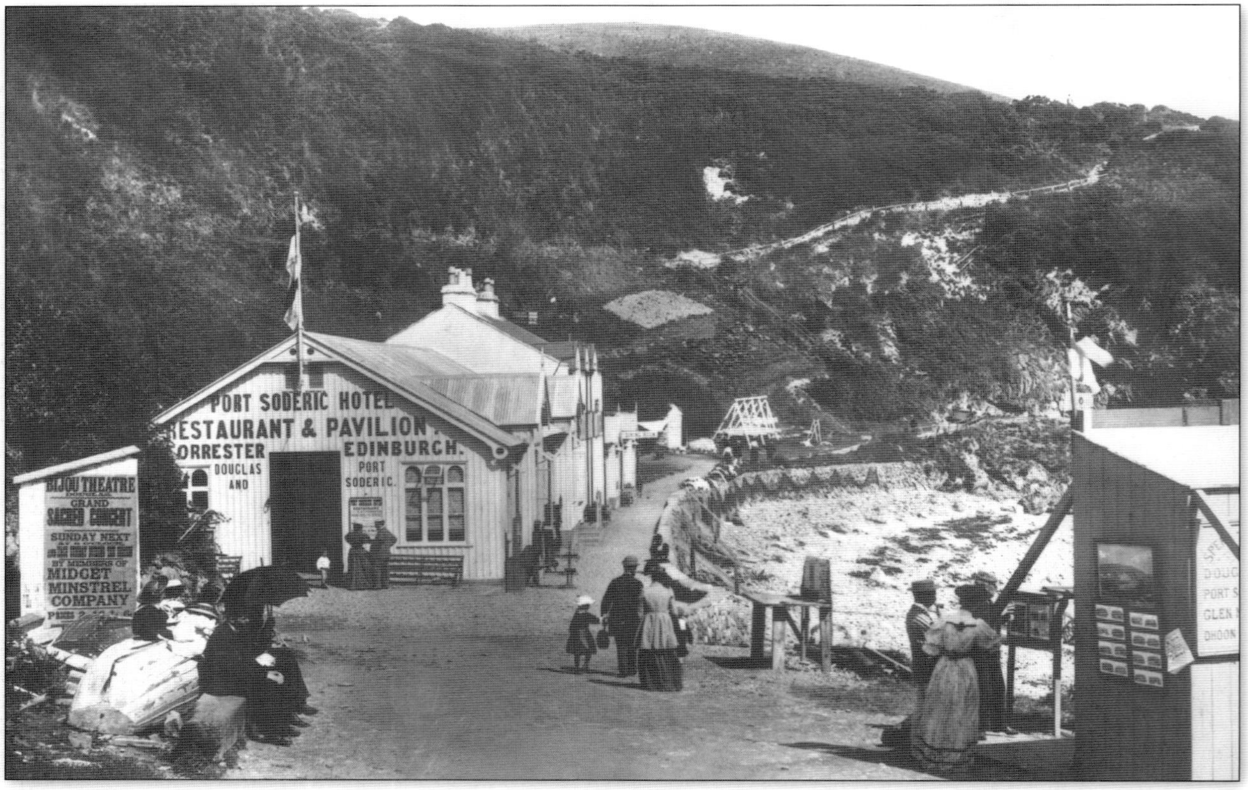

Right: PORT SODERICK, THE CAVES 1893
33029

An 1896 official guide states that Port Soderick is the most popular pleasure resort on Man, 'Romantic, Natural and the only FREE Glen on the island'. Even the smugglers' caves are free.

Below: PORT SODERICK, THE HOTEL 1903
50662

A few improvements have been made in the ten years since the previous pictures of Port Soderick were taken. The hotel has acquired a canopied front, and the inclined tramway (formally located at the Falcon Cliff Hotel, Douglas) has been rebuilt here to link the resort with the terminus of the Douglas Southern Electric Tramway. For a fare of 6d each way, the DSET offered passengers an exciting cliff-edge ride between Port Soderick and Douglas Head.

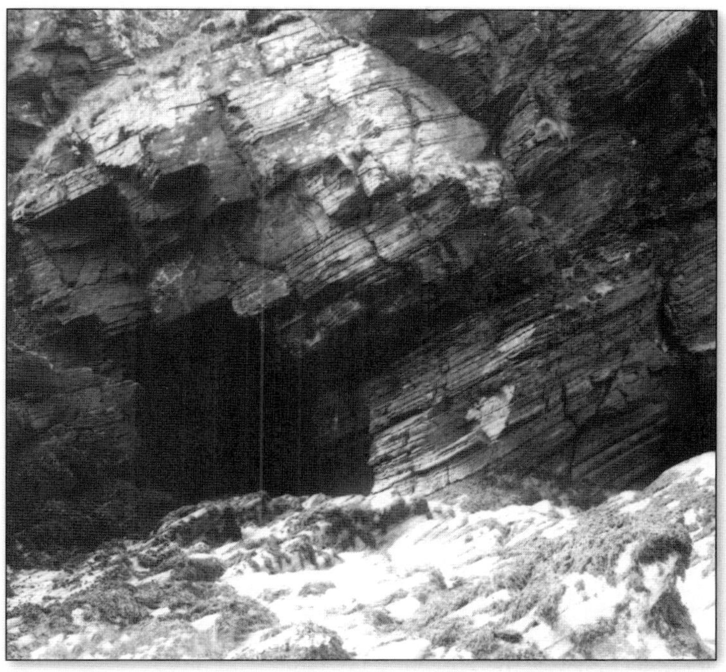

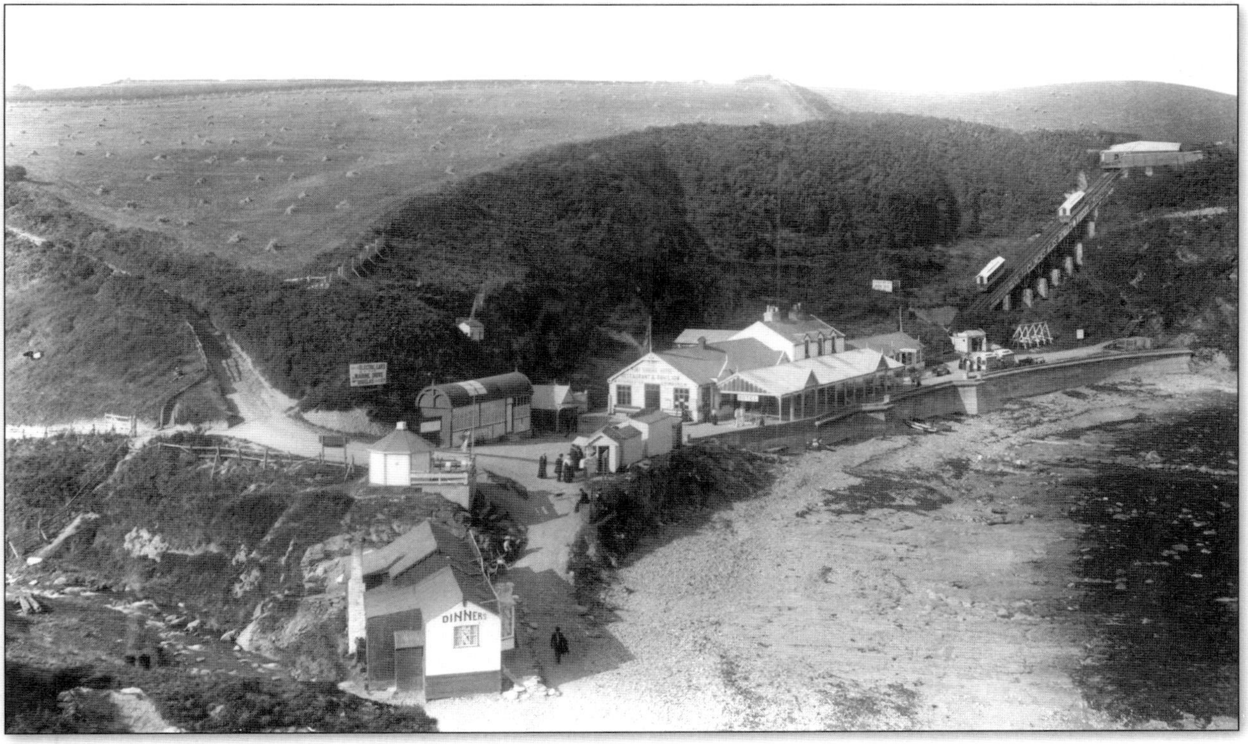

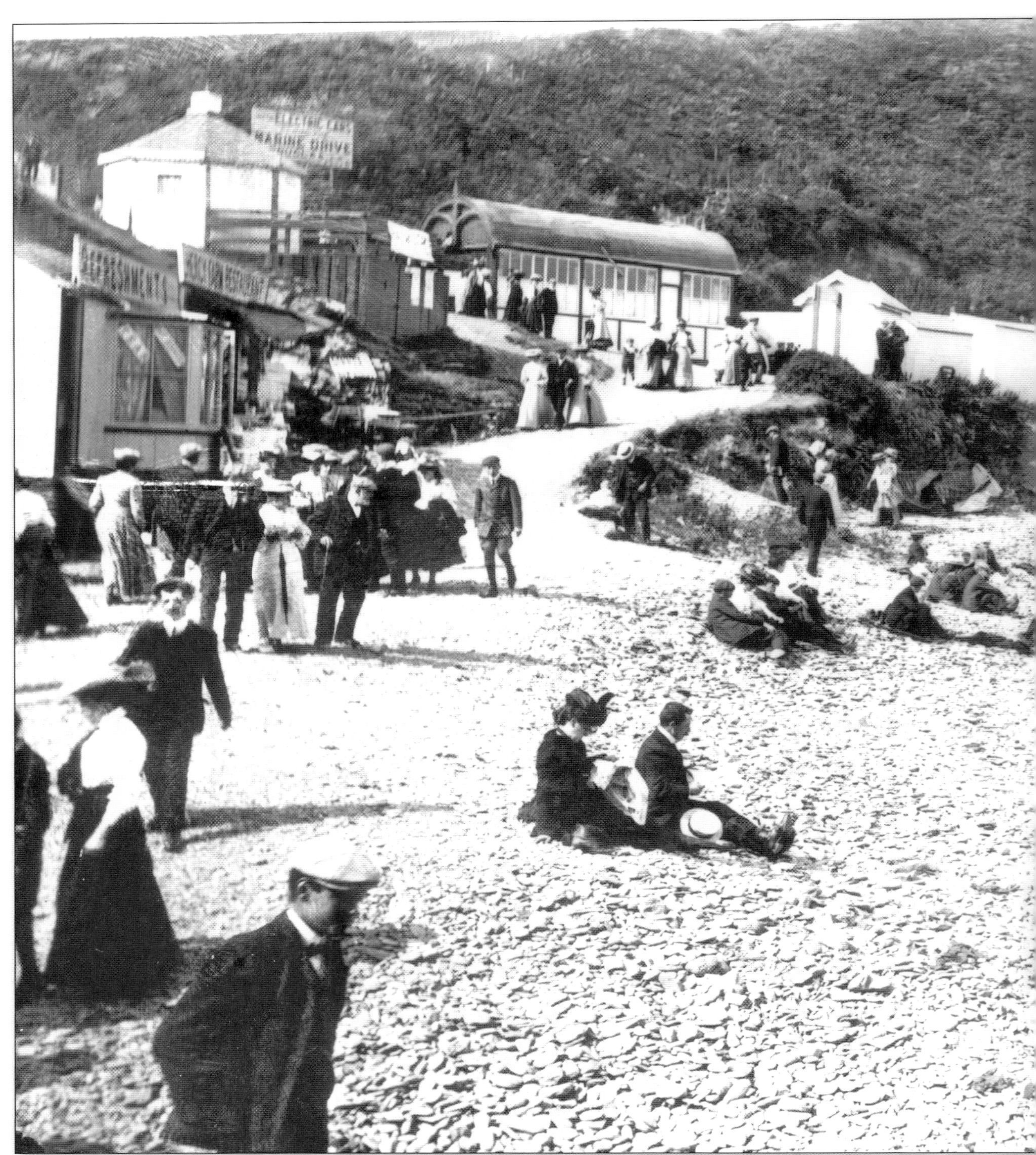
MARINE DRIVE
REFRESHMENTS

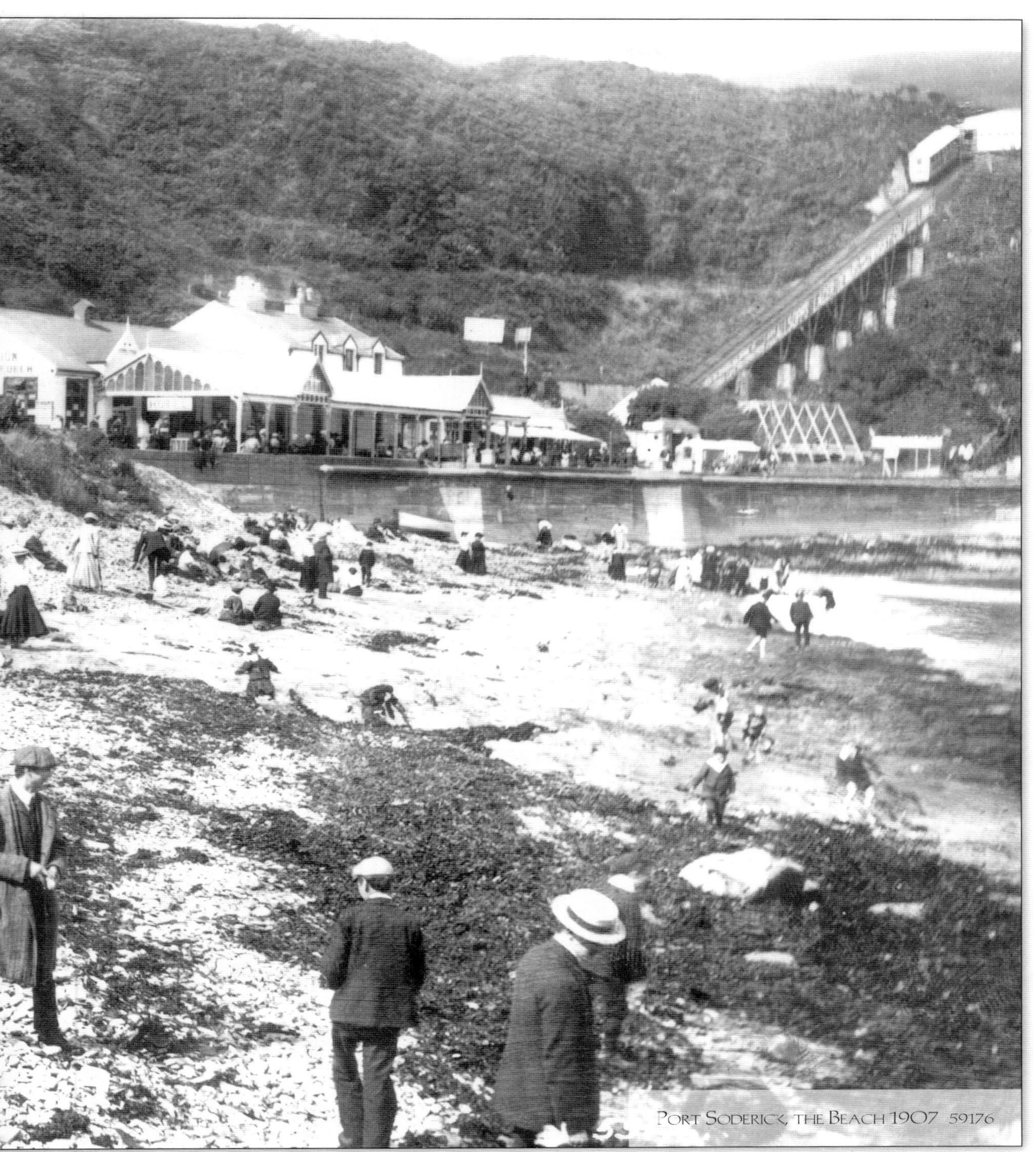

PORT SODERICK, THE BEACH 1907 59176

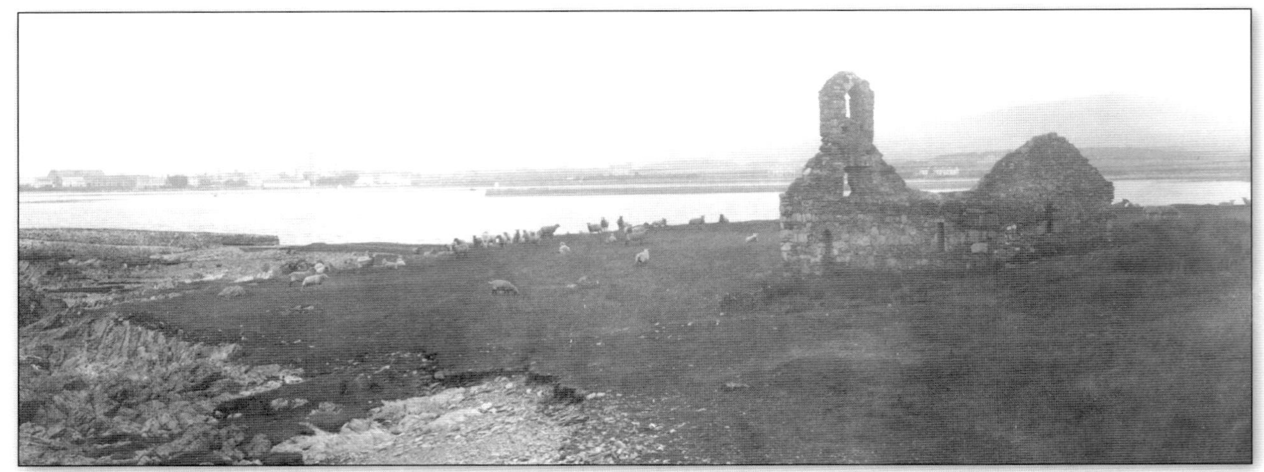

Derby Haven, Fort Island 1897 39897

The southern end of Derby Haven is protected by St Michael's Island with its ruined chapel, Derby fort and battery. In this view the Frith cameraman has included part of the broad sweep of Castletown Bay. St Michael's Island is now a Manx Heritage site.

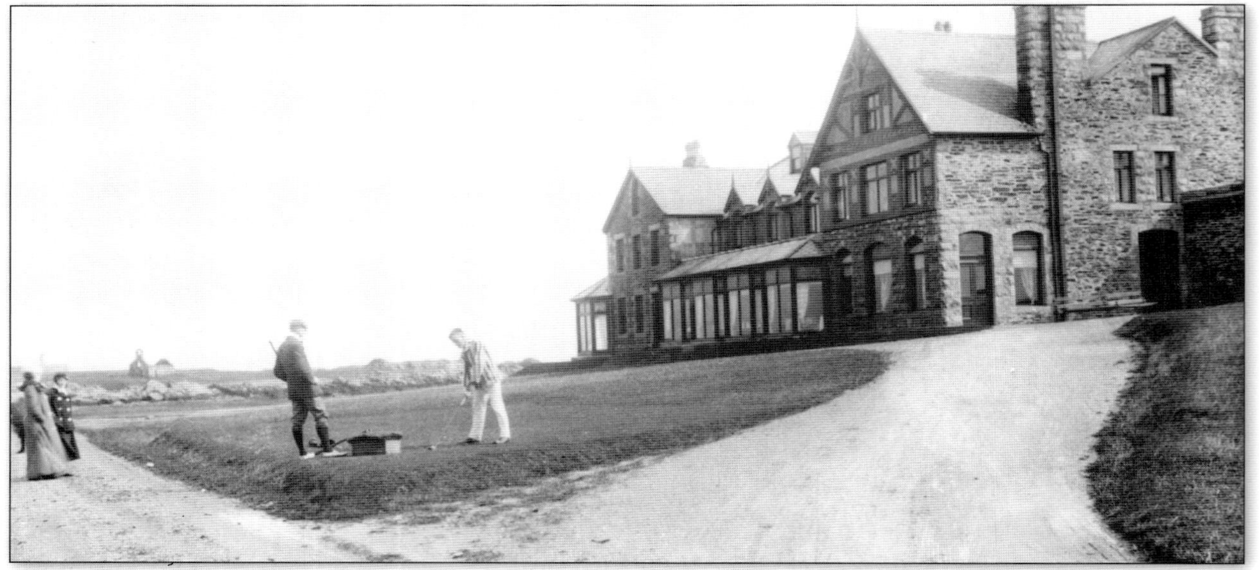

Derby Haven, The Golf Links Hotel 1903 50672

In the ten years or so prior to the Great War, golf went through a boom with a large number of courses opening throughout the UK. Professionals like James Braid were often engaged to give an exhibition match on the opening day. One such course hired a full military band - try timing shots to the strains of 'Annie Laurie' - but Braid got his own back on the last green when he put his ball straight through the big bass drum.

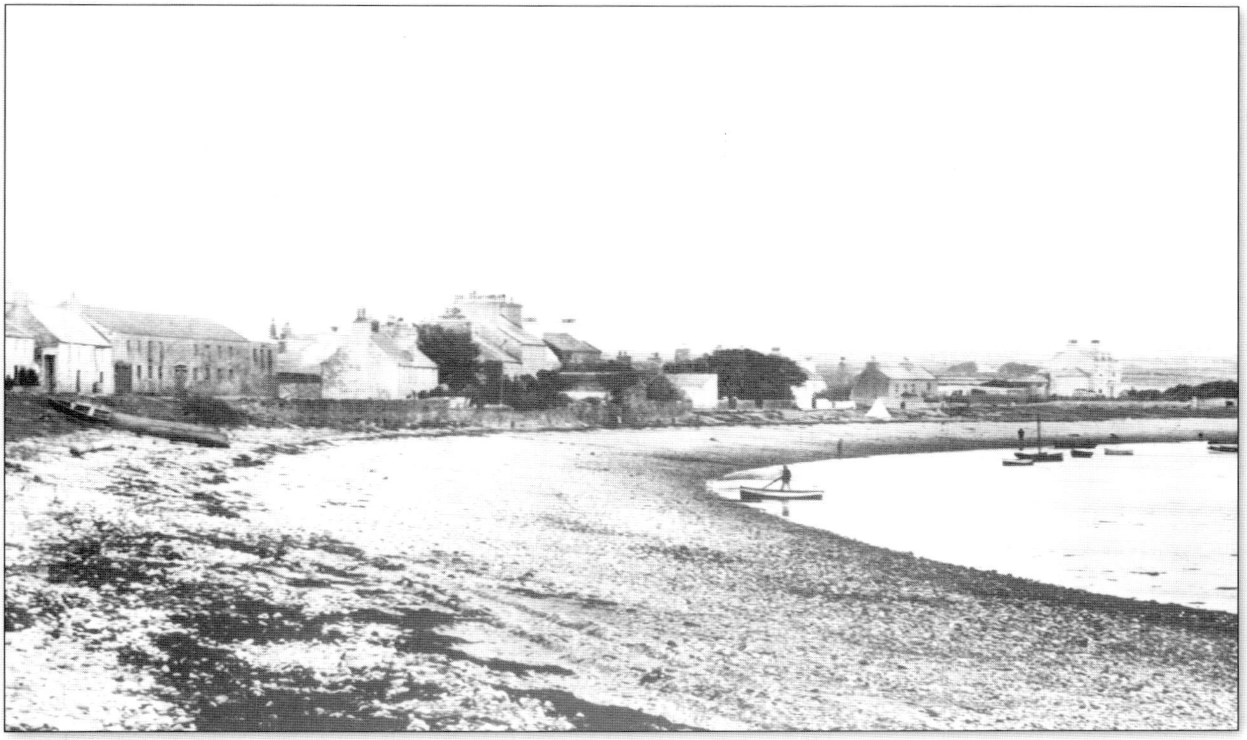

DERBY HAVEN 1897 39898

In 1823 John Butcher, a preacher from Bolton, was landed by fishing boat at Derby Haven and brought Primitive Methodism to the island. The movement's birthplace was at Mow Cop, Staffordshire, where Hugh Bourne and William Clowes held their first meetings in 1807. They were later expelled from the Methodist Conference and took the name Primitive Methodists in 1811.

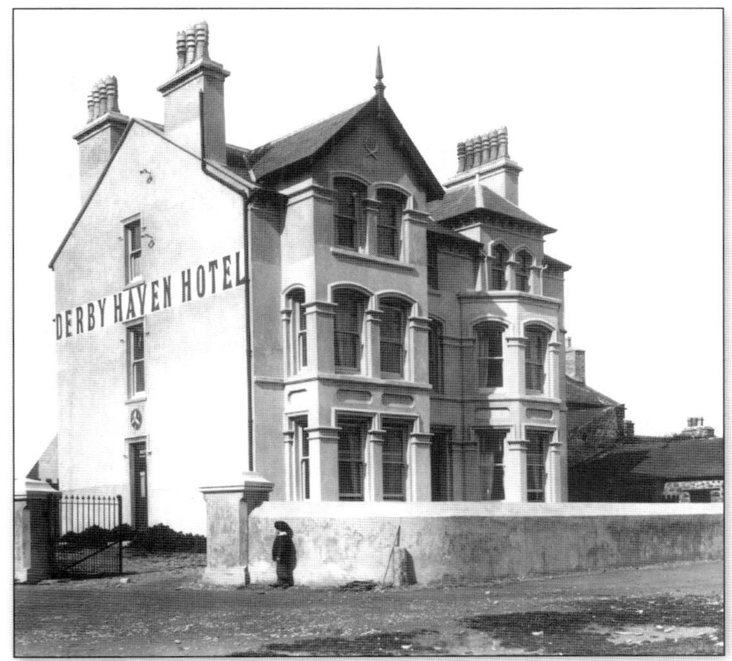

THE DERBY HAVEN HOTEL 1903 50671

Visitors to the Castletown area had a choice of hotels; the Castletown Hotel, the Derby Haven, the Marine Hydro Hotel (where hydropathic treatments could be taken), and the Golf Links Hotel which offered a pension (room, meals, service) for 6s 6d per day.

DERBY HAVEN, LOOKING TOWARDS CASTLETOWN 1897 39896

If coal was burned in these houses, it had to be imported from the mainland. There have been a number of attempts to find coal on Man, with much of the exploration work concentrated on the northern part of the island. In 1985-86 Rio Tinto Zinc carried out borings near Peel, Derby Haven and Ballasalla.

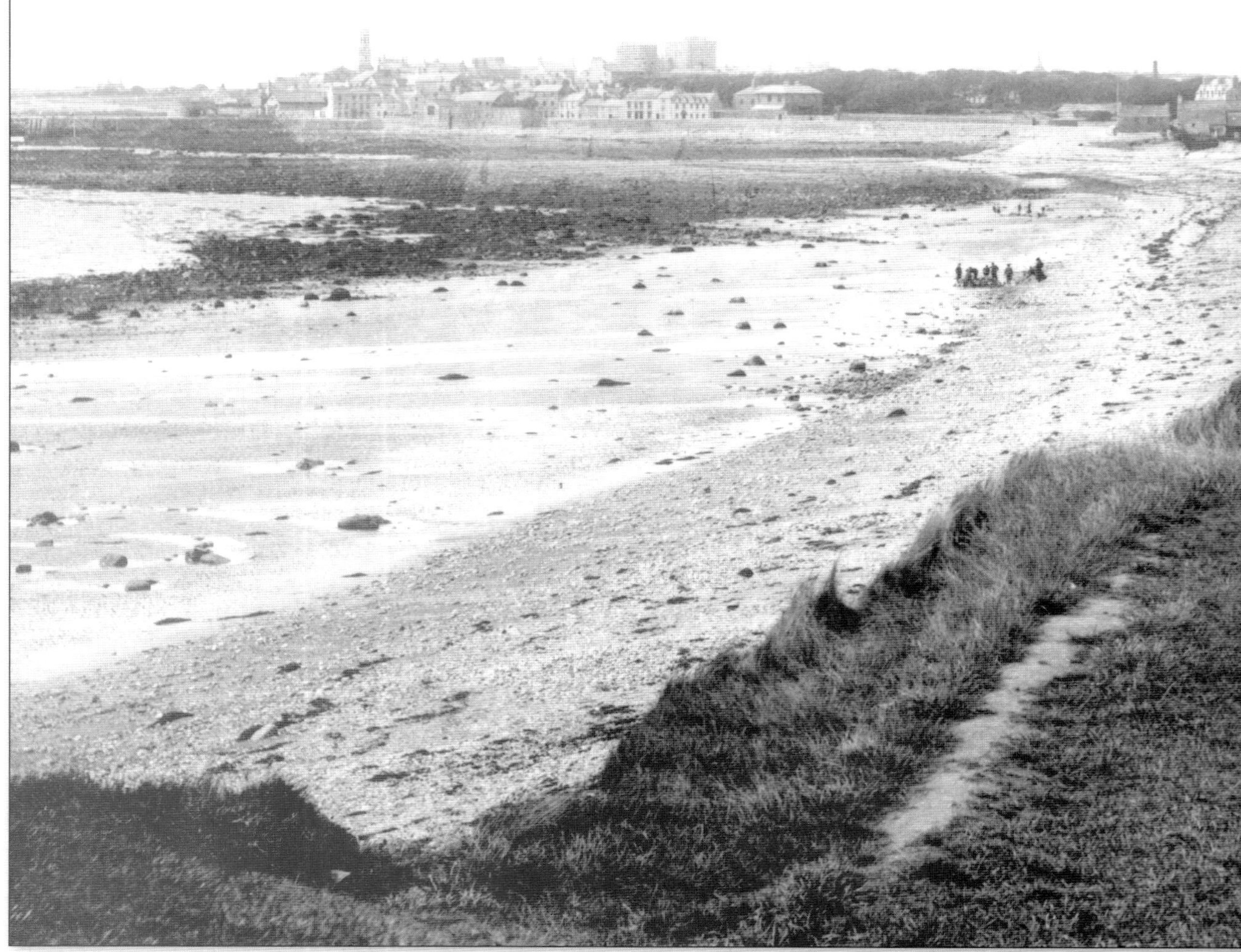

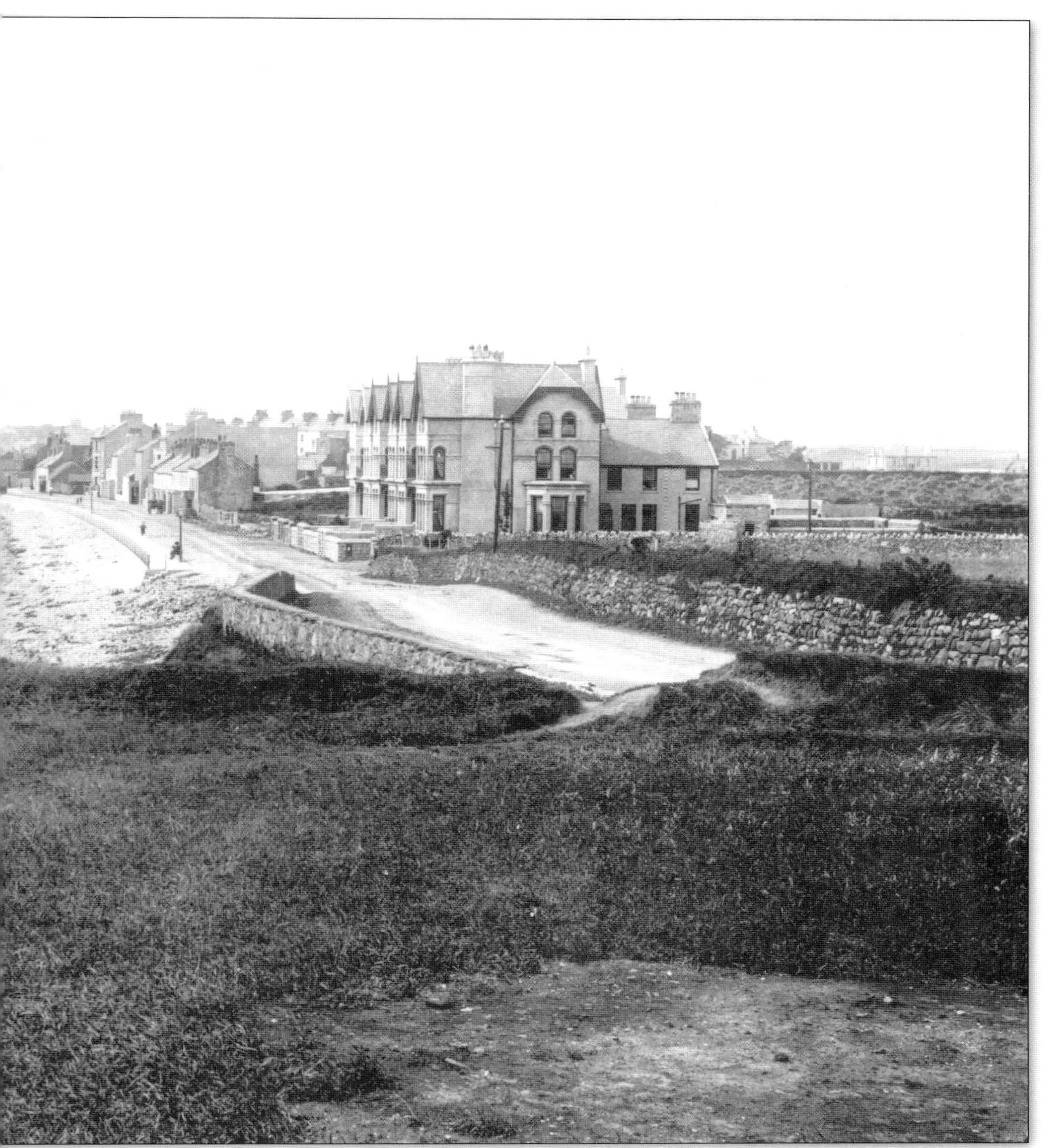

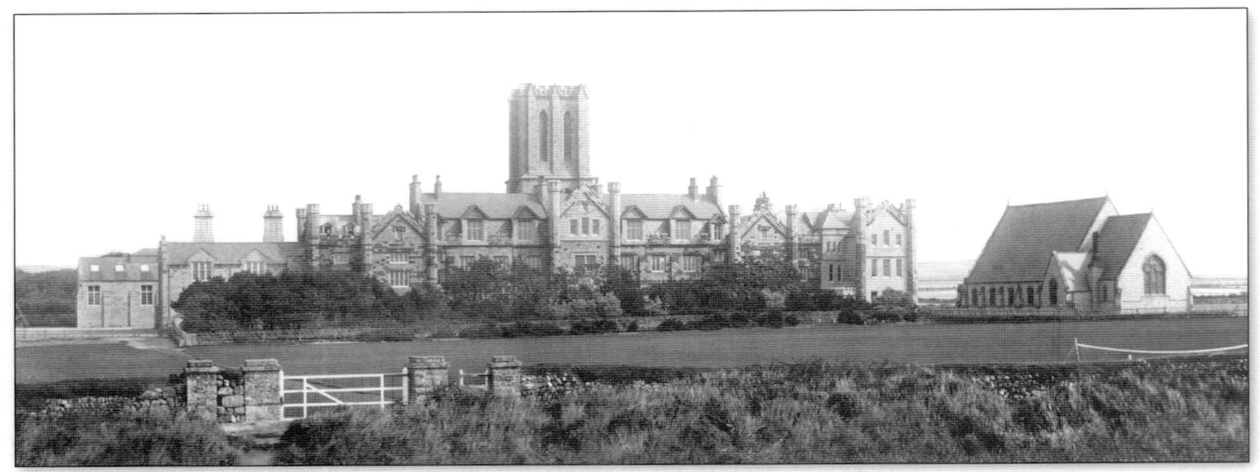

CASTLETOWN, KING WILLIAM'S COLLEGE 1897 39895

The distinctive central tower of King William's College was designed by John Welch and was a feature of a major rebuilding programme following a fire in 1844. This picture was taken the year one of the college's famous old boys, Thomas E Brown, died. Born in 1830, the year the college opened, Brown was a poet, scholar, and Fellow of Oriel College.

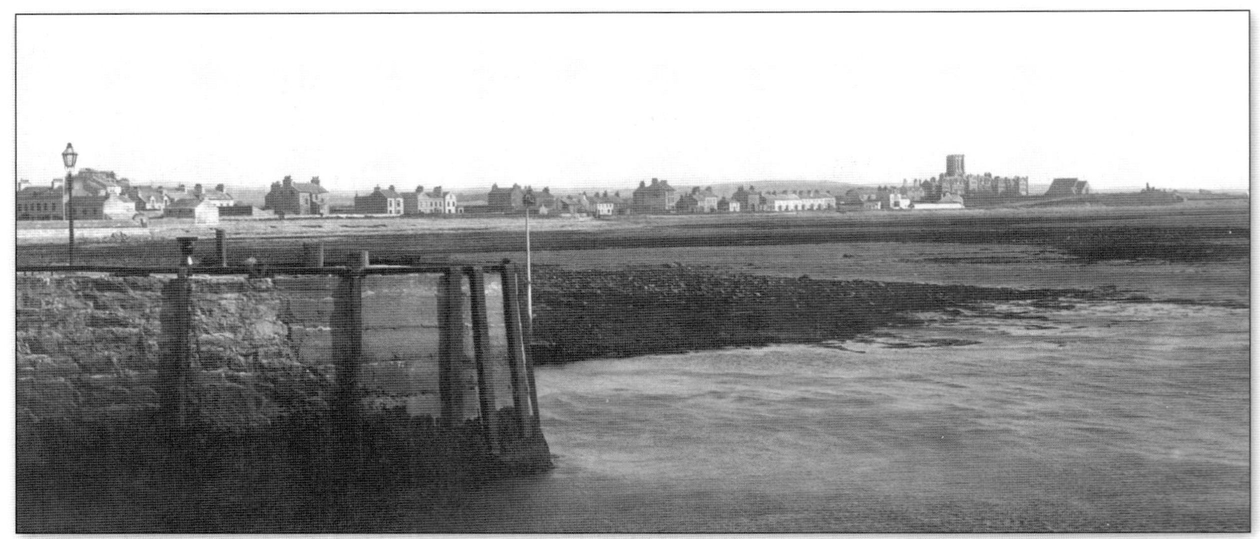

CASTLETOWN, FROM THE PIER 1893 33025

This view looks towards King William's College, Derby Haven and St Michael's Island. Near the college is Hango Hill, the scene in 1663 of the execution of the Manx patriot William Christian (Illian Dohne) for his role in the rebellion of 1651. He was sentenced to be hanged, drawn and quartered but this was commuted to shooting by a firing squad on account of his wife's 'inconsolable condition'. He was shot before news of his successful appeal to Charles II reached Man.

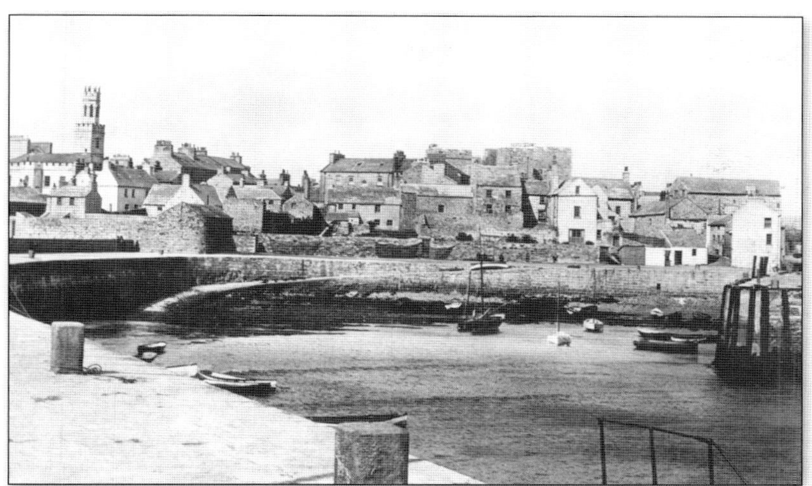

CASTLETOWN, FROM THE PIER 1893 33024

The rocky entrance to Castletown meant that the harbour remained under-developed and under-used for years. In 1955 Douglas handled around 70 per cent of the island's imports and exports, while Castletown accounted for less than 4 per cent of imports and no exports. Things improved in the mid-1970s when Castletown was upgraded to handle a container service, resulting in the port handling 15 per cent of imports and 20 per cent of exports.

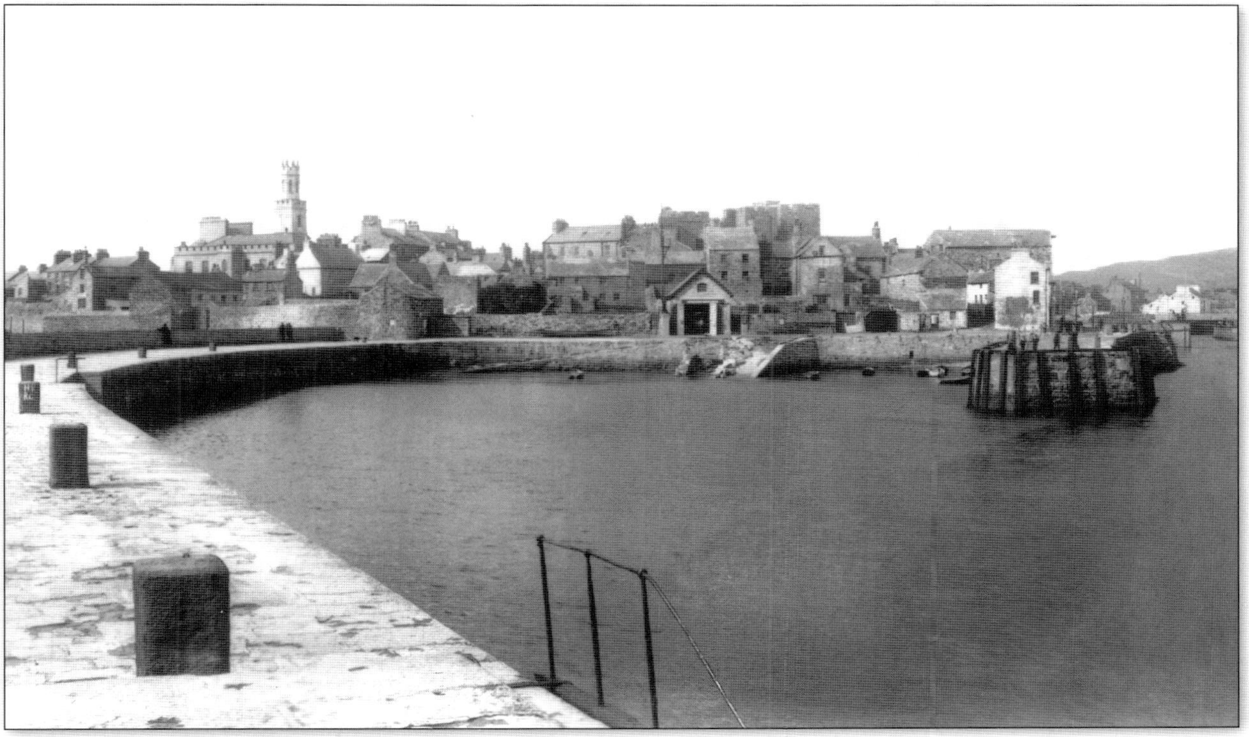

CASTLETOWN, FROM THE PIER 1903 50650

Little has changed since picture No 33024 was taken, save for the building of a lifeboat station. St Mary's was rebuilt in the 1830s, replacing the church built by Bishop Thomas Wilson in 1701. Wilson was appointed Bishop of Sodor and Man in 1698, having previously served as chaplain to the ninth Earl of Derby.

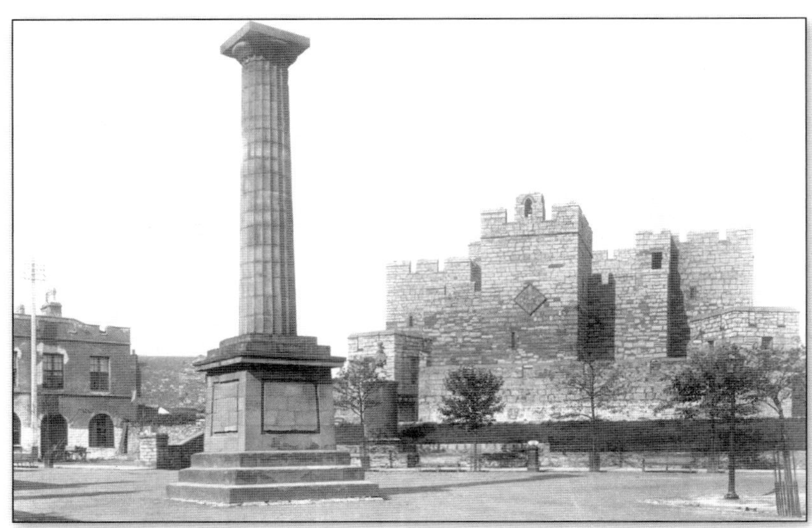

CASTLETOWN, CASTLE RUSHEN 1903 50656

The present Castle Rushen dates from the 12th to the 14th centuries. It was here in 1265 that Magnus, last of Man's Norse kings, died. With his death began nearly seventy years of Scottish rule until the island was taken by Edward III of England. The Doric column was erected as a memorial to Colonel Cornelious Smelt who was Lieutenant-Governor of the island between 1805-32.

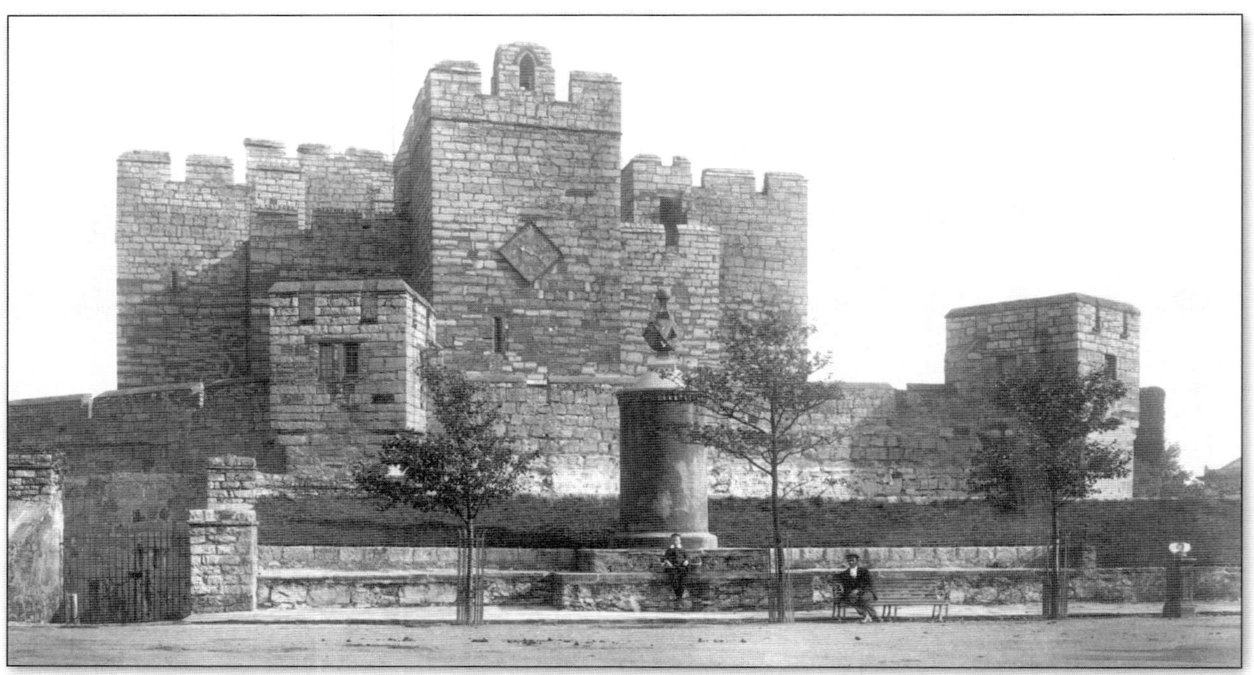

CASTLETOWN, CASTLE RUSHEN 1903 50658

When William Montacute, Earl of Salisbury, was appointed First Lord of Man he chose Castletown for his capital. Montacute strengthened the fortress defences, adding a new tower on the eastern side and a twin-towered gateway. Later 14th-century improvements included a curtain wall and the heightening of the keep. The glacis was added by Cardinal Wolsey in c1540 while he was serving as a trustee for the underage Earl of Derby.

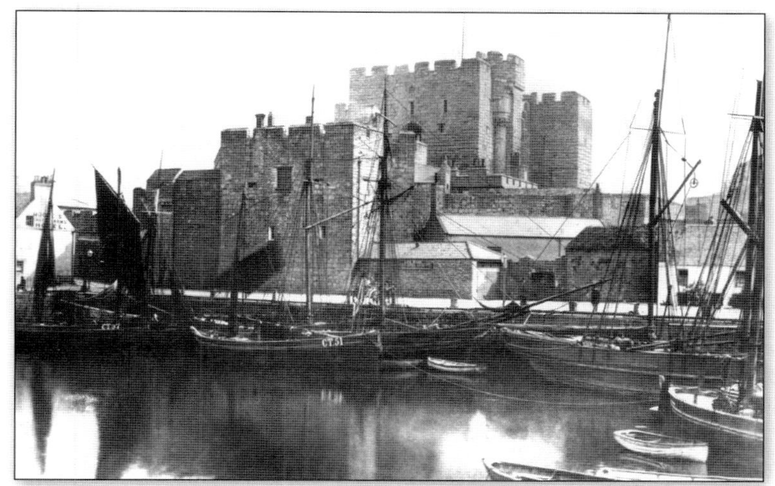

CASTLETOWN, CASTLE RUSHEN c1885 C47501

In the early 1720s Bishop Wilson was held prisoner in Castle Rushen for nine weeks for failing to pay a fine. In 1722 an ecclesiastical court found a certain Lady Horne guilty of slander. Lady Horne happened to be the wife of the Governor, who was none too pleased. The Governor declared that ecclesiastical courts were acting illegally and that they must drop all such cases. The Bishop and his vicars-general refused and finished up in jail themselves.

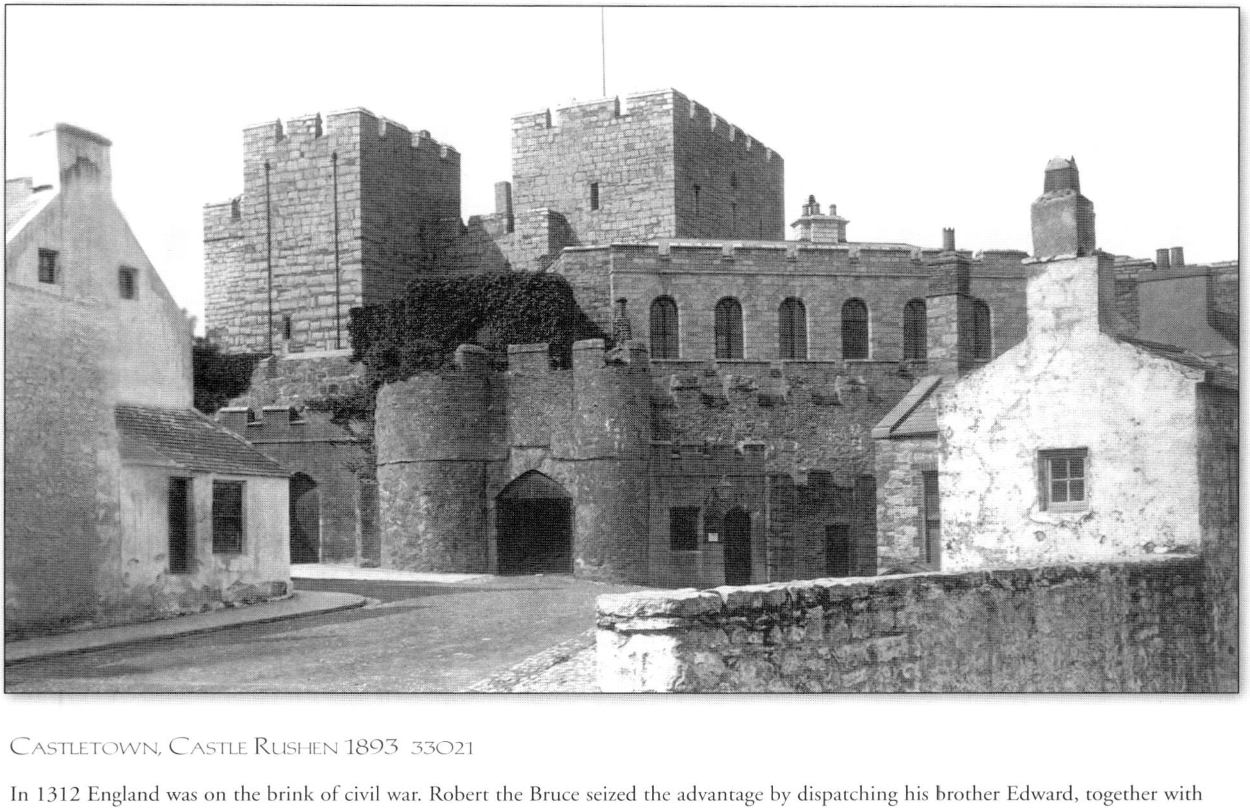

CASTLETOWN, CASTLE RUSHEN 1893 33021

In 1312 England was on the brink of civil war. Robert the Bruce seized the advantage by dispatching his brother Edward, together with James Douglas, into northern England. They sacked a number of towns, including Durham and Hartlepool, while Robert reduced England's Scottish possessions to a handful of fortresses. In 1313 Robert invaded Man, besieging and almost destroying Castle Rushen in the process.

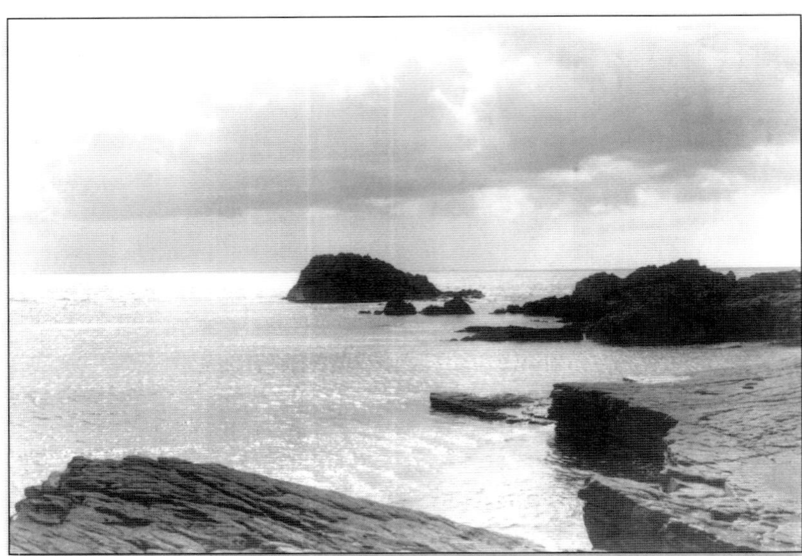

CASTLETOWN
THE STACK 1903 50653

Castletown lies within the island's carboniferous limestone area. The west side of the bay comprises Scarlett Point, which has outcrops of lava and volcanic ash, while the stack is columnar basalt.
The east side of the bay features the flat rocks of Langness Point.

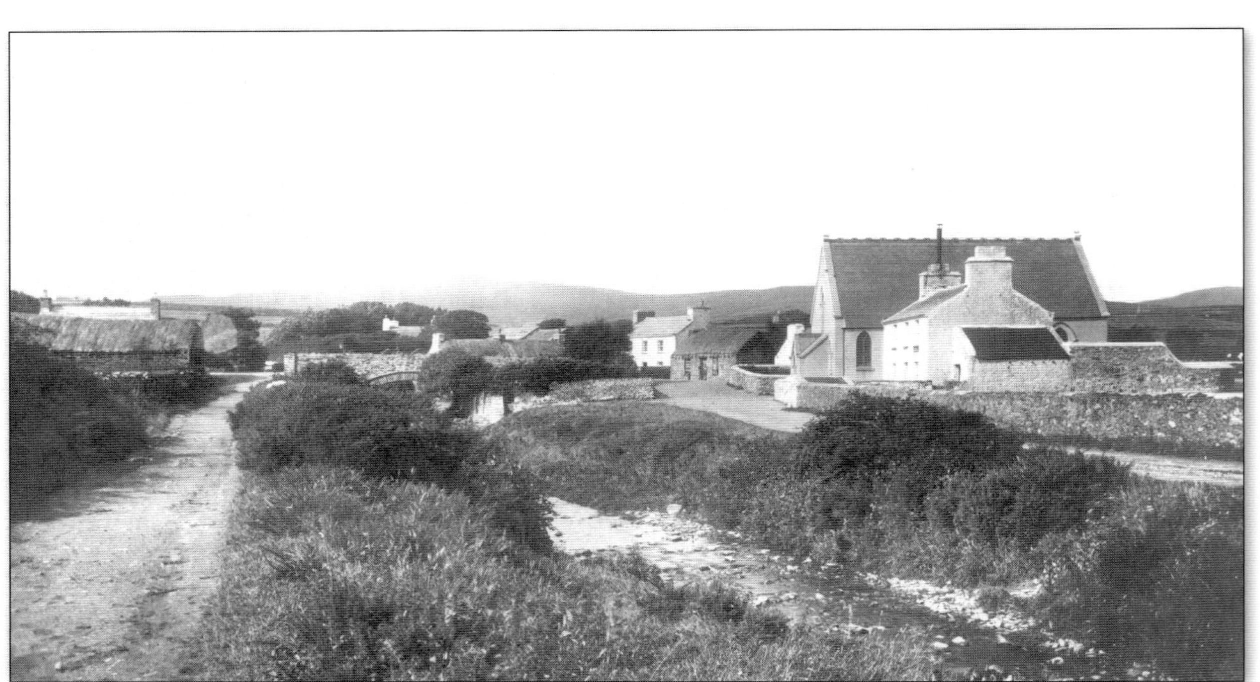

COLBY, THE VILLAGE 1897 39899

The small farming community of Colby is thought to have derived its name from Colli's farm, 'by' being a Scandinavian word for a farm or homestead. The village at this time is an unspoilt mix of traditional single-storey thatched crofts and solid-looking two-storey stone houses.

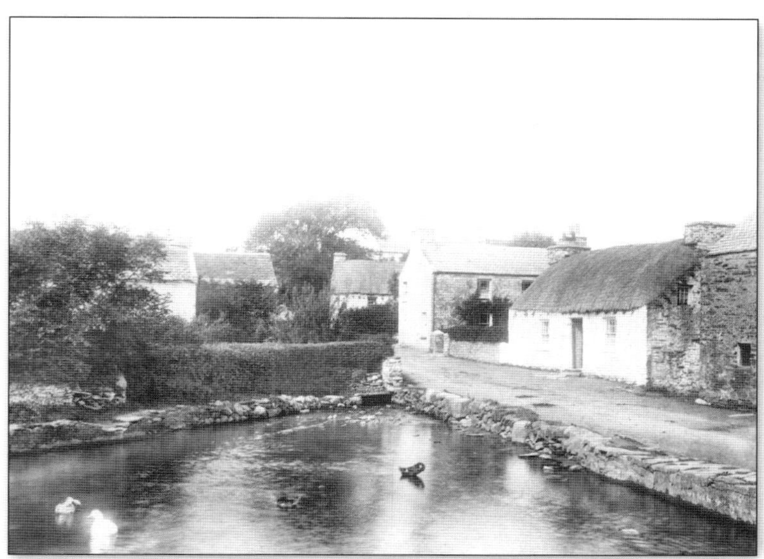

COLBY, THE VILLAGE 1897 39900

The Frith cameraman had only a few ducks for company when he took this picture in 1897, one of a series for possible use within the Frith postcard range. Postcards could be sent at half the letter rate, but in those days nothing could be written on them apart from the recipient's address. It was only after 1902 that a message could also be added.

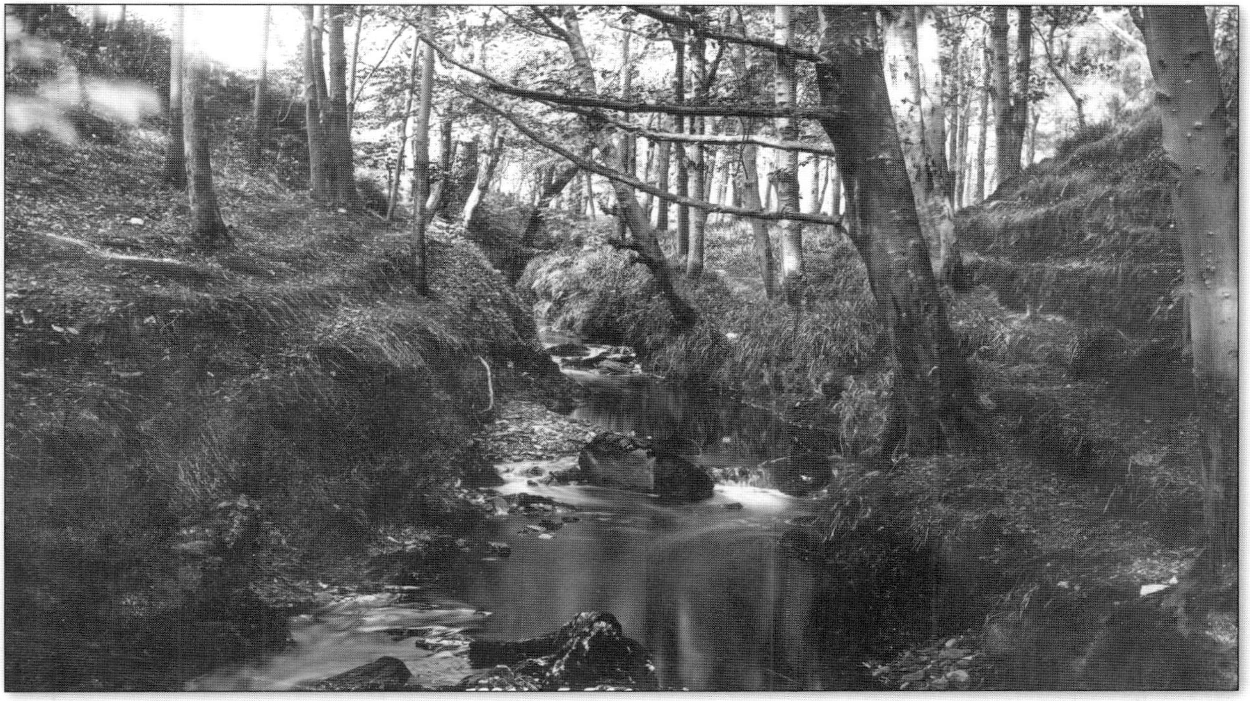

COLBY, THE GLEN 1897 39901

The opening of the IOM Railway meant that Colby Glen was within easy reach of holidaymakers based in Douglas. By rail Castletown was only seven minutes away, Port Erin eight minutes, and Port St Mary seven minutes.

DOUGLAS TO PORT ERIN

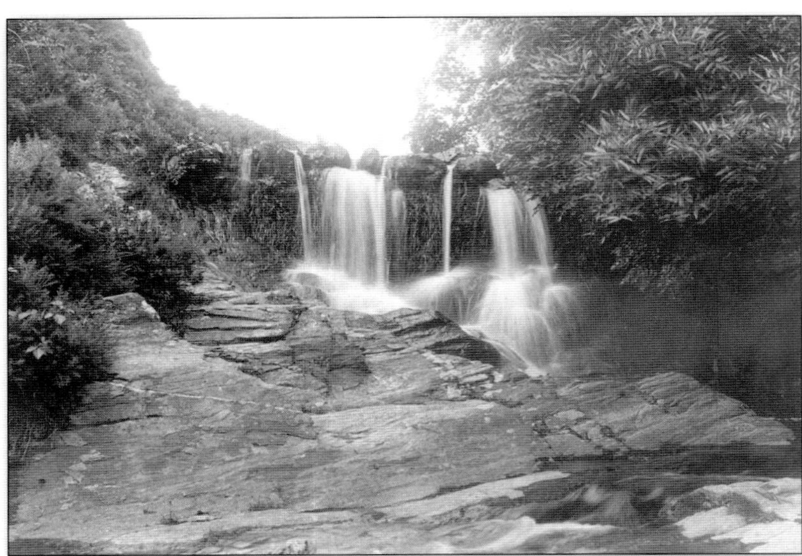

COLBY
THE WATERFALL 1897 39902

This waterfall is not as spectacular as the Rhenass falls of Glen Helen or those of Glen Meay or Dhoon Glen, but even so the Frith cameraman managed to provide us with a pleasing view of the Colby falls.

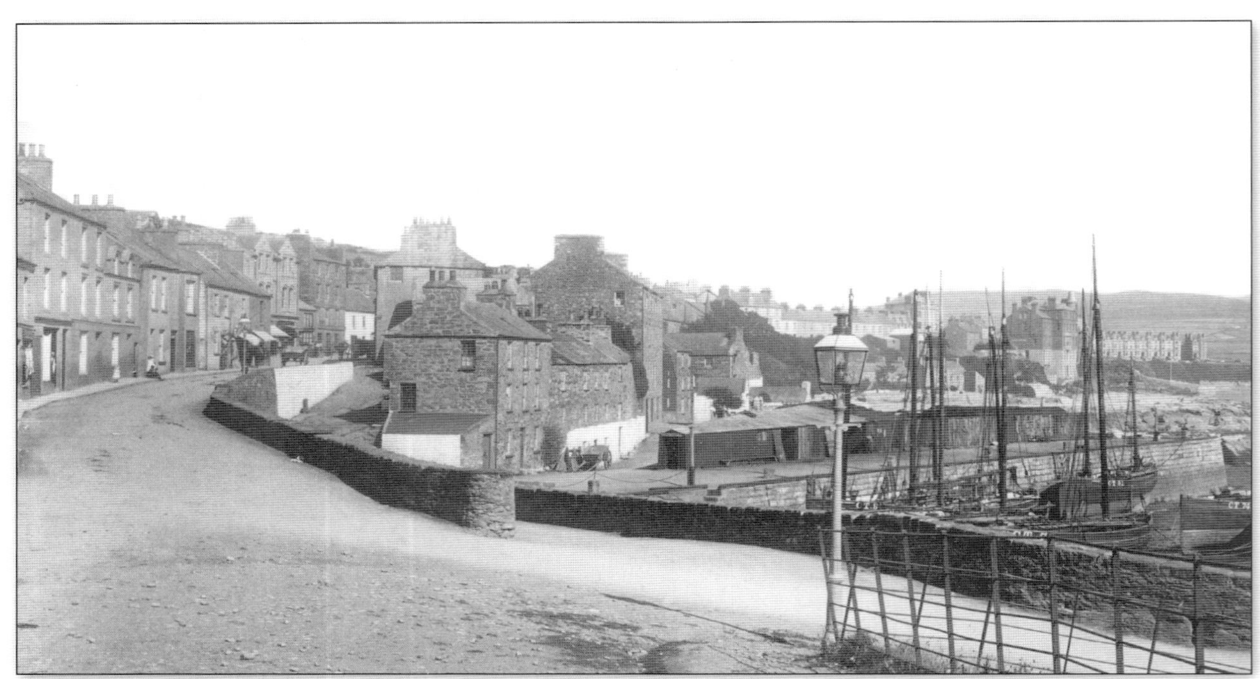

PORT ST MARY, STREET AND HARBOUR 1895 39908

In Manx folklore the village was named 'the Harbour of Mary' in honour of the Blessed Virgin by Celtic missionaries, who founded a chapel here. Missionaries from Ireland began arriving in the 5th century; it is possible that St Patrick himself founded the church on St Patrick's Isle, Peel.

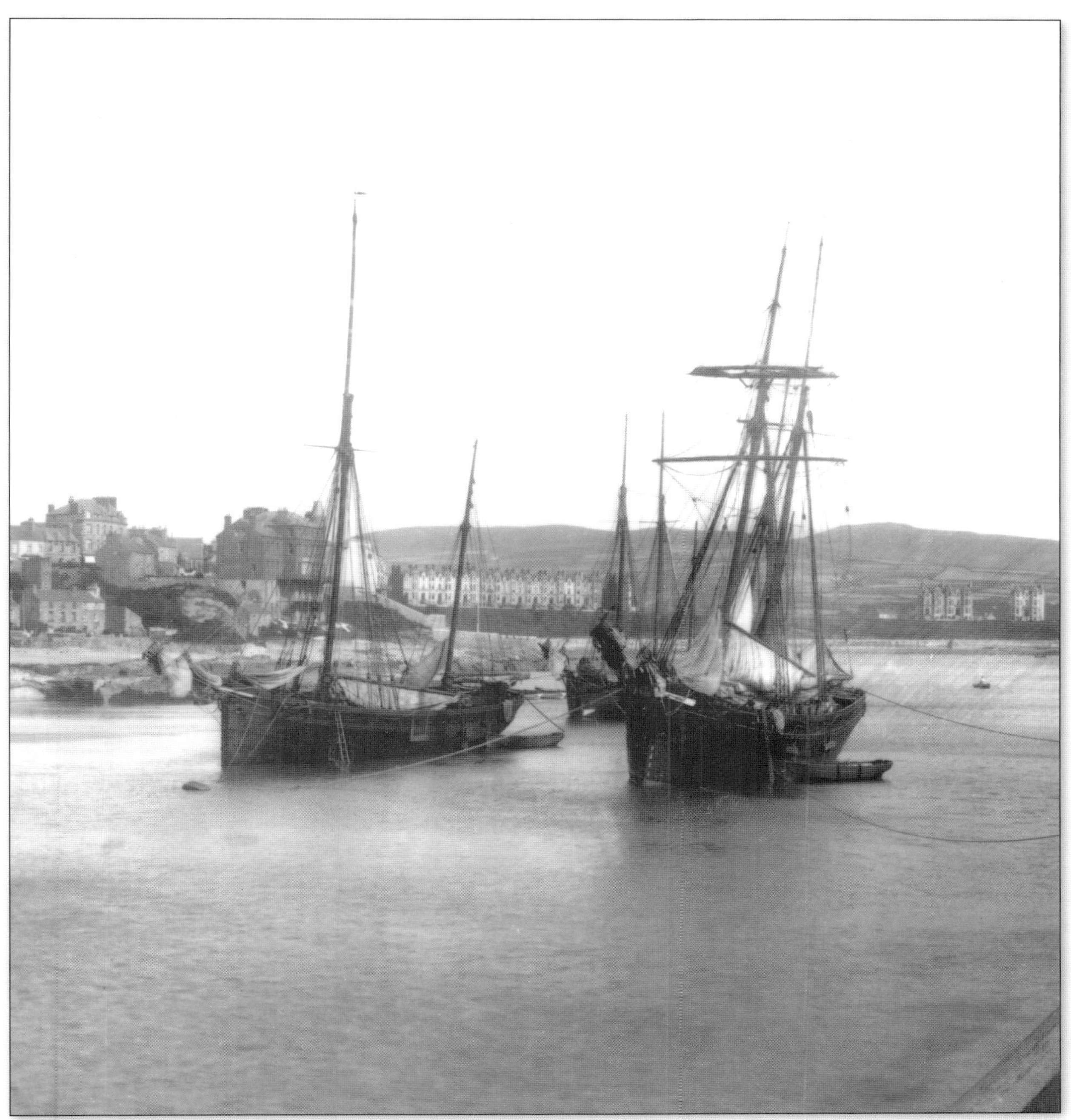

Port St Mary, The Harbour 1903 50645

It was to Port St Mary that the Scottish granite to be used in the construction of Chicken Rock Lighthouse was brought, and where each stone was cut and dressed to size before being taken out to the site. The lighthouse was built in the mid-1870s.

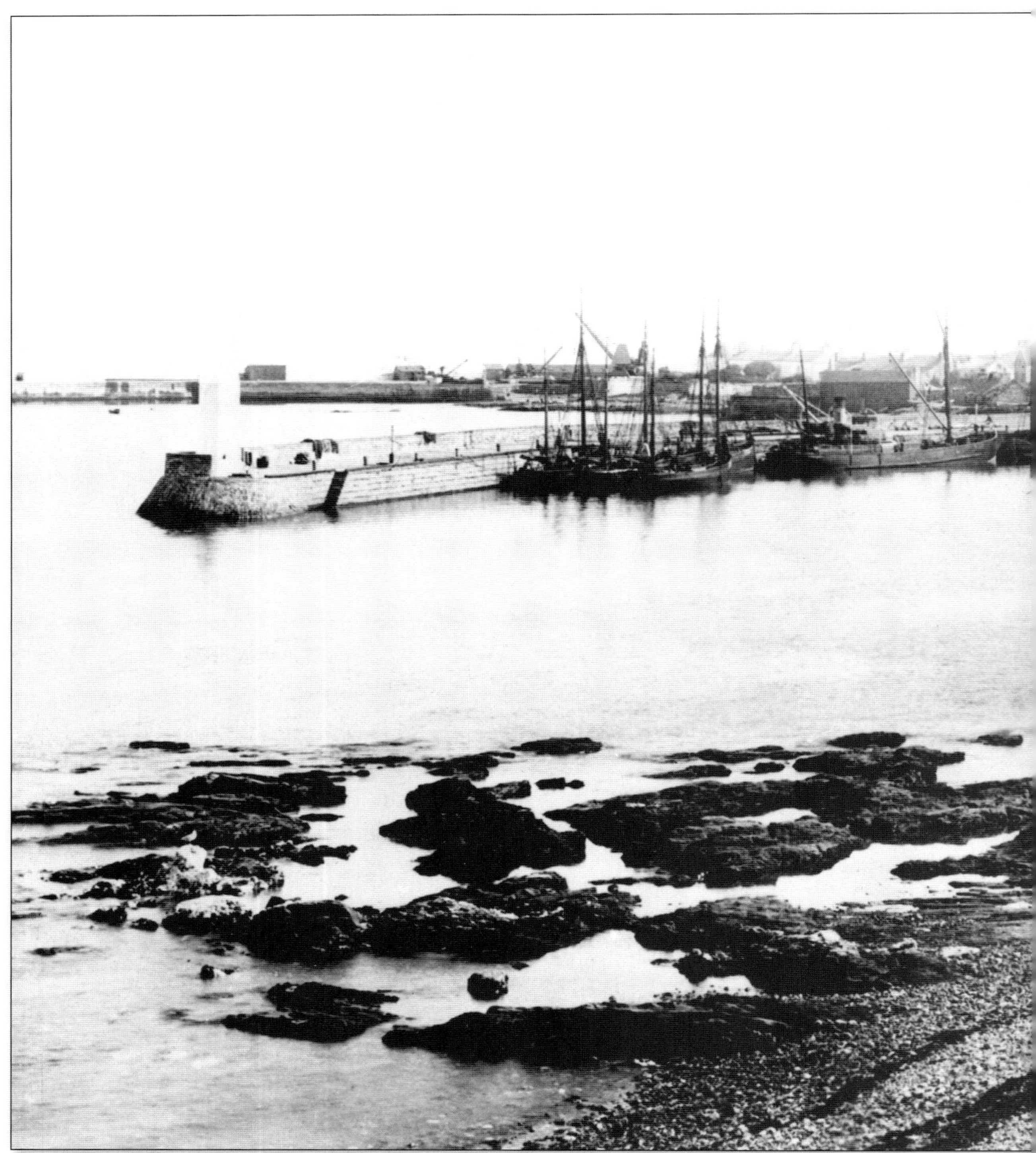

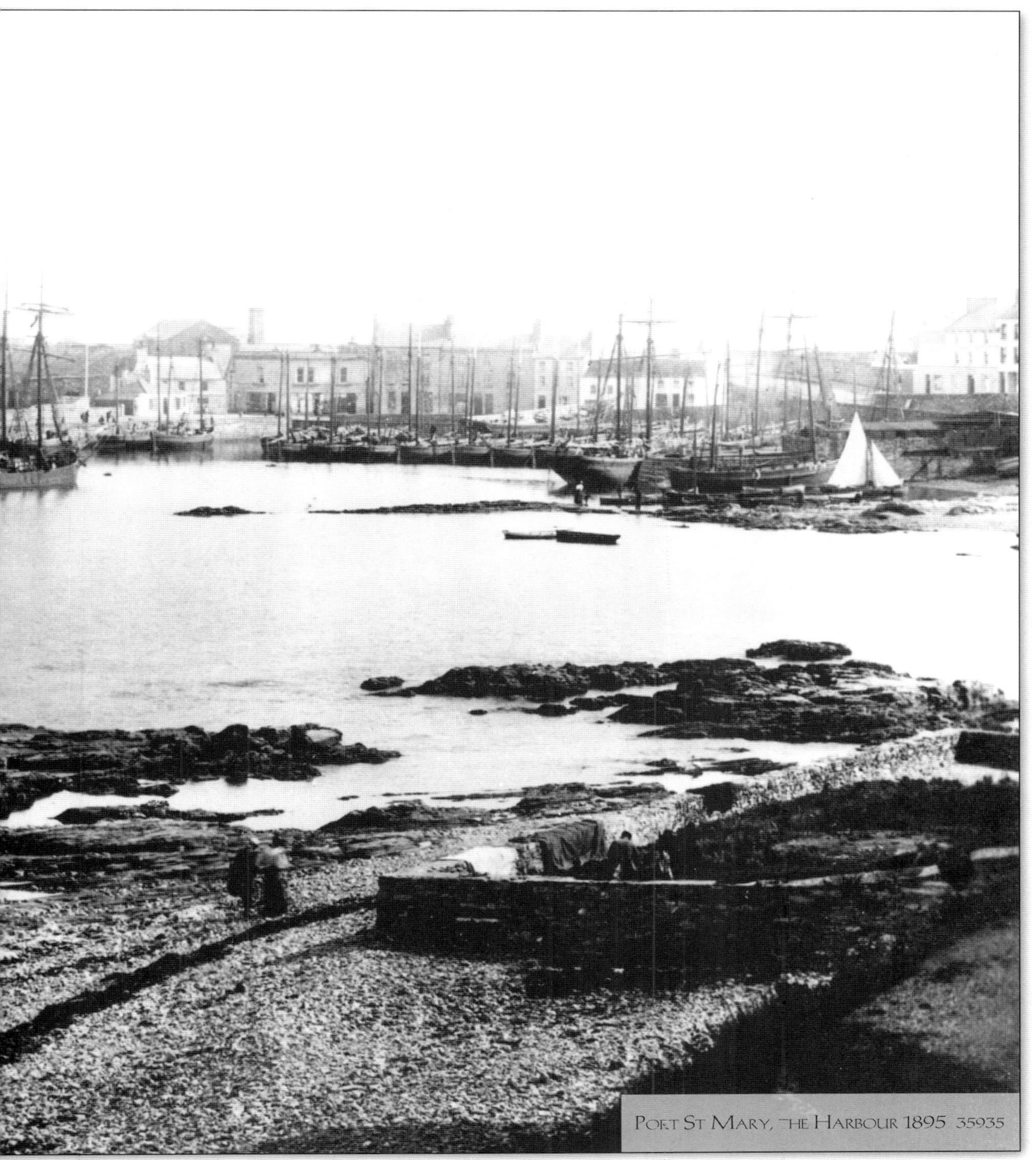

PORT ST MARY, THE HARBOUR 1895 35935

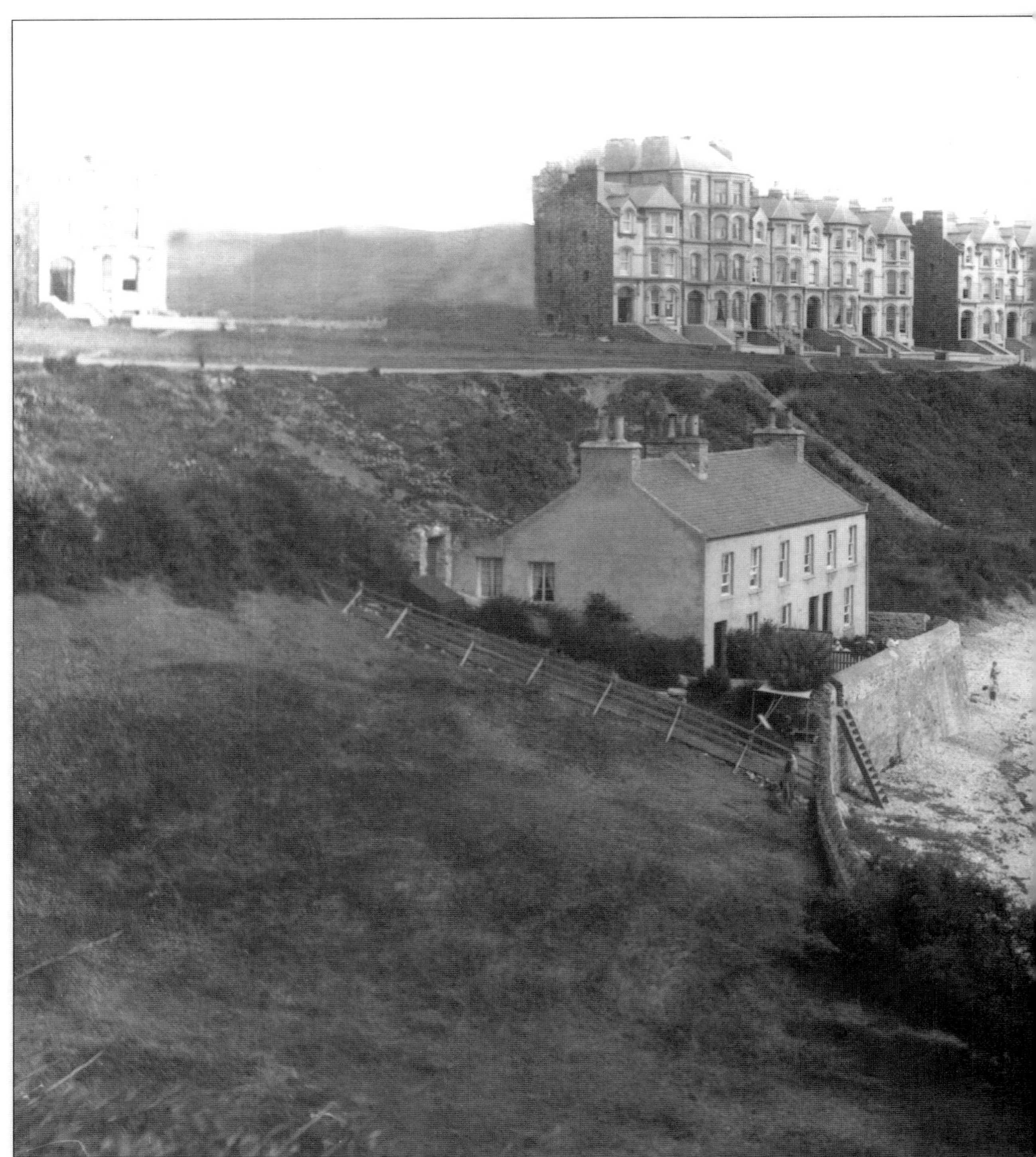

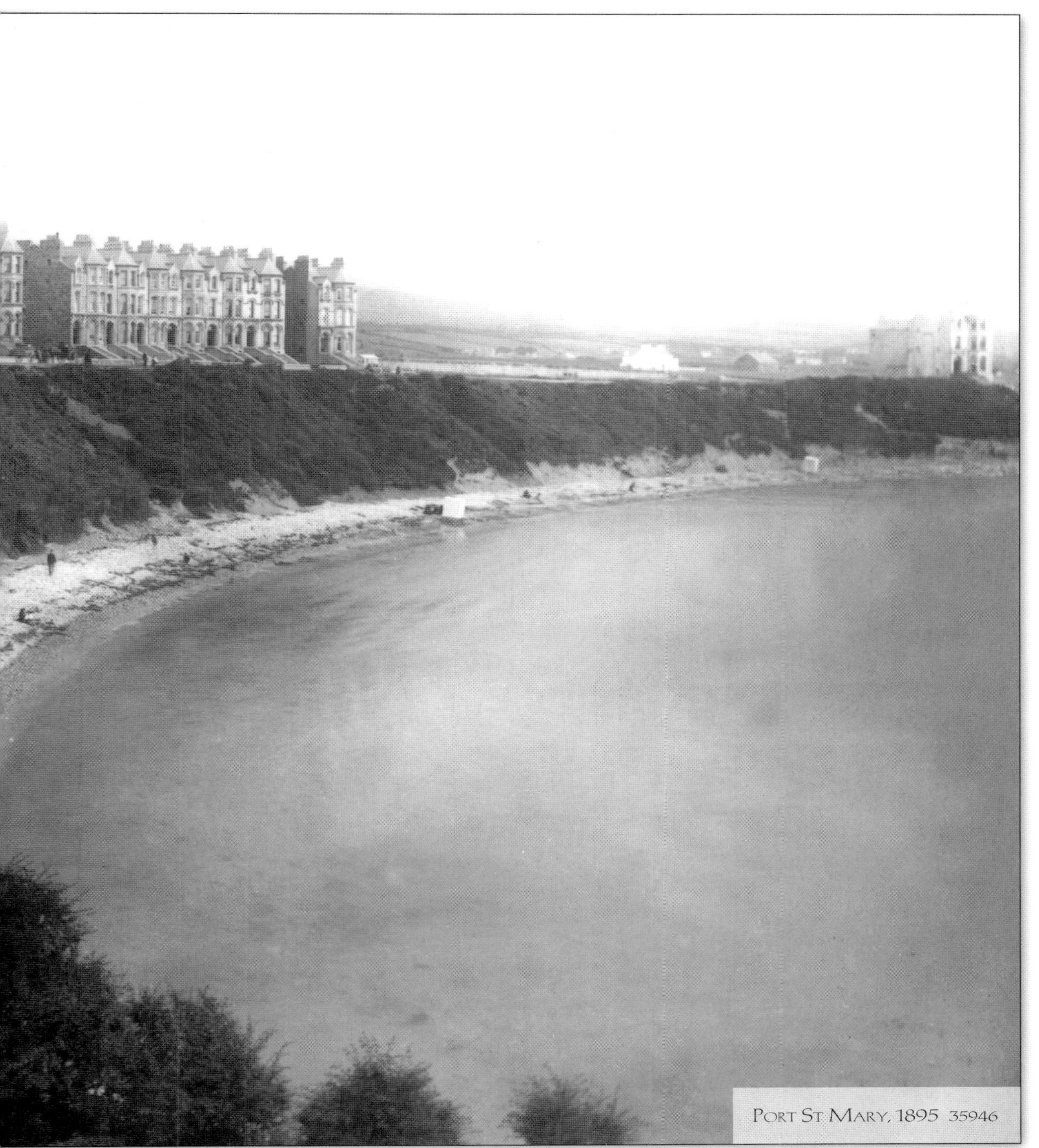

PORT ST MARY, 1895 35946

PORT ST MARY, THE BEACH 1895 35944

At this time Port St Mary was still being described as a 'pleasant little fishing port and seaside resort'. The local fishing fleet was, however, in decline. By the late 1890s the local fleet comprised 56 boats employing 346 men and boys, landing an annual catch valued at less than £3,000.

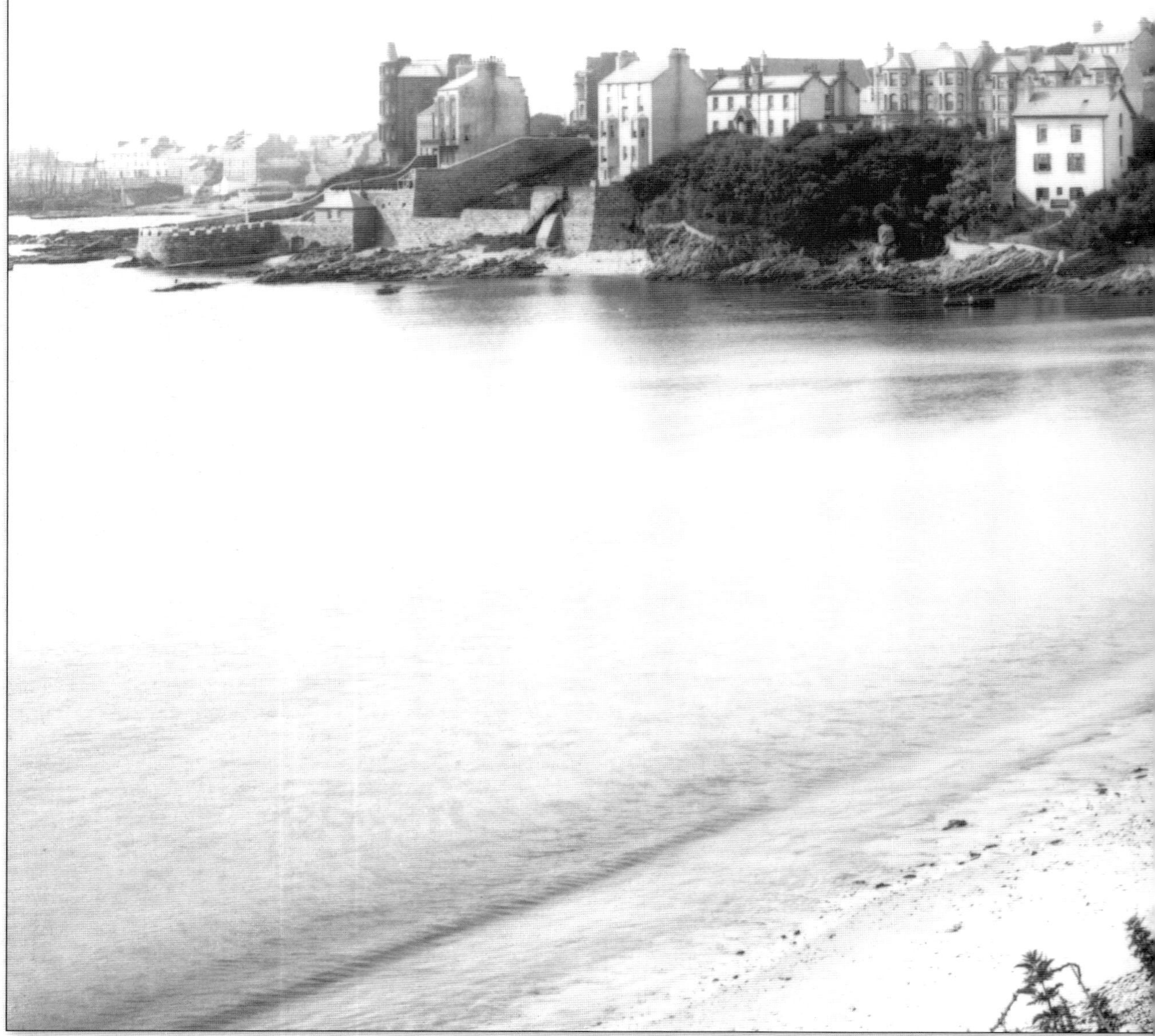

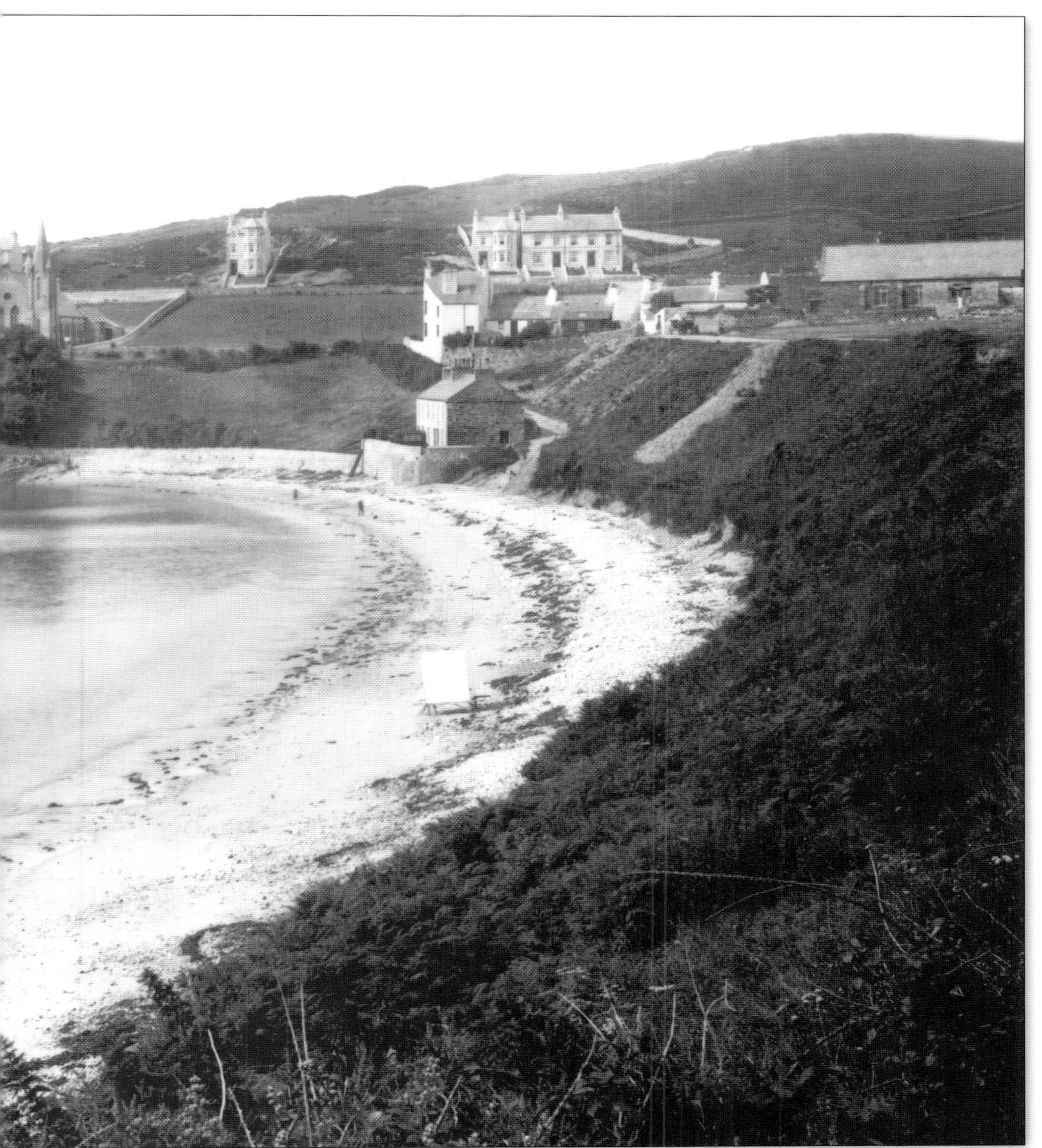

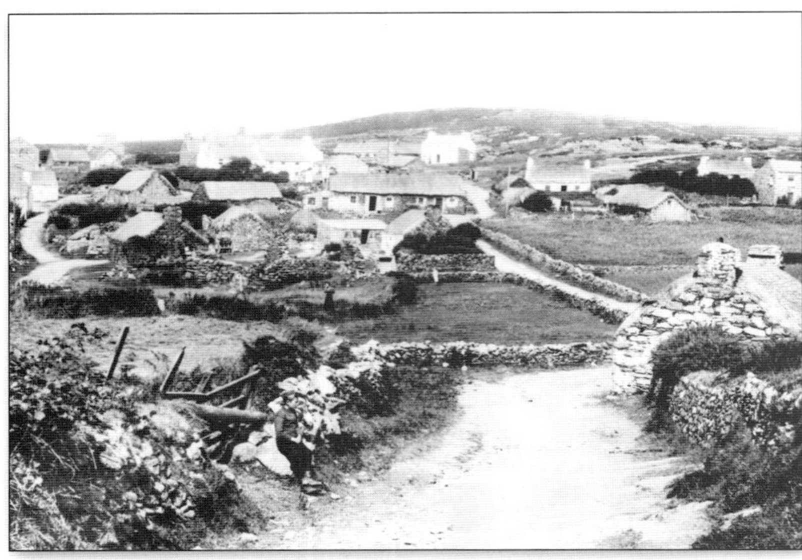

CREGNEISH, THE VILLAGE 1897 39903

Cregneish lies between Port St Mary and the Calf of Man. When this picture was taken, most of the villagers would have earned their living from agriculture or fishing, or both. A number of properties, including a weaver's cottage and a farmstead, now comprise the National Folk Museum, and are fitted out to portray village life as it was around 1900.

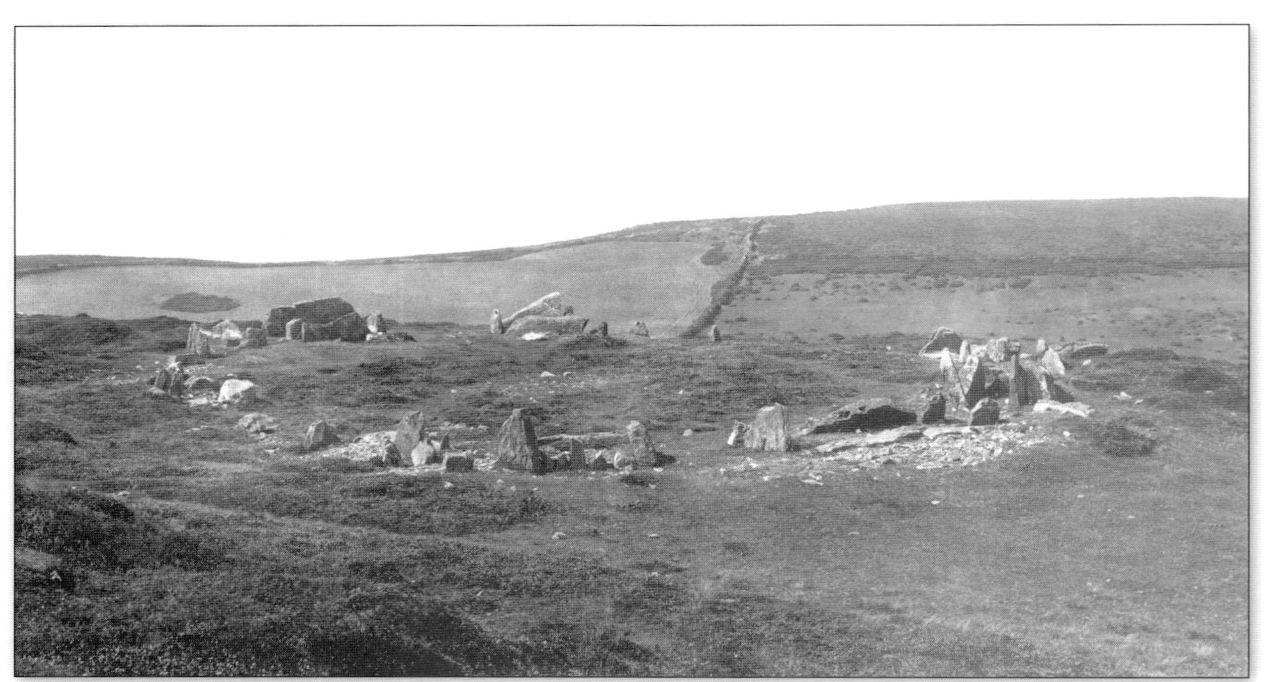

CREGNEISH, MEAYLL CIRCLE 1897 39904

There are a number of Neolithic monuments on the island; the Meayll Circle is of a unique design with six pairs of lintel graves arranged in a circle. When the site was excavated in 1893, evidence of burnt human bones were unearthed, along with Neolithic pottery. Other important sites include Cashtal-Yn-Ard and the chambered cairn near Laxey known as King Orrey's Grave.

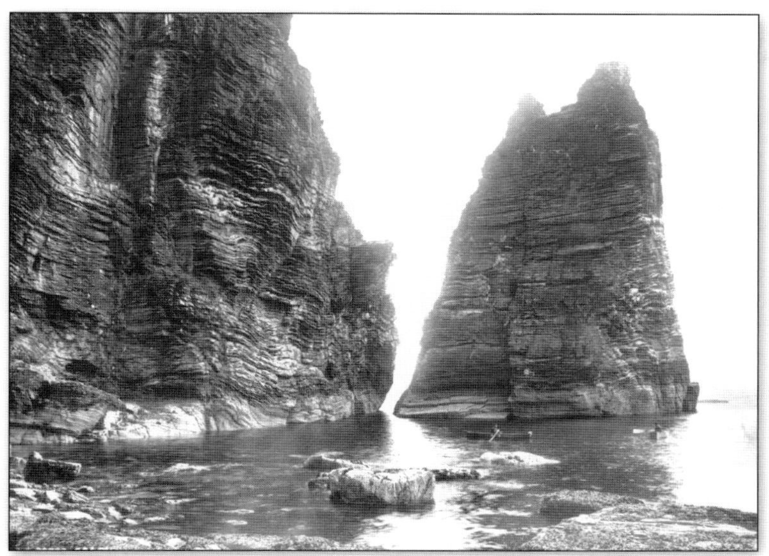

SPANISH HEAD
SUGAR LOAF ROCK 1895 36762

The cliffs in this part of the island are important breeding grounds for sea birds. Other sites include the whole of Langness (which is designated a bird sanctuary), and the Ayres conservation area in the north of the island. Ayres is a unique heathland that supports diverse plant life and colonies of birds including oystercatchers, mallards, lapwings, arctic, common and little terns, and curlews.

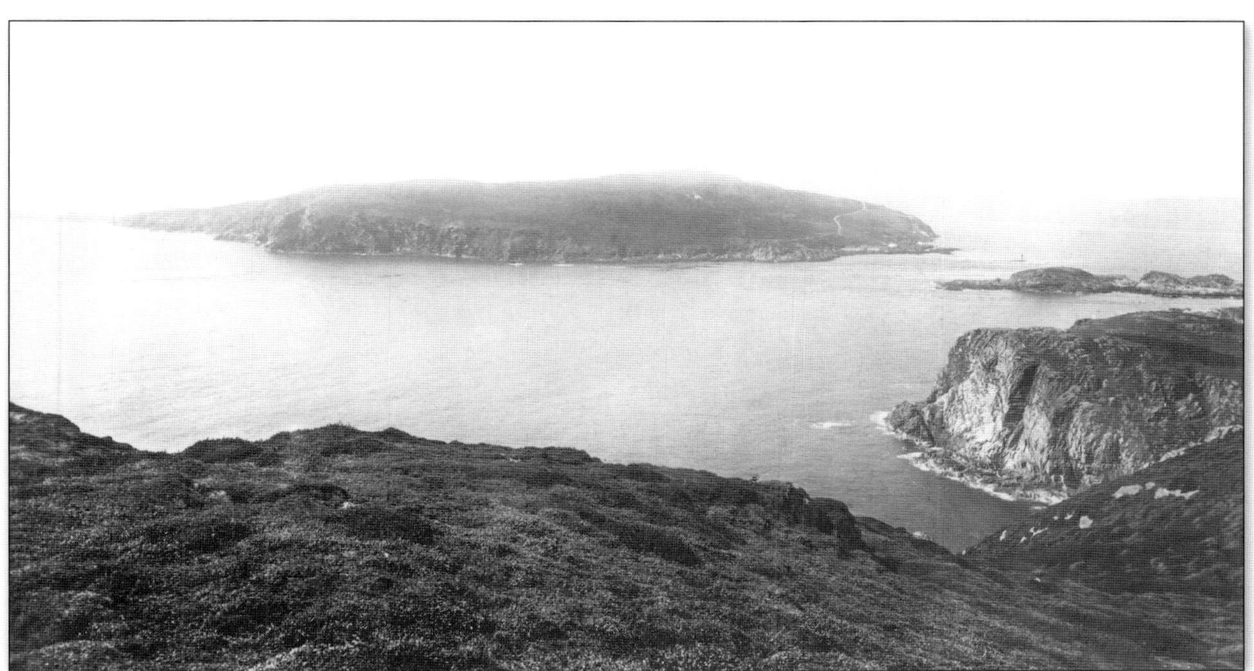

CALF OF MAN 1897 39913

In early 20th century guides, walkers were advised to leave the train at Port St Mary and go by way of the Chasms and Spanish Head to Port Erin.. The Chasms were described as fissures resembling those between Lydstep Cove and Manorbier Bay in Wales, and caused by the falling in of caves. At Spanish Head they would be offered a commanding view of the Calf of Man.

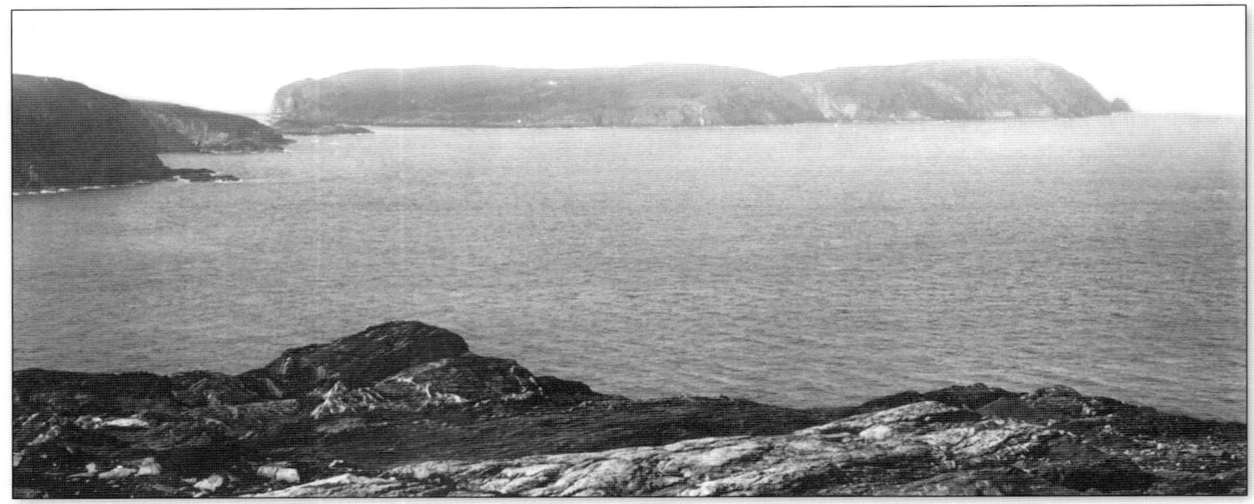

Calf of Man, from Bradda Head 1895 35932

The Calf of Man looking in the general direction of Kione Beg and Gibdale Point. The narrow channel which separates the island from Man, Calf Sound, is over on the left of the picture. There was a lighthouse on the Calf until 1875, when it was closed in favour of a new one that had been constructed on the Chicken Rocks.

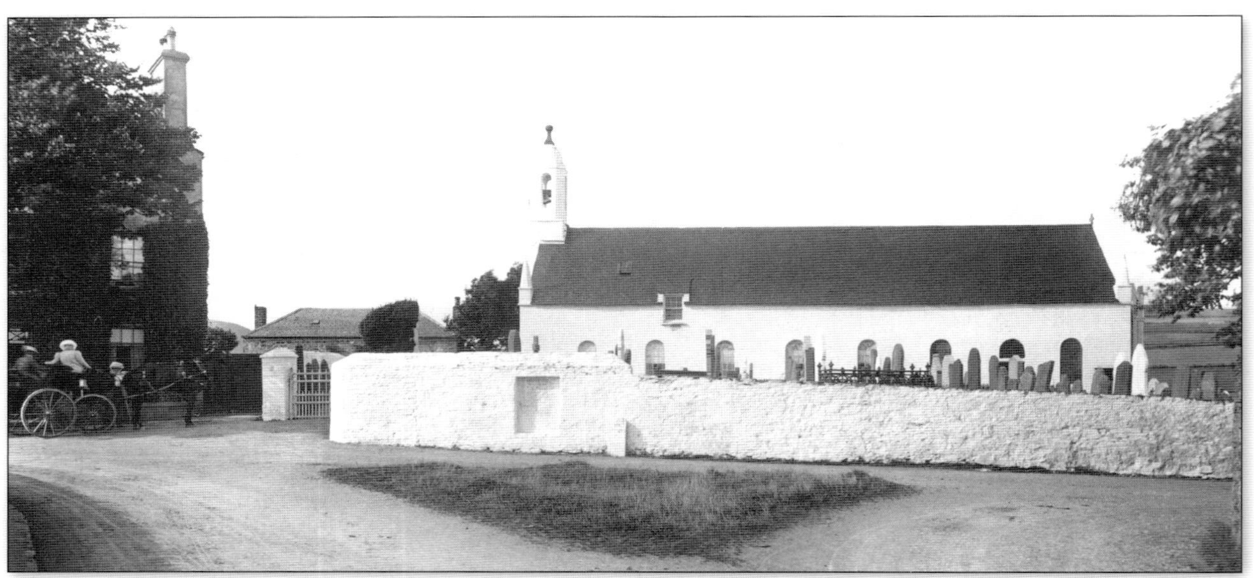

Port Erin, Rushen Church 1907 59197

Here we see Kirk Rushen (Holy Trinity) with its bell turret and the vicarage. In more recent times the vicarage has lost its chimney stacks and ivy cladding, and the tree has been felled. The church now sports a large lych-gate.

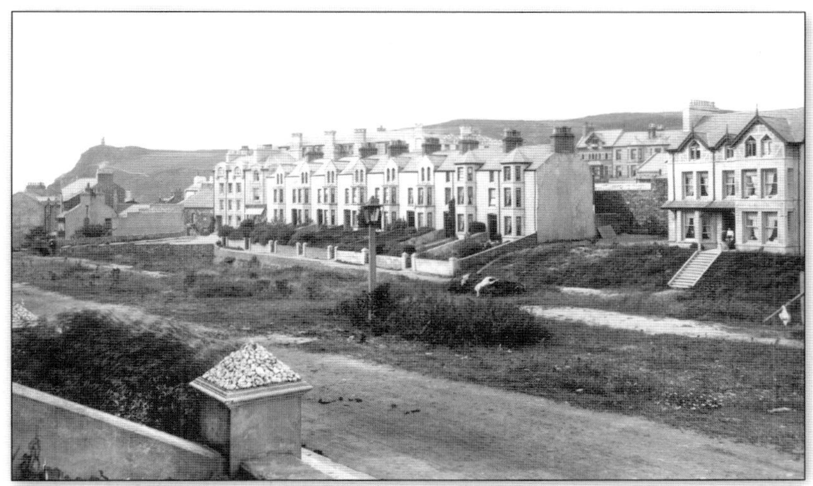

PORT ERIN
ATHOL PARK 1907 59184

This is a late-Victorian development just off the seafront; the castellated roof of the Falcon's Nest Hotel can be seen rising above the terrace. It appears that there is plenty of landscaping work still to be done, and although one street lamp is in place, it is doubtful that it will give enough light for the whole terrace.

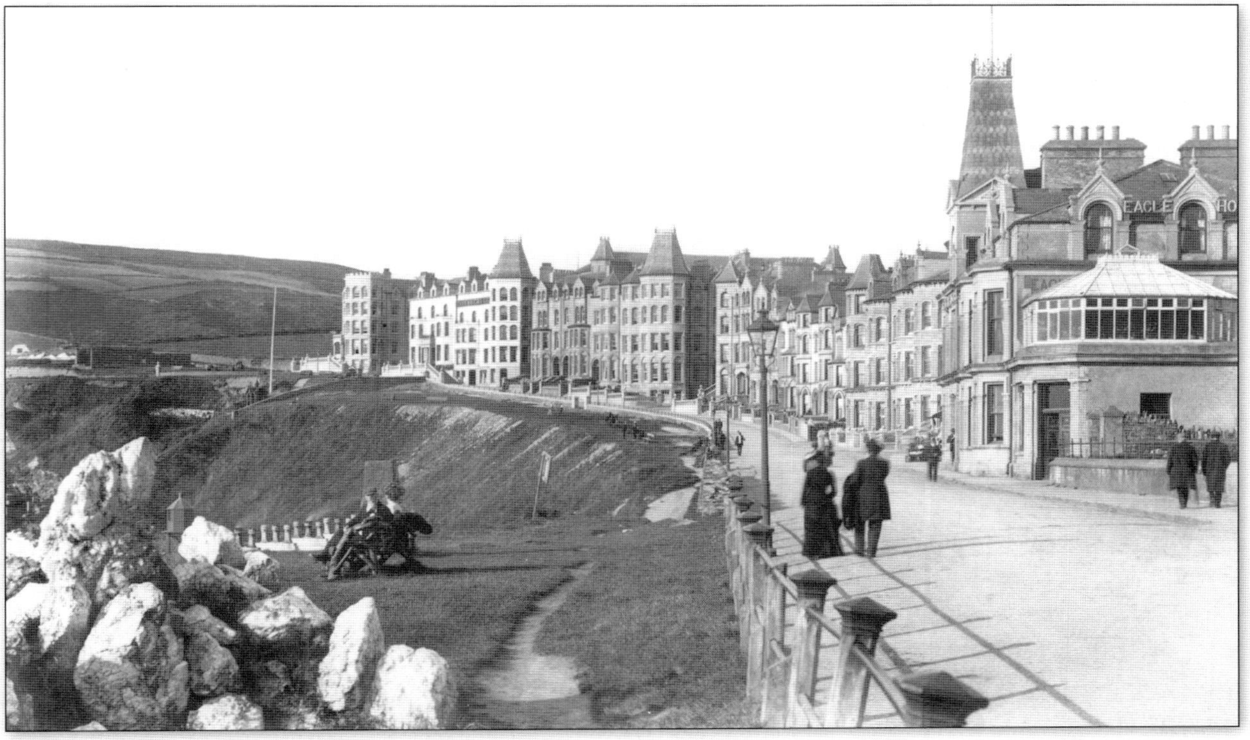

PORT ERIN, THE PROMENADE 1903 50629

This photograph gives us a good view of some of the late-Victorian seafront developments at Port Erin. The resort's popularity increased so much in the ten years or so prior to the outbreak of the Great War that the IOMR added a spacious platform during the 1904 rebuilding of the station. As passenger traffic continued to grow, the platform was extended again in 1911.

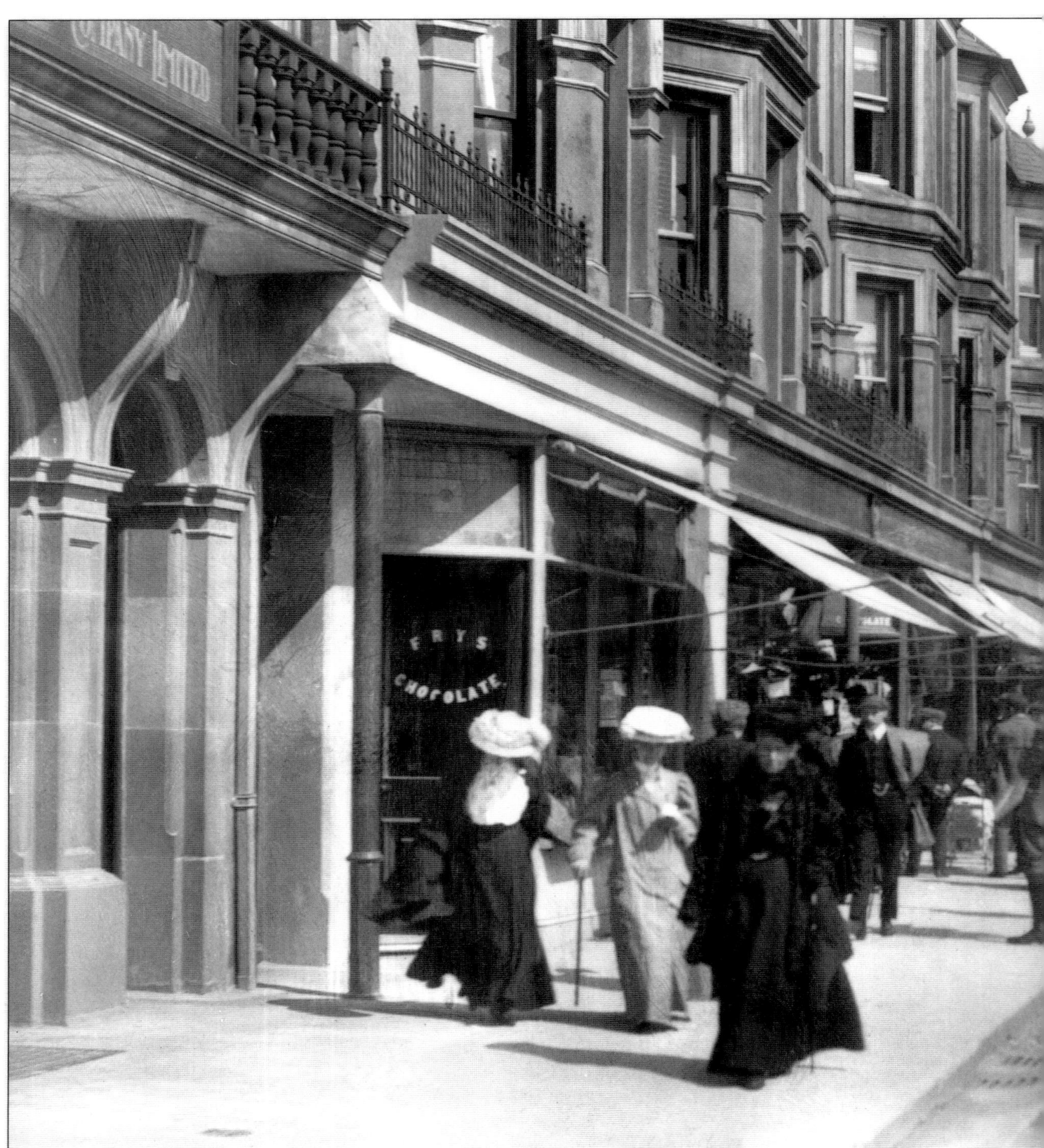
COMPANY LIMITED
FRYS
CHOCOLATE

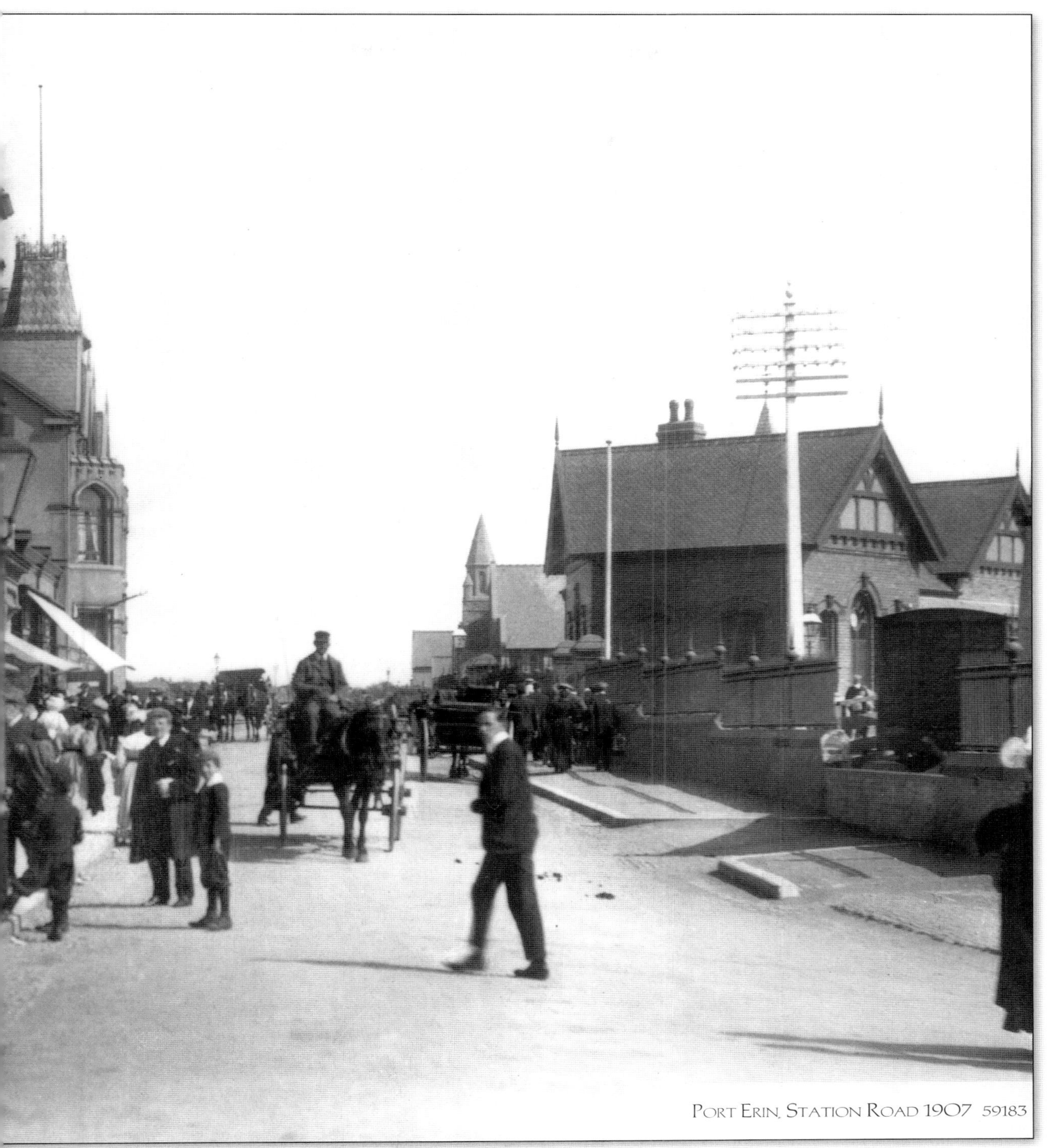

PORT ERIN, STATION ROAD 1907 59183

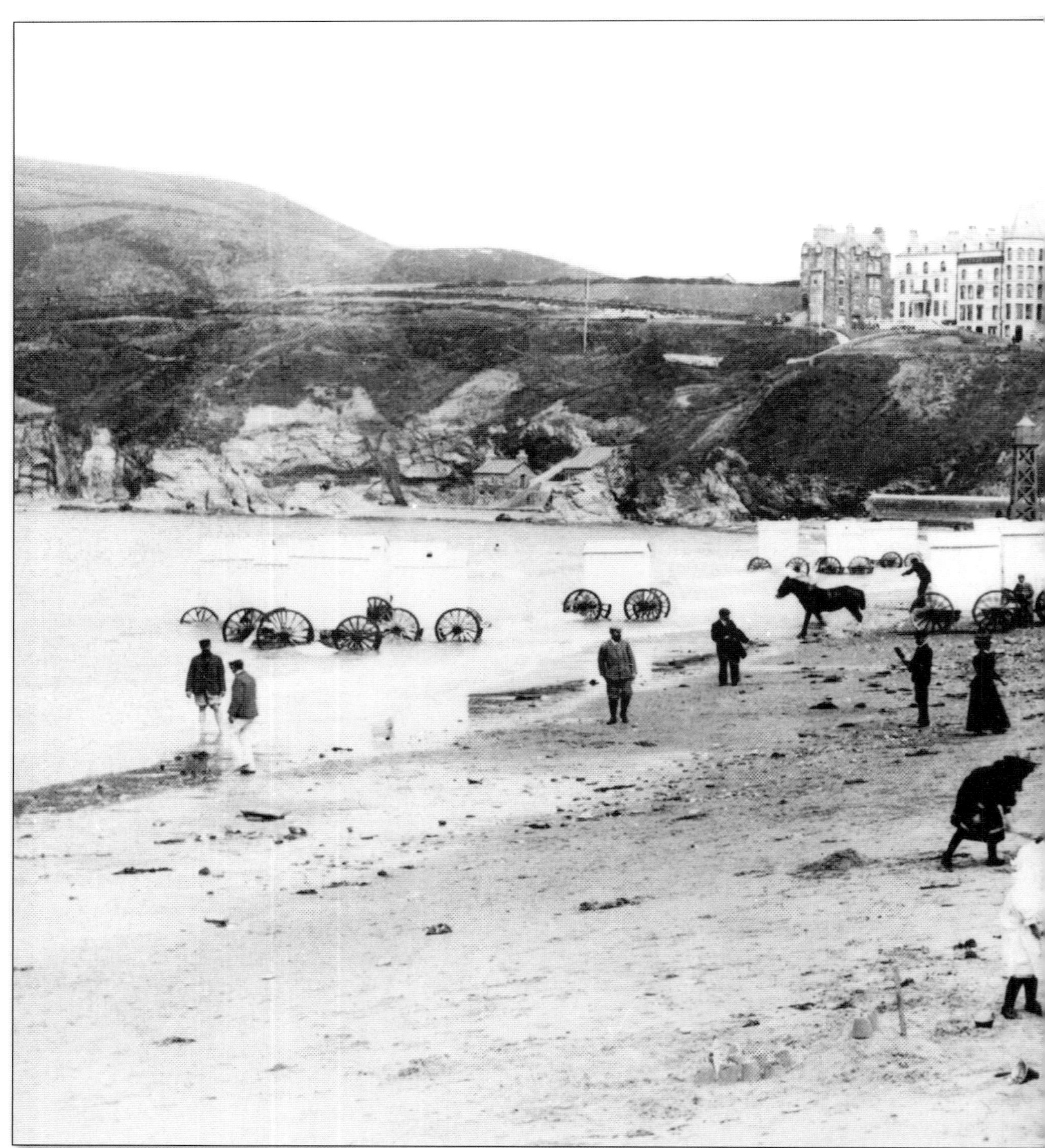

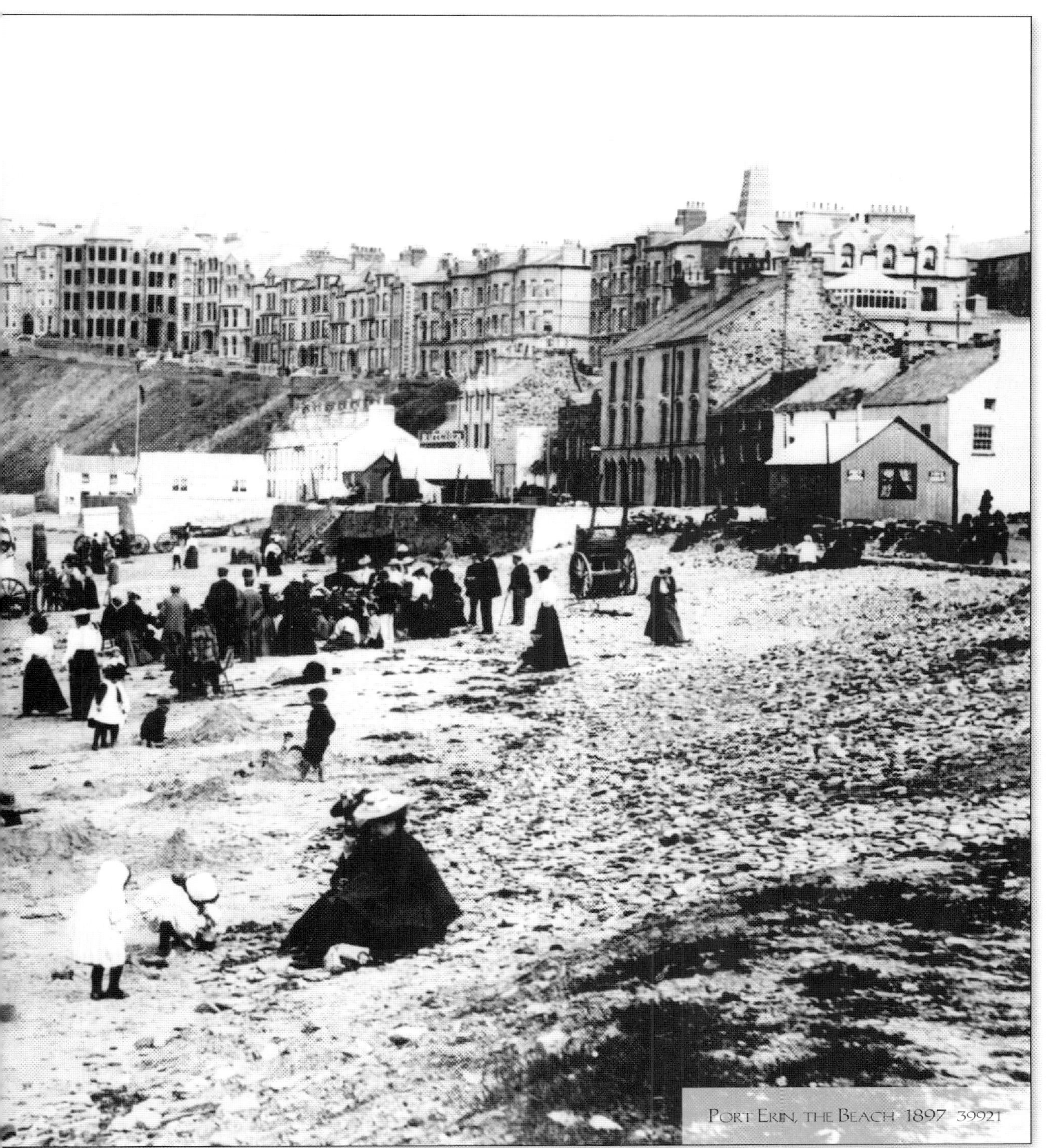

PORT ERIN, THE BEACH 1897 39921

Douglas To Port Erin

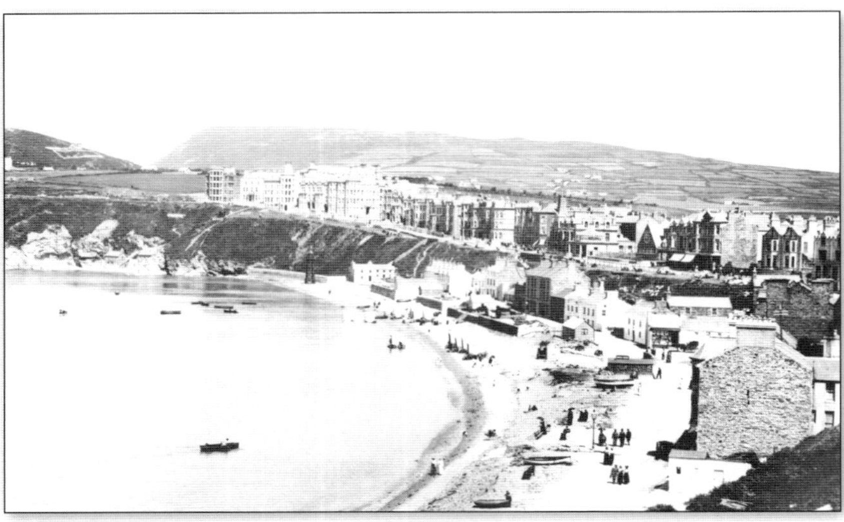

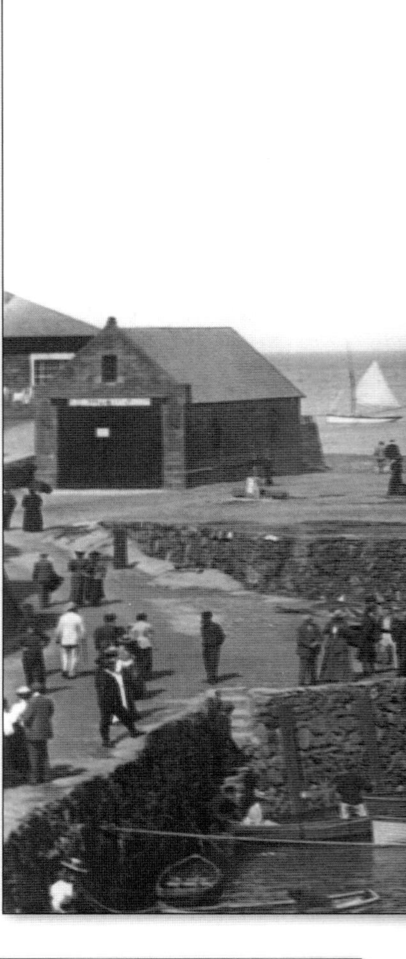

Above: Port Erin, From The Cliff 1901 47239

The cottages and buildings along the beach belong to the earliest settlement, while the later Victorian developments are strung out along the higher ground. Port Erin's increasing popularity with holidaymakers led to a number of hotels being opened, including the Falcon's Nest, the Eagle, the Bellevue, and the Bay.

Below Left: Port Erin, The Beach 1897 39922

In 1842 Port Erin was chosen as the location for a Marine Biological Station; it still exists, though these days it is a part of the University of Liverpool. One of the great pioneers in marine biology, Professor Edward Forbes, was born at Douglas in 1815. Before his untimely death in 1854 he was already the President of the Geological Society. The station can be seen here on the right on the far side of the bay.

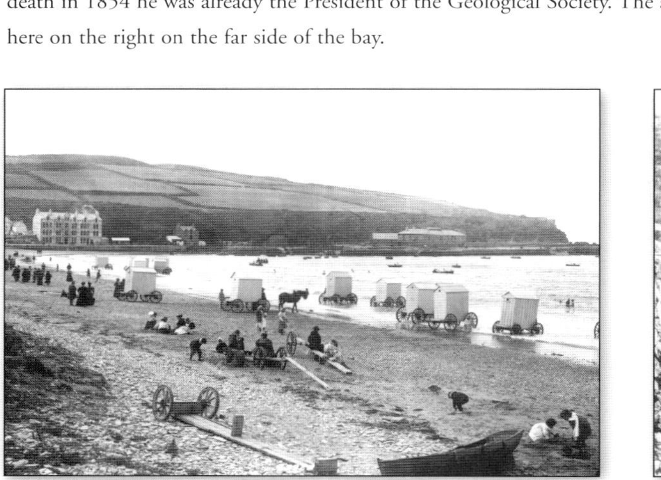

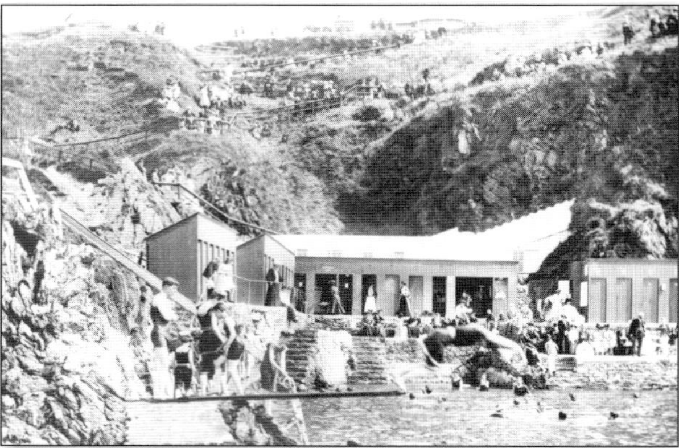

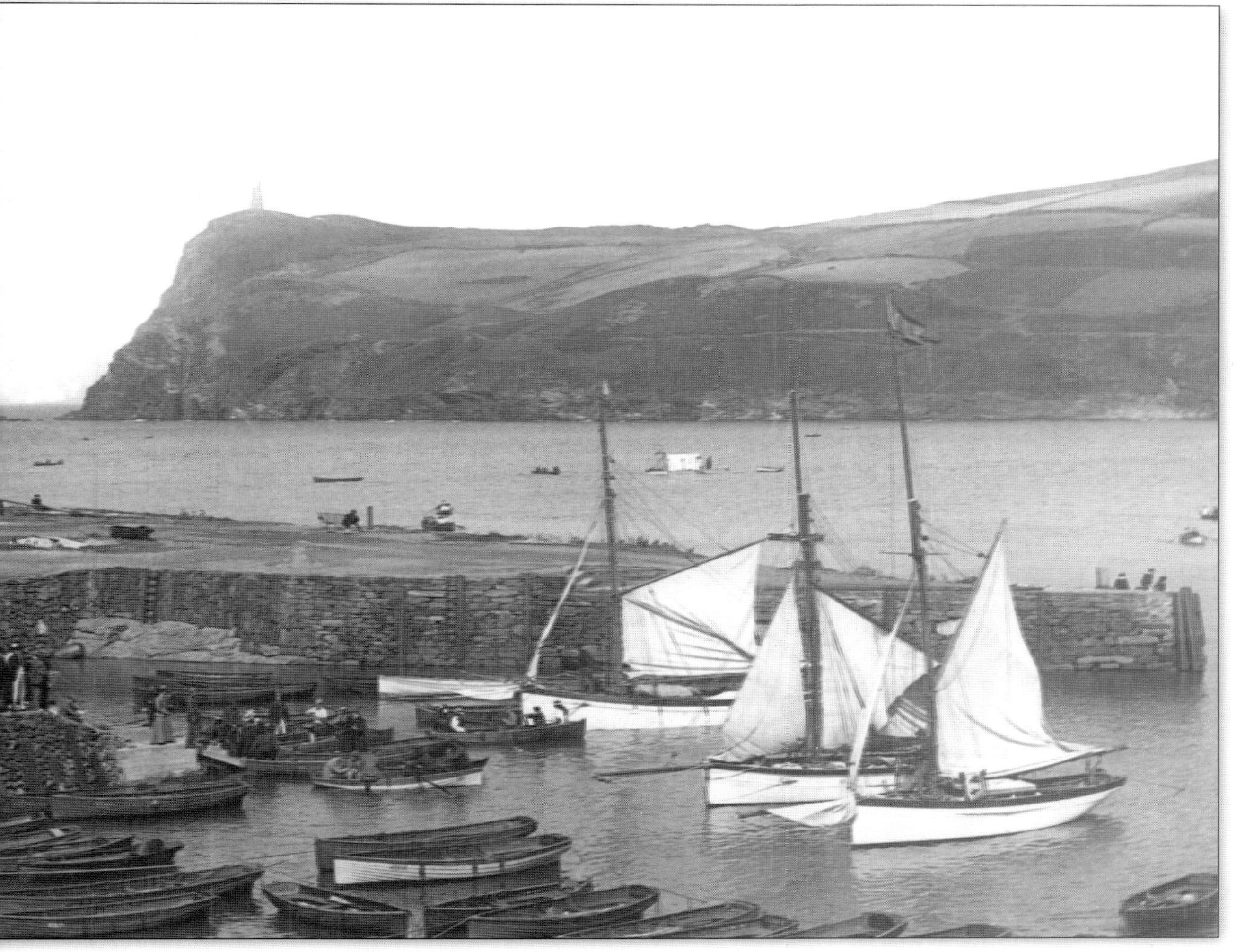

Above: PORT ERIN, THE HARBOUR 1897 39925

Whether it be Blackpool, Dunoon, Port Bannatyne, Port Erin or any of a hundred other resorts in the 1890s, holidaymakers had developed a passion for messing about in boats, mainly of the rowing variety, though there were also adventurous souls prepared to hire out yachts. With clear skies and a calm sea, it looks as though the local boatmen are in for a profitable day.

Left: PORT ERIN, THE BATHS 1907 59195

Mixed bathing - whatever next! They'll be wanting to give women the vote! But on the enlightened Isle of Man they already had it. Women were given the vote in 1881; the first woman member of the House of Keys was Mrs Marion Shimmin, elected in February 1933.

Douglas to Port Erin

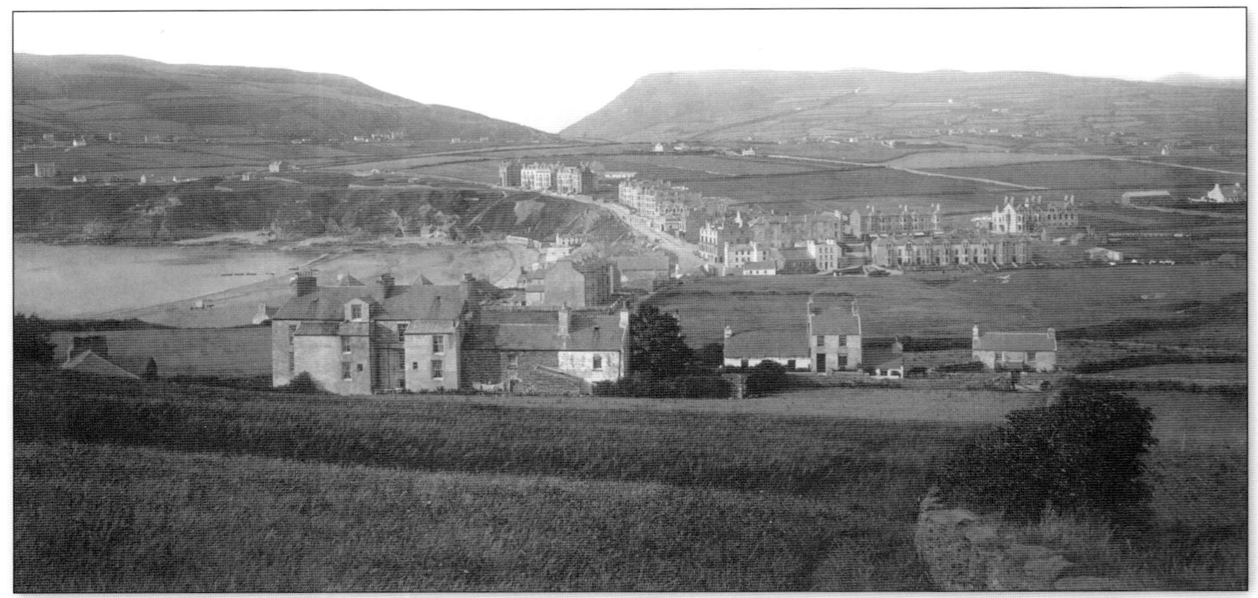

Port Erin, General View 1895 35923

As well as the development along the seafront, we can see the awnings on the shops along Station Road, the station, and the terrace known as Athol Park. In the distance is the valley leading to Fleshwick Bay.

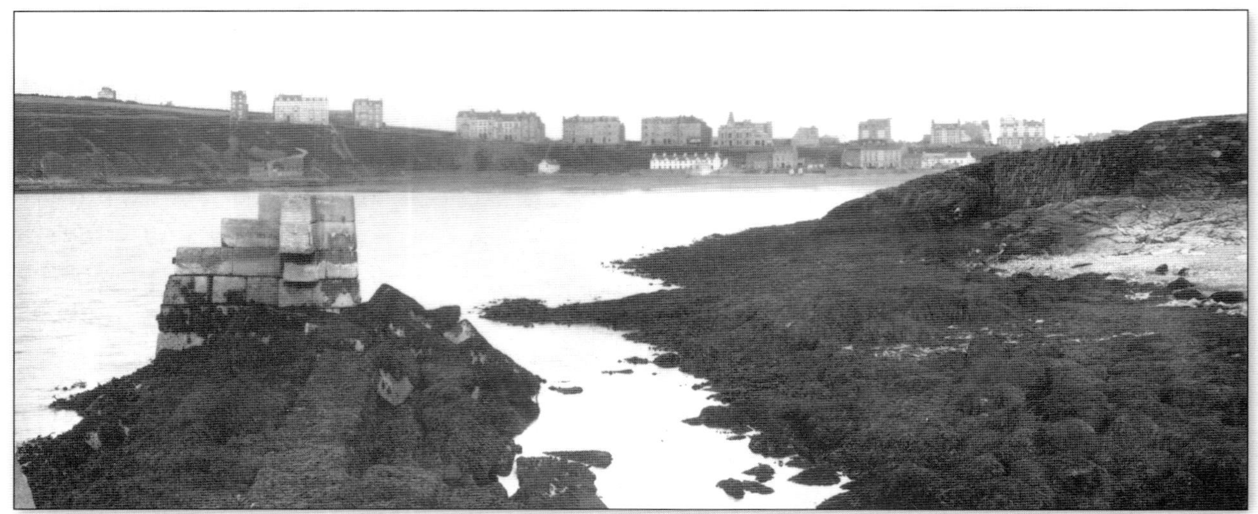

Port Erin, From the Breakwater 1894 34665

Port Erin breakwater had a short life. Work began in 1864, but in 1868, while still under construction, it was badly damaged by a storm; it was not until the following year that Tynwald voted funds for repairs and completion.

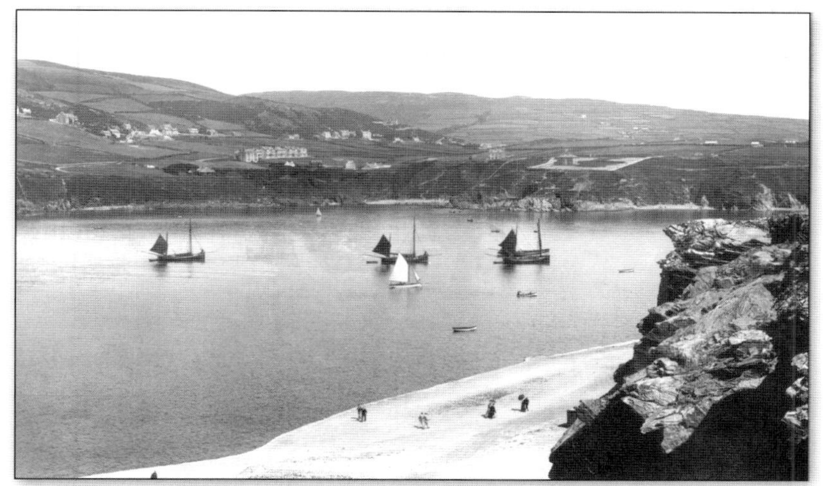

PORT ERIN, THE BAY 1901 47241

The decline of the herring fishery was offset to a certain extent by dredging for scallops and queenies. In 1937 the first dredging operations on a commercial scale were undertaken around Port Erin. It is estimated that 65 per cent of the scallop population in the Irish Sea is to be found within Manx waters. By the 1980s, half of all scallops caught in the Irish Sea were being landed in Man.

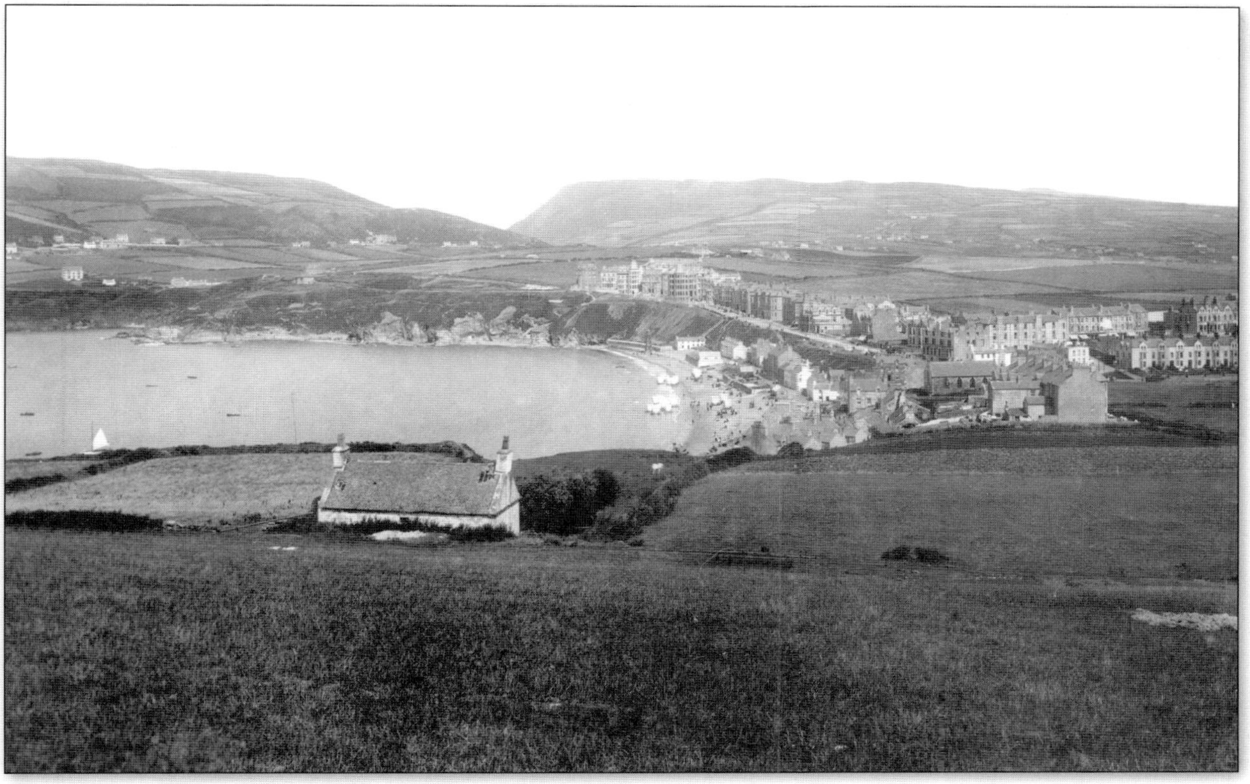

PORT ERIN, DISTANT VIEW 1897 39914

In this view we can clearly see the old fishing village at the water's edge and the later developments associated with the resort of Port Erin. In the distance to the left are Bradda Hill, Bradda West and Bradda East.

Douglas To Port Erin

Right: Port Erin, Bradda 1907 59190

By the time this picture was taken, Port Erin had been transformed from a fishing village into a popular resort. Development spread beyond the immediate area of the town to Bradda West and Bradda East; many of the houses in this picture have been built since picture No 47241 was taken in 1901 (page 113).

Below: Port Erin, From Bradda Head 1895 35931

This view looks towards Bay Fine, Aldrick and the Calf of Man. We can also see the remains of the breakwater, which by 1870 had become the subject of a wrangle between Tynwald and the Imperial Government that was not resolved until 1879. Damaged again in 1882, and repaired in 1883, the breakwater was finally destroyed by yet another storm in 1884.

Below Centre: Port Erin, The Hut 1907 59193

This charming hut has a thatched roof, leaded windows and ivy-clad walls. There is greenery inside the porch, and the old man sitting in the doorway completes the picturesque ensemble by sporting a long beard.

Below Right: Port Erin, Bradda Head 1895 35930

Some of the earliest mining on the island was carried out at Bradda Head. In 1246 King Harald Olaveson granted mining rights to the monks of both Furness Abbey and Rushen Abbey, though written records of their activities have still to be discovered.

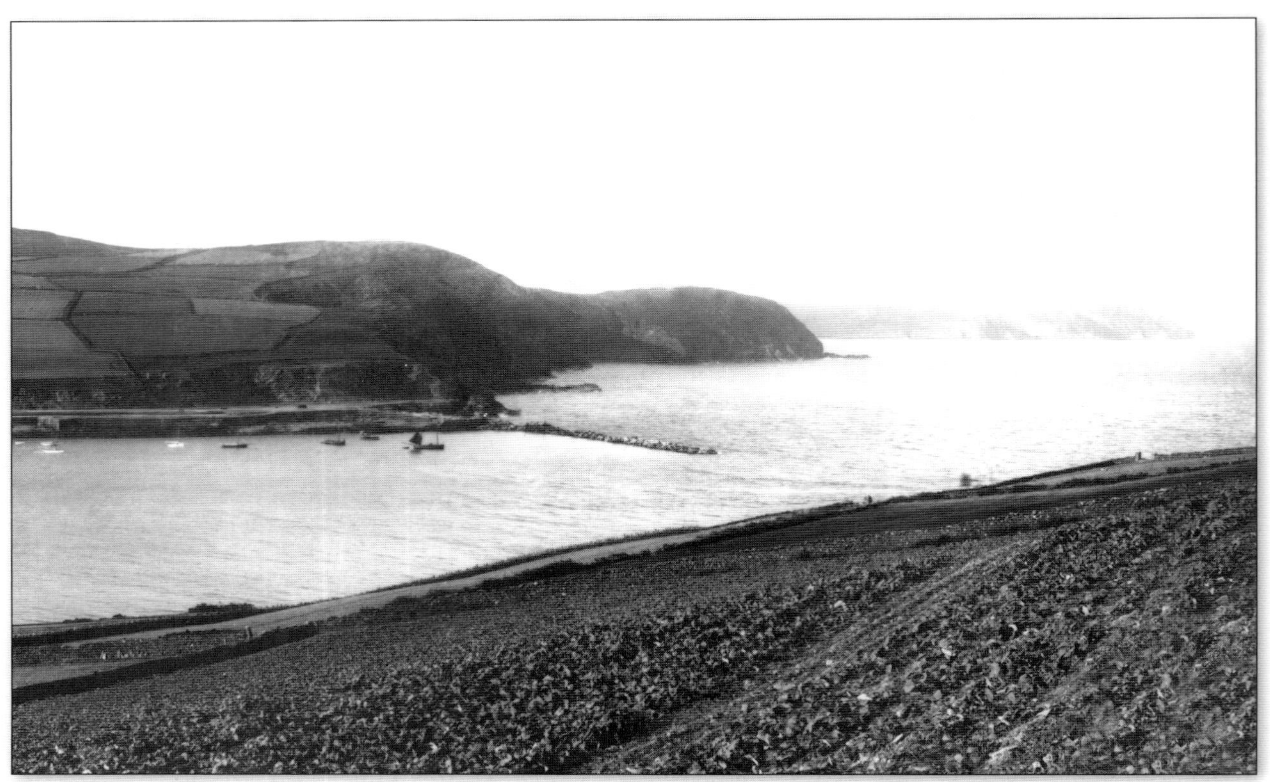

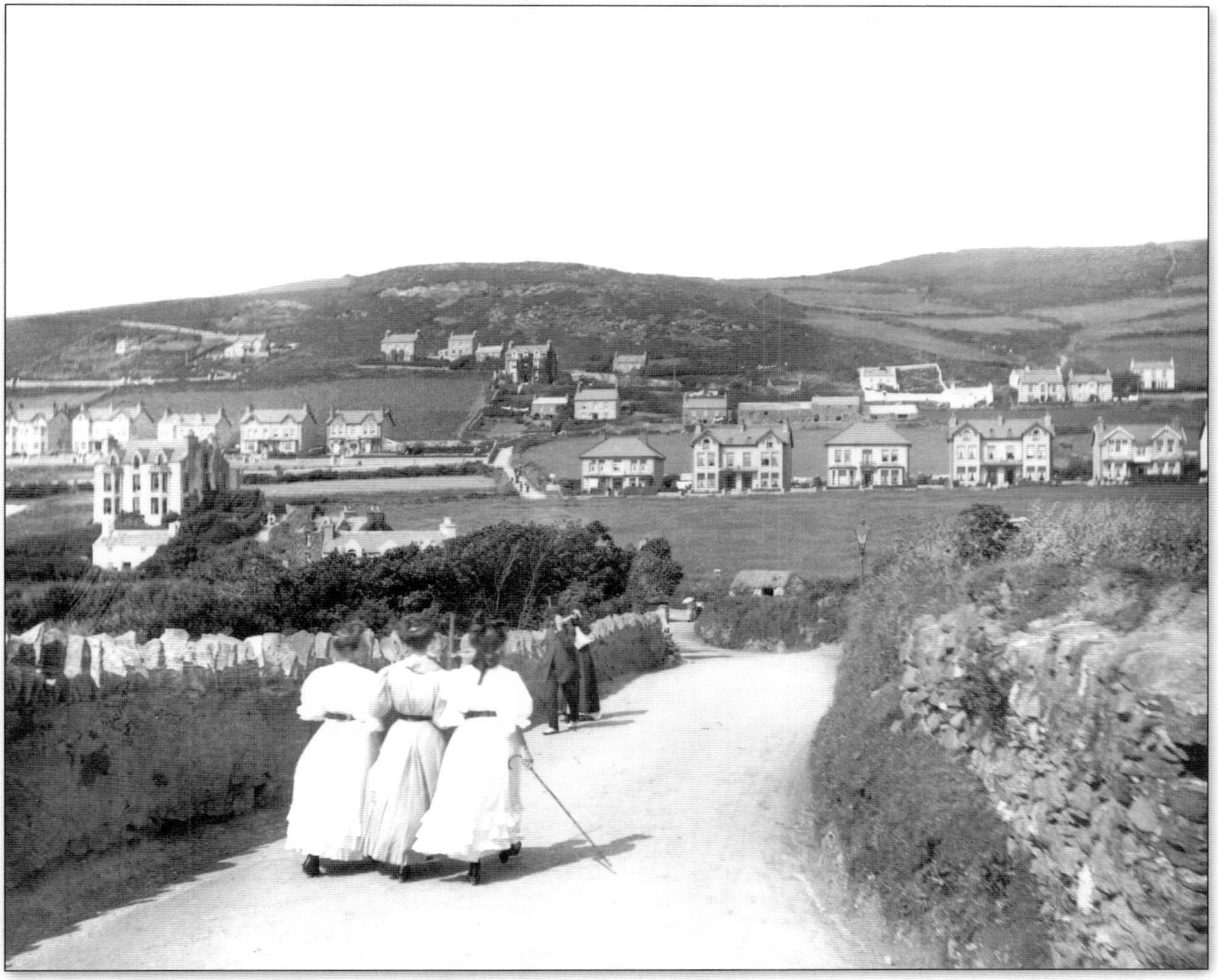

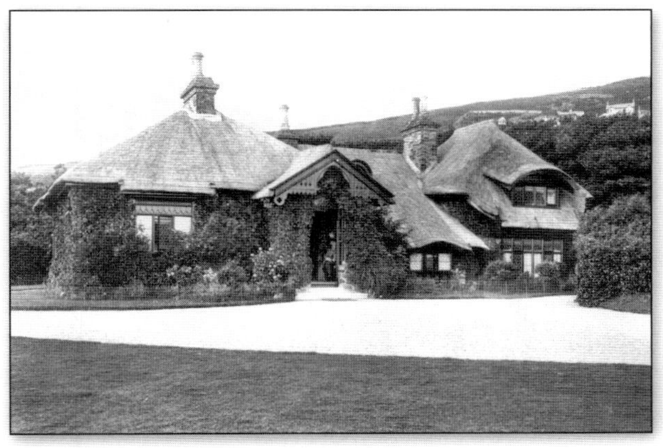

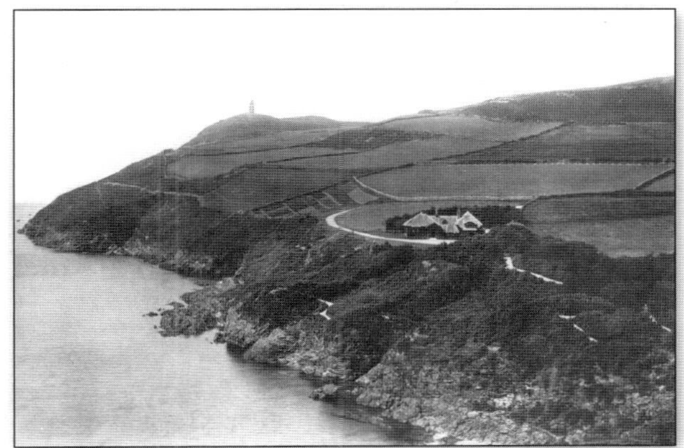

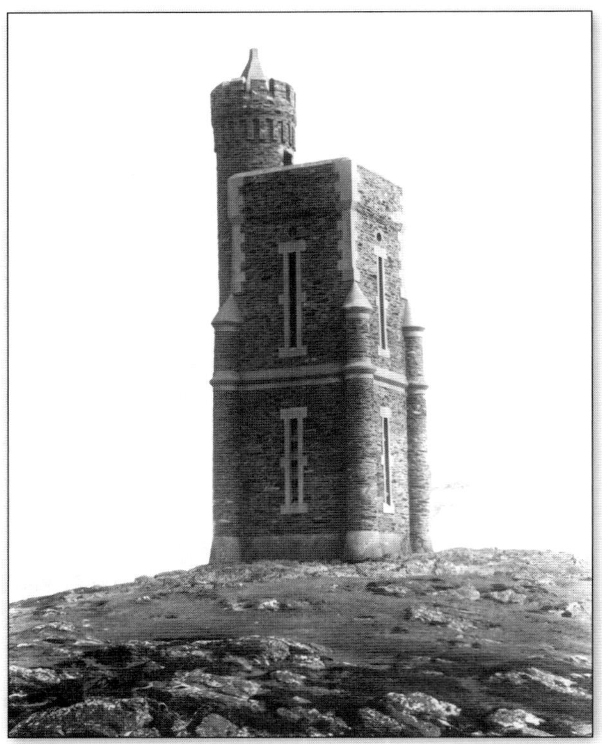

Left: PORT ERIN, MILNER TOWER 1901 47244

The tower was erected on Bradda Head in 1871 to the memory of William Milner, a Liverpool safe manufacturer who did much to ease the lot of local fishermen and their families.

Right: PORT ERIN, SUNSET AT BRADDA HEAD 1897 39927

As the sun goes down, the only activity at sea comes from fishing boats and one or two yachtsmen.

Below Left: PORT ERIN
SUNSET OFF BRADDA HEAD 1903 50636

The mine was at the foot of the cliff, and in 1656 Captain Edward Christian found Bradda contained 'lead ore with much silver'. In 1699 the mine's output was 164 tonnes.

Below Right: FLESHWICK BAY 1895 35933

Nestling between Bradda and the lower slopes of Cronk-ny-Irree-Laa, Fleshwick Bay is less than two miles north of Port Erin and reached by way of Ballaglonney. In 1895, Fleshwick presented visitors to Port Erin with an opportunity enjoy a little seclusion away from the main resort area.

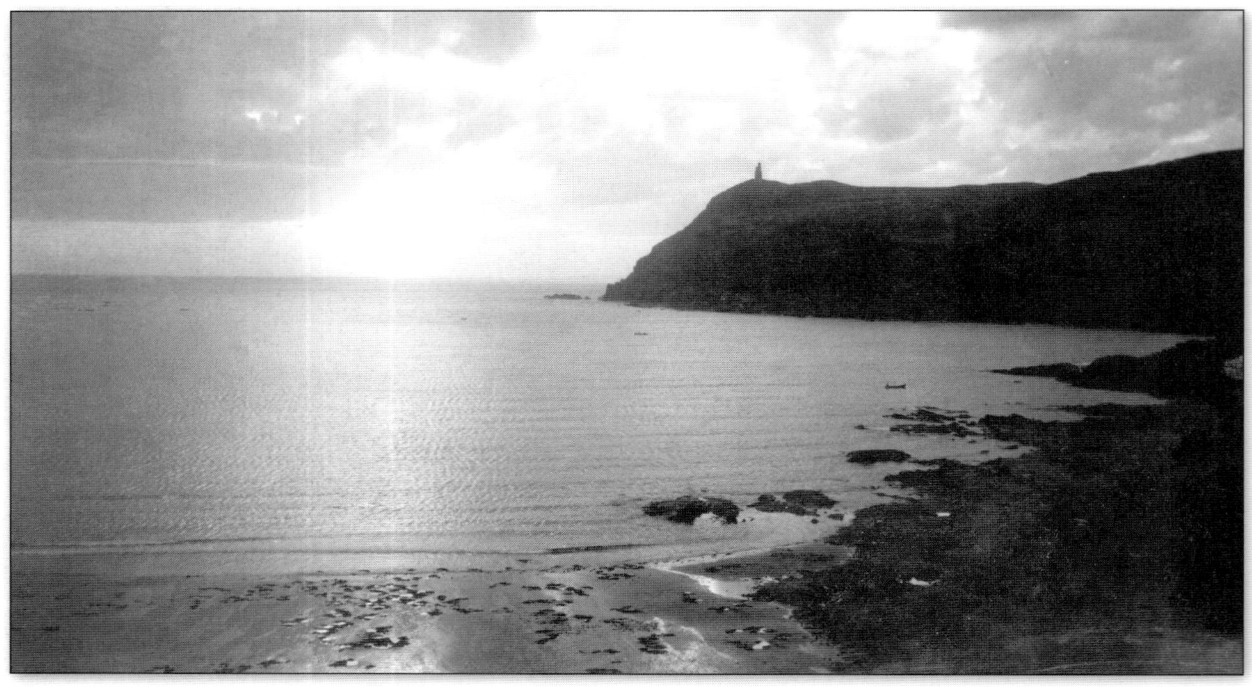

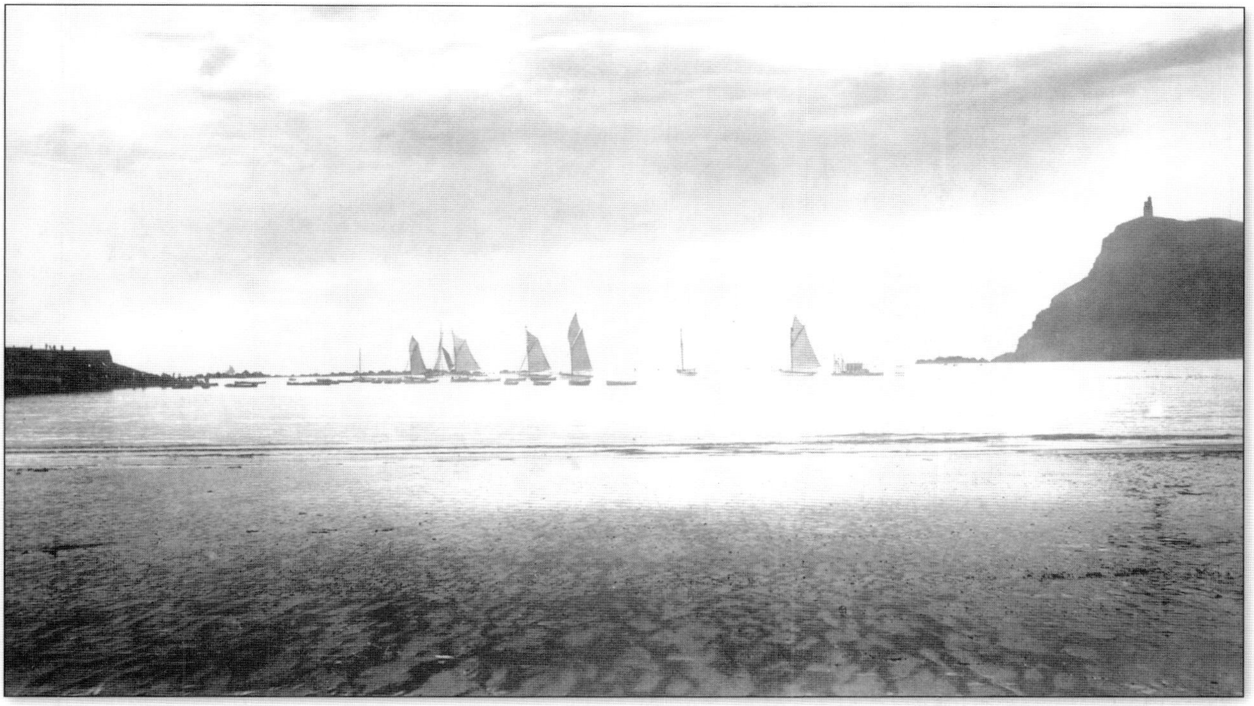

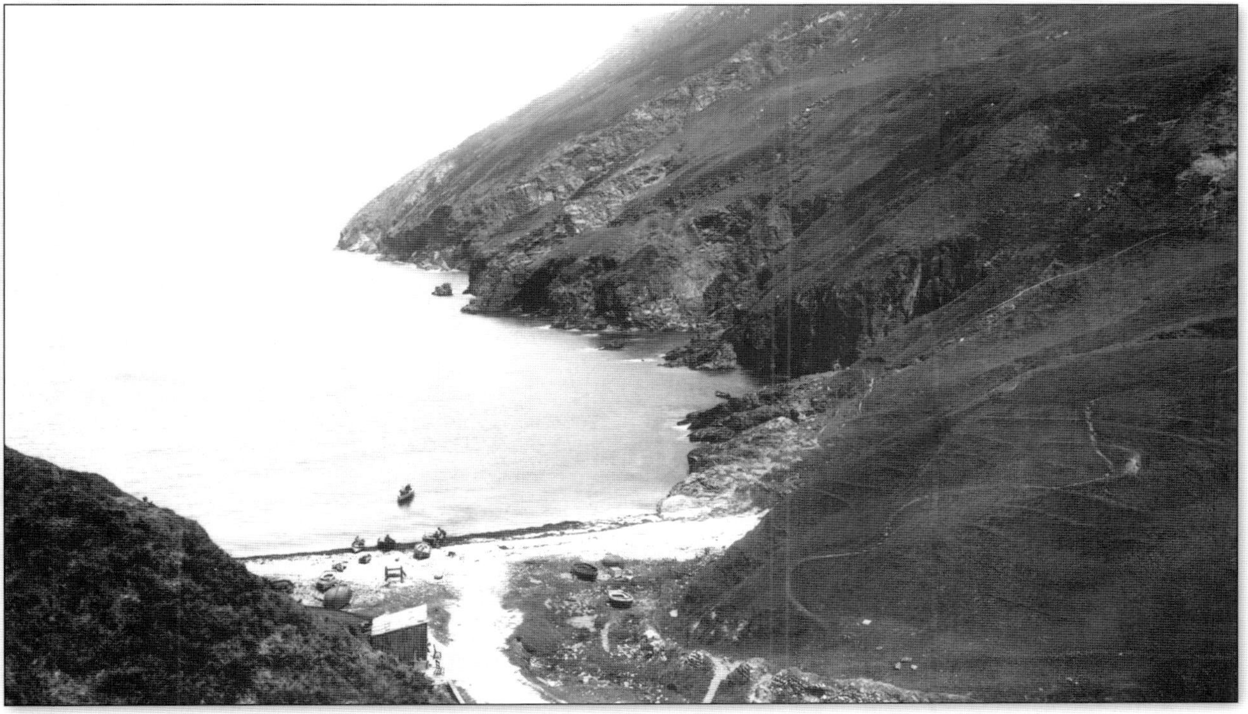

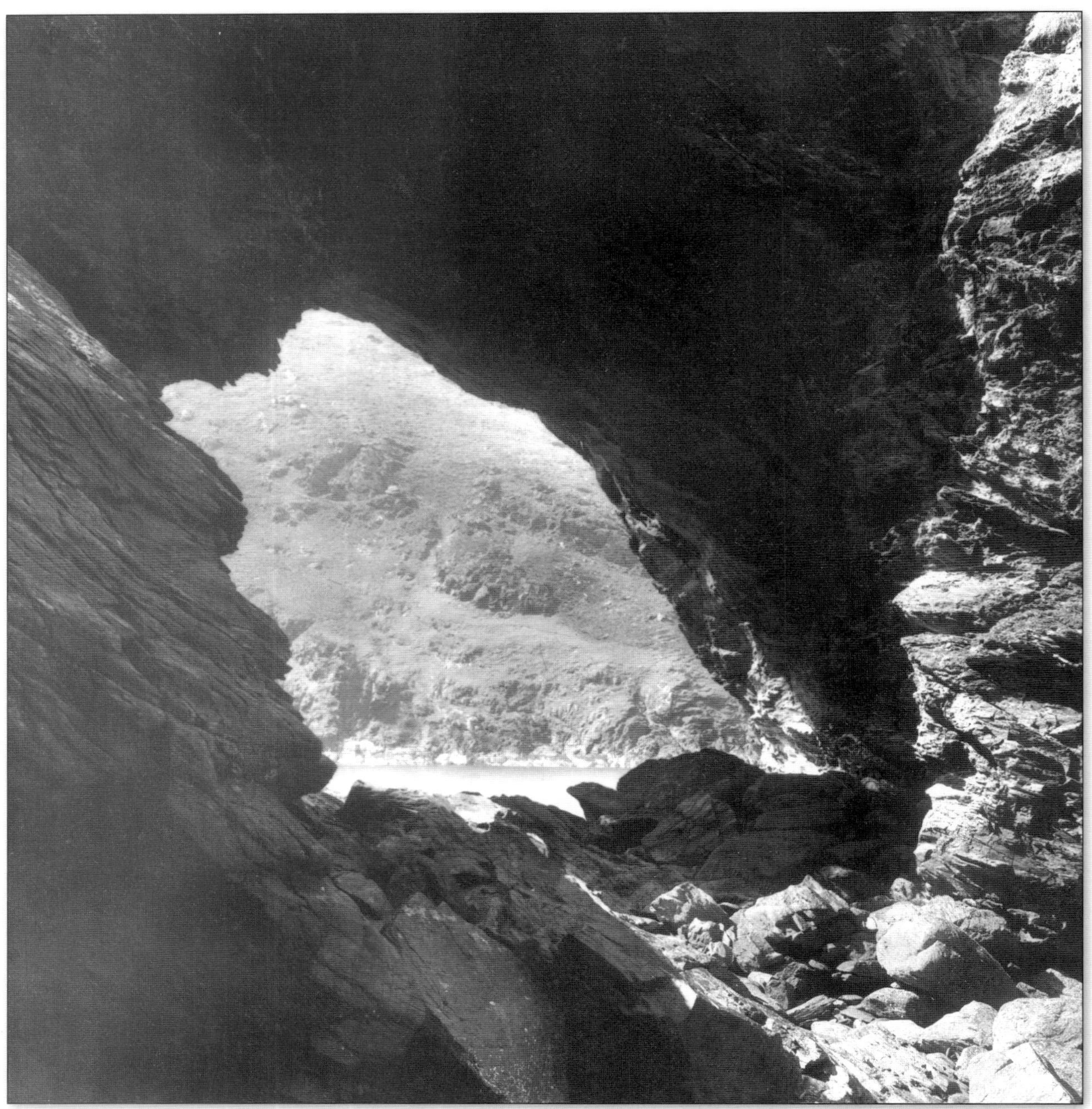

FLESHWICK BAY 1897 39928

The coastline of the Isle of Man is one of outstanding natural beauty. There is the Sugar Loaf Rock at Spanish Head, the caves at Port Soderick, and in the north east the Maughold Brooghs - a Manx Heritage site that stretches from Port e Vullen to Grob ny Strona. Here at Fleshwick, visitors can explore this superb natural arch.

Index

The Francis Frith Collection Titles

www.francisfrith.com

The Francis Frith Collection publishes over 100 new titles each year. A selection of those currently available is listed below. For latest catalogue please contact The Francis Frith Collection. ***Town Books*** 96 pages, approximately 75 photos. ***County and Themed Books*** 128 pages, approximately 135 photos (unless specified). All titles hardback with laminated case and jacket, except those indicated pb (paperback)

Accrington Old and New
Alderley Edge and Wilmslow
Amersham, Chesham and Rickmansworth
Andover
Around Abergavenny
Around Alton
Aylesbury
Barnstaple
Bedford
Bedfordshire
Berkshire Living Memories
Berkshire PA
Blackpool Pocket Album
Bognor Regis
Bournemouth
Bradford
Bridgend
Bridport
Brighton and Hove
Bristol
Buckinghamshire
Calne Living Memories
Camberley PA
Canterbury Cathedral
Cardiff Old and New
Chatham and the Medway Towns
Chelmsford
Chepstow Then and Now
Cheshire
Cheshire Living Memories
Chester
Chesterfield
Chigwell
Christchurch
Churches of East Cornwall
Clevedon
Clitheroe
Corby Living Memories
Cornish Coast
Cornwall Living Memories
Cotswold Living Memories
Cotswold Pocket Album
Coulsdon, Chipstead and Woodmanstern
County Durham
Cromer, Sheringham and Holt
Dartmoor Pocket Album
Derby
Derbyshire
Derbyshire Living Memories
Devon
Devon Churches
Dorchester
Dorset Coast PA
Dorset Living Memories
Dorset Villages
Down the Dart
Down the Severn
Down the Thames
Dunmow, Thaxted and Finchingfield
Durham
East Anglia PA
East Devon
East Grinstead
Edinburgh
Ely and The Fens
Essex PA
Essex Second Selection
Essex: The London Boroughs
Exeter
Exmoor
Falmouth
Farnborough, Fleet and Aldershot
Folkestone
Frome
Furness and Cartmel Peninsulas
Glamorgan
Glasgow
Glastonbury
Gloucester
Gloucestershire
Greater Manchester
Guildford
Hailsham
Hampshire
Harrogate
Hastings and Bexhill
Haywards Heath Living Memories
Heads of the Valleys
Heart of Lancashire PA
Helston
Herefordshire
Horsham
Humberside PA
Huntingdon, St Neots and St Ives
Hythe, Romney Marsh and Ashford
Ilfracombe
Ipswich PA
Isle of Wight
Isle of Wight Living Memories
King's Lynn
Kingston upon Thames
Lake District PA
Lancashire Living Memories
Lancashire Villages

Available from your local bookshop or from the publisher

The Francis Frith Collection Titles (continued)

Lancaster, Morecombe and Heysham Pocket Album
Leeds PA
Leicester
Leicestershire
Lincolnshire Living Memoires
Lincolnshire Pocket Album
Liverpool and Merseyside
London PA
Ludlow
Maidenhead
Maidstone
Malmesbury
Manchester PA
Marlborough
Matlock
Merseyside Living Memories
Nantwich and Crewe
New Forest
Newbury Living Memories
Newquay to St Ives
North Devon Living Memories
North London
North Wales
North Yorkshire
Northamptonshire
Northumberland
Northwich
Nottingham
Nottinghamshire PA
Oakham
Odiham Then and Now
Oxford Pocket Album
Oxfordshire
Padstow
Pembrokeshire
Penzance
Petersfield Then and Now
Plymouth
Poole and Sandbanks
Preston PA
Ramsgate Old and New
Reacing Pocket Album
Redditch Living Memories
Redhill to Reigate
Rhondda Valley Living Mems
Richmond
Ringwood
Rochdale
Romford PA
Salisbury PA
Scotland
Scottish Castles
Sevenoaks and Tonbridge
Sheffield and South Yorkshire PA
Shropshire
Somerset
South Devon Coast
South Devon Living Memories
South East London
Southampton PA
Southend PA
Southport
Southwold to Aldeburgh
Stourbridge Living Memories
Stratford upon Avon
Stroud
Suffolk
Suffolk PA
Surrey Living Memories
Sussex
Sutton
Swanage and Purbeck
Swansea Pocket Album
Swindon Living Memories
Taunton
Teignmouth
Tenby and Saundersfoot
Tiverton
Torbay
Truro
Uppingham
Villages of Kent
Villages of Surrey
Villages of Sussex PA
Wakefield and the Five Towns Living Memories
Warrington
Warwick
Warwickshire PA
Wellingborough Living Memories
Wells
Welsh Castles
West Midlands PA
West Wiltshire Towns
West Yorkshire
Weston-super-Mare
Weymouth
Widnes and Runcorn
Wiltshire Churches
Wiltshire Living memories
Wiltshire PA
Wimborne
Winchester PA
Windermere
Windsor
Wirral
Wokingham and Bracknell
Woodbridge
Worcester
Worcestershire
Worcestershire Living Memories
Wyre Forest
York PA
Yorkshire
Yorkshire Coastal Memories
Yorkshire Dales
Yorkshire Revisited

See Frith books on the internet at www.francisfrith.co.uk

Frith Products & Services

Francis Frith would doubtless be pleased to know that the pioneering publishing venture he started in 1860 still continues today. Over a hundred and forty years later, The Francis Frith Collection continues in the same innovative tradition and is now one of the foremost publishers of vintage photographs in the world. Some of the current activities include:

Interior Decoration

Today Frith's photographs can be seen framed and as giant wall murals in thousands of pubs, restaurants, hotels, banks, retail stores and other public buildings throughout the country. In every case they enhance the unique local atmosphere of the places they depict and provide reminders of gentler days in an increasingly busy and frenetic world.

Product Promotions

Frith products are used by many major companies to promote the sales of their own products or to reinforce their own history and heritage. Frith promotions have been used by Hovis bread, Courage beers, Scots Porage Oats, Colman's mustard, Cadbury's foods, Mellow Birds coffee, Dunhill pipe tobacco, Guinness, and Bulmer's Cider.

Genealogy and Family History

As the interest in family history and roots grows world-wide, more and more people are turning to Frith's photographs of Great Britain for images of the towns, villages and streets where their ancestors lived; and, of course, photographs of the churches and chapels where their ancestors were christened, married and buried are an essential part of every genealogy tree and family album.

Frith Products

All Frith photographs are available Framed or just as Mounted Prints and Posters (size 23 x 16 inches). These may be ordered from the address below. From time to time other products - Address Books, Calendars, Table Mats, etc - are available.

The Internet

Already ninety thousand Frith photographs can be viewed and purchased on the internet through the Frith websites and a myriad of partner sites.

For more detailed information on Frith companies and products, look at these sites:

www.francisfrith.co.uk
www.francisfrith.com
(for North American visitors)

See the complete list of Frith Books at:

www.francisfrith.co.uk

This web site is regularly updated with the latest list of publications from the Francis Frith Collection. If you wish to buy books relating to another part of the country that your local bookshop does not stock, you may purchase on-line.

For further information, trade, or author enquiries please contact us at the address below:

The Francis Frith Collection, Frith's Barn, Teffont, Salisbury, Wiltshire, England SP3 5QP.
Tel: +44 (0)1722 716 376 Fax: +44 (0)1722 716 881 Email: sales@francisfrith.co.uk

See Frith books on the internet at www.francisfrith.com

FREE PRINT OF YOUR CHOICE

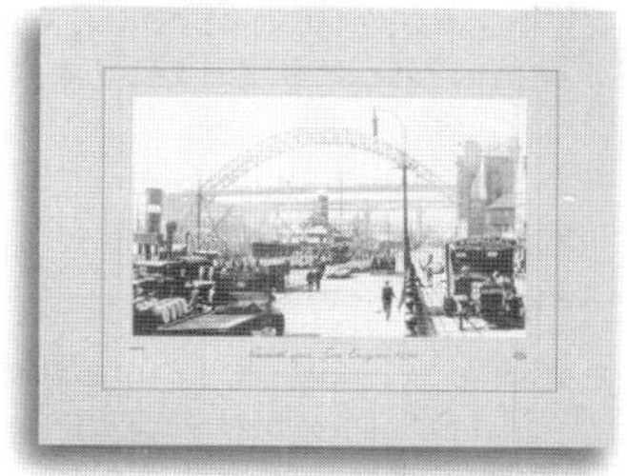

Mounted Print
Overall size 14 x 11 inches (355 x 280mm)

Choose any Frith photograph in this book. Simply complete the Voucher opposite and return it with your remittance for £3.50 (to cover postage and handling) and we will print the photograph of your choice in SEPIA (size 11 x 8 inches) and supply it in a cream mount with a burgundy rule line (overall size 14 x 11 inches). **Please note: aerial photographs and photographs with a reference number starting with a "Z" are not Frith photographs and cannot be supplied under this offer. Offer valid for delivery to one UK address only.**

***PLUS:* Order additional Mounted Prints at HALF PRICE - £9.50 each** (normally £19.00)
If you would like to order more Frith prints from this book, possibly as gifts for friends and family, you can buy them at half price (with no additional postage and handling costs).

***PLUS:* Have your Mounted Prints framed**
For an extra £18.00 per print you can have your mounted print(s) framed in an elegant polished wood and gilt moulding, overall size 16 x 13 inches (no additional postage and handling required).

IMPORTANT!

These special prices are only available if you use this form to order. You must use the ORIGINAL VOUCHER on this page (no copies permitted). We can only despatch to one UK address. This offer cannot be combined with any other offer.

Send completed Voucher form to:
The Francis Frith Collection, Frith's Barn, Teffont, Salisbury, Wiltshire SP3 5QP

CHOOSE A PHOTOGRAPH FROM THIS BOOK

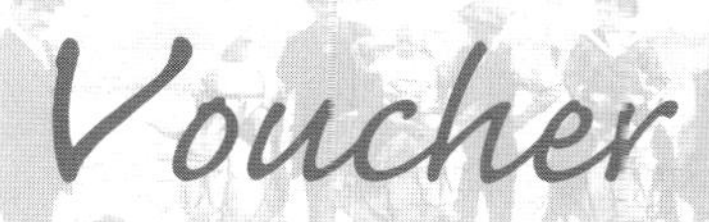

for **FREE** *and Reduced Price Frith Prints*

Please do not photocopy this voucher. Only the original is valid, so please fill it in, cut it out and return it to us with your order.

Picture ref no	Page no	Qty	Mounted @ £9.50	Framed + £18.00	Total Cost £
		1	Free of charge*	£	£
			£9.50	£	£
			£9.50	£	£
			£9.50	£	£
			£9.50	£	£
			£9.50	£	£
			* Post & handling		£3.50
			Total Order Cost		£

Please allow 28 days for delivery.
Offer available to one UK address only

Title of this book . . . .
I enclose a cheque/postal order for £ . . . .
made payable to 'The Francis Frith Collection'

OR please debit my Mastercard / Visa / Maestro card, details below

Card Number

Issue No (Maestro only) Valid from (Maestro)

Expires Signature

Name Mr/Mrs/Ms ....
Address ....
....
....
.... Postcode ....
Daytime Tel No ....
Email ....

978-1-84589-447-4 Valid to 31/12/11

Free Print - see overleaf

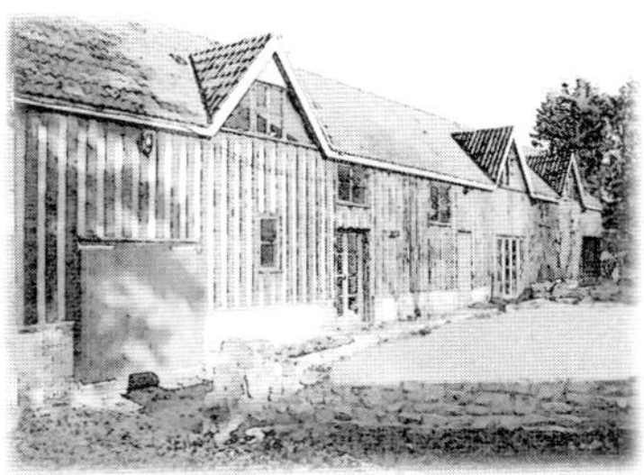

Can you help us with information about any of the Frith photographs in this book?

We are gradually compiling an historical record for each of the photographs in the Frith archive. It is always fascinating to find out the names of the people shown in the pictures, as well as insights into the shops, buildings and other features depicted.

If you recognize anyone in the photographs in this book, or if you have information not already included in the author's caption, do let us know. We would love to hear from you, and will try to publish it in future books or articles.

An Invitation from The Francis Frith Collection to Share Your Memories

The 'Share Your Memories' feature of our website allows members of the public to add personal memories relating to the places featured in our photographs, or comment on others already added. Seeing a place from your past can rekindle forgotten or long held memories. Why not visit the website, find photographs of places you know well and add YOUR story for others to read and enjoy? We would love to hear from you!

www.francisfrith.com/memories

Our production team

Frith books are produced by a small dedicated team at offices in the converted Grade II listed 18th-century barn at Teffont near Salisbury, illustrated above. Most have worked with the Frith Collection for many years. All have in common one quality: they have a passion for the Frith Collection.

Frith Books and Gifts

We have a wide range of books and gifts available on our website utilising our photographic archive, many of which can be individually personalised.

www.francisfrith.com